Uncharted

A Journey Along the Edge of

Time and Survival

Cate Cabot

Dream Press Publishing

This is a work of nonfiction. Some names and identifying details have been changed.

Copyright ©2014, 2016
by Cate Cabot
Fourth Edition 2016

Uncharted: A Journey Along the Edge of Time and Survival/Cate Cabot

ISBN-10: 0692317015

ISBN-13: 978-0692317013

Dream Press Publishing

Kelly, Wyoming

Cover painting: Stilled Life by Jeremy Morgan

Cover design: Shane Mieske Page

design and layout: Tom Cabot Author

photograph: Leslie MacKenzie

Uncharted

To my daughter, forever and for always

Contents

Part I

Part II

Part III

Part I

One does not become enlightened by imagining figures of light but by
making the darkness conscious.

Carl Gustav Jung

1

The Streets of New York

Carl Jung knew when his own psyche fractured that he had to make the crossing of the darkest inner landscape within himself, or his theories and practice held no truth or validity at all in his work with his patients. Without Jung's background or training, with no clear knowledge of Jung at all, I would navigate the extremes of my life to make a similar crossing.

This is the pathway that opened for me. This is the track I followed. Caught in the twists of a different fate, this would be my way home.

It is 1988, and I'm in New York City for the first time.

I wander along a busy sidewalk in the Soho district of Lower Manhattan, trailing behind my two companions. They pull ahead of me, mingling in the crowd. Dusk is settling. As they cross a narrow street, I step off the curb to follow them over old cobblestones and look to my left. In a shallow cul de sac, garbage cans cluster before a fence or wall. A moment of musing: The cobblestones must be historic, I think, and my foot makes contact on the old stone street.

Everything rushes out beneath me, an abrupt drop like plummeting down an open elevator shaft.

Where the wall and garbage cans stood a quiet street opens, lined with old brownstones. Voices echo, calling out as from a great distance. A repeating pattern of banistered steps leading up to front doors extends along either side of the street. The street wavers then clarifies. Only a few people are outside, each wearing fine winter clothing not of my era. Voices echo again. A girl. A father. Few others. The air is chill, fluctuates, a winter eve ... a soft summer dusk ... autumn nightfall ...

In a breath my other foot drops, hits the pavers and in a sudden upshift I startle at the abrupt solidity beneath my feet. I stagger then stumble forward, barely catching myself from a fall to the old cobbled street. Now only the darkening hulk of garbage cans lines the wall of the cul de sac. No brownstones, no stirring of seasons catch in the fading light.

Ahead my companions disappear into the dense crowd. Panic surges. I leap forward, alone in a city I don't know, rush to catch them — speak nothing of what I've seen.

A few days later, our business mostly done, we take a little time to explore the city. It's late afternoon, after we've spent hours in galleries, museums and with fabric designers. We're making our way on public transit back to the apartment where we're staying. Lingering at a bus stop, waiting for our last connection, I feel exuberant, full of restless energy.

Stepping away from my companions, I turn to see a squat, dated stucco building. Three nondescript business fronts link together. Curious, drawn to the sign above the middle shop, I cross over and try the door. It's locked. One of my companions has trailed behind me but wanders away to return to the bus stop.

I step back and look up at the sign. I can't read the script. It's indecipherable. The characters almost fade before my eyes. A pull like an undertow draws me back to the window. The interior is dark. Cupping my hands I press my face to the glass. Inside a shadowed density, dark wooden figures fill walls, shelves and floor, all neatly arranged. The figures clarify, startling me to my core. African masks, totems and spears, things I can't name. Terror flashes.

The sidewalk plunges away as before, down down down an endless chute.

Abruptly, the sidewalk snaps solid beneath me. Shaken, disoriented I fling back from the window. I turn to see my friends moving to the steps of a bus that has just pulled up to the stop. Speechless, I run to catch them.

Two days later, we fly back to Wyoming. The experiences in New York travel back with me, haunting. Logic fights against what I've experienced. But I'm irrevocably changed. A long strange journey has begun. There will be no turning back.

———

Our lives are a crossing and recrossing of old paths and, sometimes, ancient paths. When the timing and sensing is just right, time pops open. So here is my story. Your conclusions will be your own.

2

Rainbow

As a child, I loved the world. I was a porous one, open with deep sensitivities. I did not know what this meant then or what it would come to mean. I was a child, simply myself, whole with the greater heartbeat of the world. I felt no separation from my family, or from sun and rain, soil or grass or bee, nor the prairie that wrapped our town. All was me and I was all, happy and sad. Storm and shine.

My earliest childhood was a pattern of generosity. The world felt unstinting to me. Open. Fine. Strong. My parents were happy. Their spell of falling in love was paired to the magical thrall of being in love with a world they were creating. Our family was mostly a ricochet pattern of goodness and content. We lived in a neighborhood along the edge of the open sage steppes of central Wyoming, where we thrived for a time. My mother had been raised on a second language of open space and horse breath, the lonely only child of a single divorced mother who at last with my father lived some large part of her dream of family, and belonging. My father, a newcomer from Michigan, was the only boy among three siblings and the oldest, born to a father embittered by life and the struggle to feed his family through the Great Depression.

In my earliest memory of my father I am tiny and look up to the sound of his voice, high above in a forest of suit panted legs. Other man voices rumble. There is laughter. My father swings down, sweeps me up in his arms, tucks me in close and rises. "This is Cathi," his voice croons, proud and soft. "Our generous one." I feel his warmth. I am close in the circle of things.

Life was a good thing then. But times change, and life beats its way into us. In an abrupt shift my family moved to Mexico. It was 1957. I was five years old. My father leased a large hotel complex called the Monte Mar along the Baja. My parents had no idea what they were kicking up, old currents asleep in the soil of that place. They strode south with utter confidence.

For me, Mexico became a place of great generosity — beauty and thrill, flavor and texture, brilliance and strangeness. It was a place of great mystery. It would also become a place of crushing fear and threatening darkness. My whole life would be fired in the clay and the questions of Mexico.

———

It is 1956, before my family makes the move. Before my best friend Petie's hand slips from my grasp outside the car window as we back out of our driveway. Gone. Good-bye forever and tears streaming. It is before that. It is the first time, when we take the train to Disneyland and visit Mexico. I'm four years old. My family is together in a car that drives and drives, until we cross over something called a border. The young woman who helps my mother, Sharon, is still with us then. My daddy doesn't want to stop. He never wants to stop. Even if I'm carsick and everybody knows it, he doesn't want to stop until it's too late. But this time he does stop, at a motel along a white beach to spend the night, because everyone is cranky. There are burros made of stone, life size, three of them in front of the motel. Big. Middle. Small. I'm too little to get on the big by myself. My brother won't help me. He takes it for himself. I want to get on the middle. My sister takes it. Even though it's hard, I scramble up on the smallest burro. I love all these stone burros. They fit in a perfect place inside me. Happy. I grin at my brother and sister. *Baby. Baby, baby*, they say. I love the little burro. But my face is covered with tears. I'm not a baby. Our little brother is the baby. He's too little to even be out here. He can't climb on a stone burro at all.

We get up the next morning, fight over the burros. This time I get up on the big by myself somehow. The stone is hard on my bottom. The small is a perfect fit. But I don't say so. I look all around from this high point, at the sand and sea and the sky. It seems like a blink and I'm off the stone burro, in the backseat of the car again, moving away. *Where did the stone burros go?* I want them. But they're gone like the clouds fleeing outside the windows. We drive and we drive. It's hot.

Within the year, we move from Wyoming to live in Mexico. We're no longer visitors. My sister, brothers and I are a puppy pile, roving and happy, always on the move. Everything sings of adventure.

When the grunion run Daddy drives us to a wild beach after dark, and we race with flashlights along wet sand. An old shipwreck hangs ghostly and creaking out in the roaring surf. We drop from roadside cliffs onto banks of white seashells — so deep it's hard to walk through the shifting grind of their salty tang. Their bleached fracturing bites in my nose. We find hidden beaches pulsing with waves, glistening with giant kelp. The waves slap us. We skip in the spray. When the red tides come we no longer play in the ocean. We find new adventures in town.

And the mystery of Mexico's promise begins to change.

———————

Five years old and I'm running on a street through this town that is new and big and bright, senses streaming. Ensenada, my mommy calls it. I can't understand anyone except my brothers and sister and the boy, Pepé, all running ahead. I barely keep up with my older sister. She is fast so fast too fast. People are everywhere — this way and that — they are all directions. My heart is fast too fast it is pounding and pounding. I trip but my sister doesn't. She wants to keep up with the big boys and has our little brother by the hand. Our big brother is running with Pepé, who washes cars for our daddy.

I don't like it behind them. I step off a curb. People and buses whizz everywhere. My heart squeezes up in my throat. My sister is six. Our big brother, Tommy, is seven. I'm not the baby. Our little brother is the baby. My head spins and I lurch past a car and run. I don't know how old Pepé is. He's bigger than all of us. I make it across the street in two dodges to tag my sister.

Pepé wheedled and wheedled our mommy to let him take us to the movie. Lots of wheedling — Pepé is good at that — and finally she gave in. "Ok," she said, as she looked him over. "There's a Walt Disney you can go to. It's the only one the little kids can see."

Now we are alone. We've never been alone like this before. I don't know where Daddy is. Taking a nap, maybe. Voices gabble everywhere. Daddy says that when we speak the Spanish it will be easier. I don't know.

"Come on! Hurry up!" our big brother yells. We run in the theater together. The boys stop at a long row of empty seats. We sit on scratchy velvet and I laugh. I look down the row, all smiley at my big brother.

"Shut up. Be quiet. No matter what! Be quiet!" his snarly voice growls. "This is a different movie. *Tarzan, King of the Jungle.* It's better." He looks at us with demon eyes, fists cocked. "You better not tell mother!" Both the big boys laugh at each other then at us. "You're all babies, if you make any noise. Just shut up!"

My sister and I look at our little brother in the seat next to me. He gets mad when Tommy says, "Baby. You better not be a bunch of babies!" then puffs up and grins. "I'm not a baby!" our little brother cries. We look at each other and smile. He's only three!

The velvet curtains whoosh open. It is huge and white behind them. I look at my sister. We wiggle back in our seats.

Music blares. I stuff my fingers in my ears. A yodel song breaks out. I drop my hands. Tarzan swings in on a vine to grab a woman who swings away with him. My blood jumps up.

A group of explorers, several men with one woman, talk dandily to each other, pack up a bunch of gear, hack through jungle, dodge poisonous darts, fight off giant spiders, slinking jaguars, huge swinging snakes, roaring lions, leap over hidden pits with spikes after one man falls and dies on them, run from spears that kill some of them. I flinch, lurch, buckle, cringe, gag and nearly jump out of my skin.

The explorers meet Tarzan and fight with him over something. The woman smiles at Tarzan. They go different ways. The explorers get captured by a group of men wearing almost nothing but shiny, glossy skin. My throat catches.

They are taken deeper into the jungle. Drumbeats are pounding, louder and louder. I don't like them. A giant black cauldron smokes over a raging fire. The glossy people dance and wail then gather in a knot, glistening. I feel like I'm on fire.

The explorers are all tied up. They're afraid. Afraid. The glossy-skinned people shake things at the men. One man is yanked away, forced to the crossed poles, pushed high up and bound to them. He twists and yells. The drums get crazy. I can't breathe.

The glossy people cry out in wavy screams. A glossy man with a big knife climbs the poles. He hacks the vines. The poles spring apart, a terrible scream. The bound man is ripped in two. I crumple in my seat.

Through tears I feel the glossy people go wild. A yodel calls. The glossy people look around excited and crazy, shoot darts from their mouths through long tubes. I can't breathe. I sit up rigid in my seat. Tarzan swings in on a vine. Everyone goes crazy. The big curtains whoosh closed.

I can't breathe. The split man is still in my eyes. So are the spiders, the bloody man in the pit and the snakes and the big white teeth of the jaguar. I feel sick. I look at my big brother. I try to stand up to go and not cry. The big boys ignore us.

"Tommy," I whimper, "Tommy, I want to go home!" My throat feels like sharp glass.

"Shut up!" his savage eyes cleave to me. "We're not going yet. It's a double feature!"

I feel cold. "But the movie is over." I start to shake. "I want to go home."

"There's another movie, dummy!" His face is all shiny. Pepé is smiling. "You better not tell mother!" They hoot. "You're all just a bunch of babies."

"I'm not a baby," my voice quavers. "I want to go home."

The theater goes dark. The big boys stop bouncing. They shove back in their seats. Eerie music creeps through the theater. The curtains creak open. My skin crawls. I climb back on the scratchy velvet. I can't stop shivering. The screen goes all grey and murky.

Two scientists in a room talk to each other. They are afraid of something. Something they can't see. The music gets creepier. A couple out walking under trees get spooky, look around and all at once grab their necks, squirm and fall to the ground. Something invisible has sucked out their life. The alive people find them. The same thing happens over and over again. Eerie music! Grab your neck! I writhe in my seat. There is nowhere to hide. The creeping things come faster and faster. The music always tells when they're near. The people never hear it in time. I hear it. I nearly climb out of my seat. Scientists find a way to make visible the gruesome slithering things, with bulbous heads on long spines and no eyes that suck out people's brains. Now when they drop out of trees we can see them. You don't need the music. I want it to stop. The things leap out of nowhere. Everywhere. The world is breaking. The scientists find a way to destroy them. The world is saved but they know it is not safe. It is just a matter of time.

The curtains smash closed.

Light blasts in my eyes.

I can't stand. I want out. I want to run, hide. My legs buckle. I can't move. There is nowhere.

"C'mon! C'mon!" my brother yells. "Are you a bunch of babies?"

My little brother shoves past me. I try to follow. I stumble and push my sister out the end of the aisle. The big boys race away and out of the theater. They look back at us. I try to run with my sister. We are all running. We are running forever. Then we are back at the Monte Mar and mommy is scolding us.

"Where have you been? It's five o'clock," her voice snaps. Her eyes are wide and slitty at the same time. I want to wrap her red and white checked skirt all around me but I don't dare.

Mommy gives me morsels of fresh buttered lobster from her dinner with daddy. No one but me wants to try it. But then we have to leave them. The mariachi band in glittering suits serenades us as we climb the stairs.

After dinner, after bedtime stories, my sister and I are in our pink beds in our pink room and mommy is tucking us in. I don't want her to go. "Are you alright?" she asks. She smoothes back my curly hair. I want her hand to stay. My eyes get heavy.

Later I wake. The room is dark. I hear something. Rustling. I feel something. Slithering. My sister is quiet in her bed across the room. The floor squeaks. *It's the invisible brain-sucking things. They're on the walls.* I feel them sliding along the ceiling. I want to run to my sister. They creep along the floor. They are everywhere. They are coming. My sister is not waking up. They ooze down my wall.

I scream and scream and scream.

I will wake up screaming for the next ten years of my life. The havoc these night terrors create in my family will push the screams to silence. They will become soundless screams. Then they will gnaw from the inside out.

Something terrible has made its way inside my porous nature, something that will not leave, not for a long, long time.

A careless moment by neglectful parents and everything is changed. What was my mother thinking, letting her youngest children go alone to a movie with two boys not much older, no local knowledge or language, unattended in a strange new culture? When I look back, I see an overwhelmed and naïve young woman, no clue to what she had bitten off, my father unnerved and fast losing confidence.

They had crossed into unknown territory.

The violation of fear too great to handle at five years old sullies my nature. I still have expansion, whole world communion. But my journey has begun. Mexico is now the place of first terror, first contraction. I'm too young to know this, to know anything but the wonder of the world with its first lock of fear. Too young to know my family teeters on a threshold.

My father has no stomach for his hotel ambition. He will not stay in Mexico but will run from its weight, leaving us alone again and again until he deserts us there. Though he'll meet us at the border on our return to Wyoming later, a new pattern will have set its course by then. But there is more. And out of that ruffled disturbance a dark hand is rising.

Had I been set on a path clear and true as a child, aligned with purpose and meaning? Was the porosity of my nature a generative field, a gift? Or had life violated my innocence with its unquenchable forces, my openness a curse that would take me apart? At five years old I could only be in the great openness that was the world and trust it to be as it had been.

Who guides us helps make us what we become.

———

We move in and out of memory, the spatial fields of time and dimension. Such is our human nature. Splendid wonder opened for me in those southern lands, and within each extreme the whirling mystery.

My nature, fluid to eras, outer reaches of temporal order, was always calling the world. What was it that called my parents? I remember how my mother sang to us as children, the most beautiful voice.

"Somewhere over the rainbow, blue birds fly. Birds fly over the rainbow. Why then, oh why can't I? Someday you'll wish upon a star and wake up where the clouds are far behind you. Where troubles melt like lemon drops, away above the chimney tops, and that's where you'll find me. ..."

3

Ranch

It is 1958. I'm six years old. It's morning. We've been driving to a ranch somewhere outside of Ensenada. Daddy pulls onto bare, hard-packed earth between two long adobe buildings. There are no other cars. Many people gather. The men are mostly dressed in white under large straw hats or with rags tied 'round their heads. Some women are more colorful, but not all. There is nothing that grows here, except two dried-out old trees. Dust permeates ragged white canopies that sag along cracked walls in brilliant sun. A few people crouch against the walls, watching.

I hear my mommy in the front seat call out in Spanish to a woman who rushes toward us. Daddy stops the car. Mommy leaps out and the Spanish woman grabs her, words babbling between them. One word falls from the crush off our mother's tongue. *Chanchitos!* I lock eyes with my brother, who's two years older. *Baby pigs!* We are out of the car faster than sound, racing along the dusty earth toward a group of men gathered in a knot ahead of us.

Mommy's voice cries out sharp to block my tracks. "Cathi, Cathi, no, Cathi, no!" Another voice follows, tracking my mother's. "No, muchacha, muchacha, muchacha, Catarina, no!" but I'm faster than the words and stay ahead of them. I'm faster than Tommy, who chases behind.

Baby pigs! I race toward a group of clustered men.

A man is crouched on the hard-packed earth in front of me. His sharp features sear in my direction. I veer wide to go around him. Creased skin shines around dark luminous eyes. Jet-black hair falls over brows that knit weathered above that brilliant piercing. Eyes of fire. They burn to my face. They flick to the knot of men ahead, flick back to me. A slow cruel smile twists on his weathered lips. I flinch, veer wide then wider, pass him by.

I race toward the gathered men. Their backs are to me. I see a great white sow lying on the earth. I run in close, smiling, lean forward to look for pink wiggling babies. And stop. A cloying copper odor assaults my nostrils. It is sharp and warm, and I shudder. At my feet, narrow red rivulets sink into dry soil. Dry. Dry. So dry. I look to the sow. She is split throat-to-tail. From bloody inner reaches men pull still, tiny forms, hold them aloft like prizes. They're laughing. Pleasure ripples through the crowd. I stagger back, struggling to reverse. Revulsion rises against the terrible. The smell. My brother flashes past me several paces to crouch in the dust before the bloody sow. His face turns to me, eyes lit. He's grinning. He looks into my eyes and nods with pleasure. He turns back to the cavernous gutted form and leans forward, arms crossed on one raised knee. I can't turn away fast enough. In a panting zigzag lurch, I reel back the way I've come.

The crouched, fire-eyed man captures me in his gaze. His eyes reach for my face. Pleasure ruptures in a brilliant smile and his white teeth flash. His head throws back. Sharp guffaws cuff the morning air. A dagger of laughter howls, flung up from that gaping mouth. I cringe, balk and swerve to cut around him. His eyes devour me. Shame launches me blind toward the blue metallic glint of our station wagon ahead. The back door wrenches open in my hand. I claw my way to the open platform on the flattened backseats, right to the middle where no hand can reach me. My mother's voice calls from an open window, hands reaching. I scramble away.

It is later. I wake sweaty and feel the weight of the morning before we came to this ranch. It lies heavy on my mind. This weighted feeling — it's a guide I haven't learned yet to follow. I lie at exact center of the flattened backseats. My daddy's promise wrenches inside me, as screaming monkeys arrow through my mind. This promise of my daddy — roadside monkeys to see up-close — they're trapped by filthy chicken wire next to a shack where we stopped on the road to the ranch, halfway from our morning start. They screech out from some not-so-faraway near-blind curve bad dream. My sister scoots into the car beside me. She whispers a miracle. *Horse.* I feel a spark and then I don't care. She pulls on me and we slide from the car. A swaybacked white horse stands nearby. Two other girls jump around with my sister. I move to the opposite side of the horse, close to the wiry flecked hide. Pain slides up against my own. The girls lead the old broken horse away from our mother along a road of dry yellowed mud gone to powder. Dry. Dry. So dry. The girls fight for turns, shimmy up to slide on and off the wrecked animal. I wince, drag along by its side, head feeling squeezed. I don't want to be here. I don't want to be anywhere.

My sister grabs me. "Mother made me promise," she cries.

I don't want it. I don't want to sit on the old tired back. Tears choke in my throat. She pushes me to the other side of the horse. I'm so tired. I don't want, I don't want, I don't want. My head spins. My heart feels cracked. The girls shove me up until I have to straddle the horse or go over the other side. I grab at the shock of coarse mane. I swing my legs wide. The horse lurches on. Elation leaps sharp in my heart, surprise filtering through the swaying rhythm. It feels good to be on the horse.

In forever we curve around a bend. The horse halts stock-still. My sister grabs my hand and I slide off. We follow the road to the edge of a precipice. There's the road, then no road. Pebbles and grit trickle-ricochet down a steep pitch. A stone rolls to where the road picks up again below. My eyes follow and rise to a blasted landscape. I fall out of myself into the strange. It spreads out forever. I expand and expand and expand. Dry cutouts of hard naked mountains march out of sight. Desolation goes on forever. A flash of fear rips through me, *how can the people live out there?* The fear snaps me back in the blink of an eye, mind crushed and gone, wonder flayed to withering shreds.

The child I was shatters into fractional form, pieces flying. Permeable to the world, completely in the moment, each as it expands, she is diminished. Life has set its stage, stumbled across itself, no guarantees. How long will it take her to find all the missing pieces, how long to recover each flying shard? Extreme events, as yet far ahead, filter down through the years to winnow on the outbreath of time. Was life preparing me for what lay ahead? The girl that I was had no idea of the worlds trying to open in her, nor of the great forces about to work from without. Earthquakes were melting into place. Hers would be a long journey home.

The first shifting sands of my family in Mexico braid through timeless time. Natural order fluctuates. I am the world. I am its whisper and speak. And I am caught in a web of forces that begin to buckle and roll. There are conduits of history to which we each belong. Had my parents unwittingly stumbled into unfinished business from times past? Had I chosen my parents? Had they chosen me? Where do we all begin, where does the tapestry end?

One memory buried deep in my childhood bursts into full consciousness, slicing open long-held grief out of all proportion to the moment I am in. Within it lies a marker to a past that precedes the child that I was, and the woman I am today. There was a family in Mexico to whom I was tied briefly as a child. When I remember them at all, I split open on sharp unexpected loss. Times past, times present, time slips.

Mommy wants me to play with the girl in the tiny casa hidden behind the bushes across from the Monte Mar. I don't want to go there. The girl can't play. She can only lie in bed. She won't look at me. Her eyes are angry. Mommy makes me go there every day. The girl's momma is friendly. She has dark hair and smiles big. We talk with our hands. Sometimes I help with the broom on their dirt floor and throw water from a pan out the door. Our words are too different, but sometimes we're chattery together anyway. Sometimes I lean against the silent girl's bed and tell stories. She ignores me. She can't understand me. Her momma smiles at me anyway.

But then the girl starts to look when I come through the door, and I start to be very glad. I run to the tiny house every day. One day her daddy comes home. I feel him before I see him. His unhappy. His mad. When he comes in the room and sees me he steps away fast through the door, says some hard words to the momma, disappears.

My momma is making us go to school. I don't want to. I miss my kindergarten class where we lived before. I miss starting first grade with my best friend, Petie. Mommy takes us in the car to a bus one morning. She walks us to the steps. I don't want to go. I cry for her. My sister pulls me up the steps onto a cracked seat. The bus drives us away. It leaves us at the school. My older brother and sister go into a room together. None of the rooms have any doors. I can't understand anyone. I'm marched down the length of the long building by myself, with a teacher pulling my hand. We go into the last room on the end. My little brother has disappeared with the bus driver. Why do I have to be here? This is a baby's class. I'm supposed to be in first grade!

The next day, mommy walks us across the street from the Monte Mar and over the empty field. The field is full of broken glass and poop, and we have to hop over it. She shows us where to wait for the bus. I cry and cry to stay with her. She is sad but she walks away. The day after that we cross the dirty field by ourselves. My heart hurts.

Another day, I run out of the door of my classroom and away, because my little brother is never with me in this baby class. He always goes with the bus driver in the morning after we get dropped off. I'm mad. Nobody listens to me. I run out of class to the middle of a cactus patch at the end of the building. I scream and scream. After that my little brother comes to the baby class every day, too. I'm starting to understand some words. The teacher says, "Gato! Gato! Gato!" all the day, hitting a curled tailed cat drawn on the chalkboard with her long stick. Every day, "Gato! gato! gato!" She makes everyone say it. I start to hate that gato.

The girls at school are mean to me when we have recess. They are mostly older. There's a candy stand on the playground. Sometimes they steal my candy. Sometimes they steal my coin. One day the older ones bring a dirty wrinkly old man in baggy pants over to me saying, "Amor, amor, amor," and they laugh. Their faces are flushed and look sneaky, but they make friendly sounds. I want them to like me. I smile. They shove the man at me. His mouth has no teeth and is stinky. He opens his long coat. His peepee waggles out of his pants. I turn away. My face burns. The girls scream with laughter.

I tell my mommy. She doesn't listen. She doesn't listen to anything anymore. She doesn't tell stories or read to us. She is always tight in her face. She never has time. No matter what. She doesn't seem like my mommy.

One day there is a fire at the school. A bell clangs. Everyone rushes out on the playground. Smoke billows from the building next to the school. It smells sticky and sweet. The candy factory is on fire. Everyone is running and screaming. I can't find my sister and brothers. Scared, I spin around and around. Then a little voice inside me says, *Hold still. Hold still.* I hear it. I stop. I let myself go soft. And then I feel it — I know my mommy will find me. I stand in the middle of the rushing and clanging. And then there she is. I see her coming. She yells my name. I run to her.

When we get back to the Monte Mar I go to see the girl and her momma in the tiny casita, like I always do. When I get to the little house it's empty. There is nothing there at all. The room is completely bare. Nothing. I can't breathe. Where have my people gone? I run to the Monte Mar and find my mommy. I tell her. I tell her through my cracked voice. I feel like I might die. She shrugs. She walks away. *Where are they? Where are they?* My voice squeaks. She looks back, shrugs and keeps walking. My tears get crushed into the nightmares, where no one is home anymore.

————

We move away from Mexico. We move back to our old home in Wyoming. When it is time for second grade I have to stay back in first. Petie goes on to second. All my old kindergarten class goes on to second grade. I beg to go, too. But no, no one will let me.

My best friend, Leslie, doesn't go at all. She and her family have moved away again. I miss her. I miss our horse games. She is sick all the time. That is why they move. They move and move. And then they come back. We play horses. And then they move again. She gets to adopt a horse orphan one of the times they come back. I don't like to go to the smelly stable to see it. I don't want a horse. I want to *be* a horse. Then Leslie is gone again. I worry about her being sick and being gone. I miss her.

———

The puppy pile of my brothers, sister and me isn't the same. We play more with other kids now. Out on the prairie beyond our neighborhood we roam and sled and explore. I love to be alone on the prairie, but now I'm afraid to be alone on the prairie.

I feel my small girl self on that high desert prairie, me yet no longer me. She is a subatomic particle that has joined to other particles, a long chain of events in reaction that implode and become something new.

I'm eight or nine years old, crouched in morning sun among sagebrush and prairie grass, spare breeze lilting. Crooning over a mystery held within my steady hands, fingers laced into a cup, my heart beats calm ecstasy. Breath mingles with parched soil and breath of lichens. Song hums through my body, light dazzling into the hold of my cupped hands. A streak of gray darts, butts against sparest of openings between my fingers, tiny legs scrambling.

A taste of stone fills my nostrils with the scorch of yesterday's sun, yet morning lies cool around my bare ankles. Communion with the being cradled in my hands shifts to a changing cadence, our skins opening to further knowledge of the day. Gale force winds will rise on the dry belly of the afternoon, race loose all things untethered for miles beyond morning origins. This change is a given. Bodies within the body of this place are full of wind knowledge; backbite to sun-warmed soil and pungent sage.

Pulse of stone, sage, wind and soil whispers, as my blood throbs tender toward the slight gray being resting on one palm. There's a shift within cupped hands, a settling. And my head rises on an up note, eyes squinting. Poorwill calls. Killdeer answers. Horned toad softens, as meadowlark morning soliloquy ripples, thrilling. Thumb drops to caress the scaly outer fringe of the little ridged body from its head to the half-moon comma of a tail. Slightest sigh rises. Body swaying, I rock back on my heels, universe thrumming.

Tiny claws flex and still me to silence. From one held breath to two, I curb back my love and fascination. Gazing into the cave of my hands, I bend to listen. Soft ululation rifles deep knowing. Tiny black eyes dart from my gaze to the cracks of light slicing between my fingers. Flash of tongue flickers. My sigh floats free. And I know.

This one stays. I glance up. Diffuse morning light illuminates rabbitbrush, greasewood and sage in softest gray to palest jade green. Tumbleweeds lift and settle, rattling. Horned toad hovers on the swells of my closed fingers as I survey light, stone and shadow. Song gathers low in my belly, sweeps dusty soil into rhythm. Pebbles dig into soft skin and bone of my bare knees. Mercy unlaces my fingers as I lower my hands to the tabled surface of a large, flat stone. But my body thrusts upward, cupped hands swinging aloft. Myriad flitting birds, prairie expanse, cloud and sunshine burst on my upward arc, and I spin one complete rapture. Praise beats in my blood.

As quick as my rise, I bend low on a spare singsong whisper. Half shadowed by brush, warm rock receives the weight of my hands unfolding. The small oval form flows out. I crouch as my hands lift away, quick deference to the slight pause of the horned toad's unknown course. One swift dart and the center of the stone lies vacant, ancient, mottled hush. Breeze witches through rabbitbrush. Another flash. At the edge of stone meeting earth there is movement, rapid shimmer in a confusion of root and stem. Stone moves on stone, soil itself sudden brief undulation. And the horned toad is gone.

I hover. Regret pulls against freedom unloosing in my limbs. Traveling sun blinks down. Reaching for a small cardboard box lying on sandy soil, I tuck it beneath one arm, and on the next breath of the day I rise. Arching in a backward crescent I twist then wander toward home, song cooing beneath breath beneath sun beneath the hard, soft body of the world.

───────

On a cold rainy day our mother lets my sister and me bring in a stray calico kitten. We play with it on my bed. A stream of diarrhea squirts out of the kitten onto my bedspread. My sister and I look at each other disgusted and scared. Our mother runs in yelling. She grabs the kitten and runs away down the hall to the back door of our house. Standing at my bedroom window I see the kitten hurl out the back door and hit the wet pavement hard, then limp away mewing in the cold and drizzle. It cries and cries. I watch, crying and crying.

───────

And then I am ten years old. My little cousin wants to learn to roller skate. He wants to so bad. My head hurts, and I feel heavy. But I try to turn the skate key to get the skates to hook on his shoes while he wiggles around. He is afraid I won't get them on. He is afraid I won't teach him. He is afraid we will all skate without him again today. I try and try, but the skates come off every time he lowers his foot. He's crying. I try again. "Mikey, don't cry," I beg.

My mother comes to the door. "Cathi!" She stands behind the screen. I shush my cousin. I turn to look up at her and Mike whimpers. He begs me to hurry. My mother's face is angry.

I flinch at her hard, tight voice. "Leslie died this morning."

"What?" I say. She stands looking at me with her angry eyes. "What?"

"Leslie is dead." She turns and disappears inside the house.

Mikey is crying now, frantic. "Please, please, you promised," his little voice squeals through tears. I drop to my knees and pick up his foot, pick up a skate. I fumble and drop them both. He begs, crying harder. "You promised," his wheezy breath blows past my ear.

"I know, Mikey, I know." I try again. I try the skate key. My hand is shaking. And suddenly I'm on my feet, pushing through the screen door, running for my bedroom, a terrible wail careening out of my mouth. It cuts above the wail of my little cousin out on the porch. I fall on my bed.

My mother comes to the bedroom door. "What's the matter?" she asks.

Sobbing, face buried in my pillow, I manage to stammer, "Leslie."

"Oh." She sits on the bed beside me. "I didn't think you'd care."

I cry myself to sleep. It is the last time I will cry in front of my mother and the last time I will cry out loud for uncountable years. I do not understand that my mother is disappearing. I cannot yet grasp the crisis taking hold in my family. Too young to understand the burden inside the thrill inside the terror that Mexico has become in my life. Too young to know that a child's spirit can be crushed, that mine is crushing inside a vise, inside adventure, inside hope laid bare.

I cherish Mexico. It lives vivid, alive inside me. But Mexico is also circling unease. I can't imagine needing the first touches of guiding spirit I've experienced there. I can't grasp that I've had them. I don't need to yet. In my family the kind still outweighs the mean. I'm too young to imagine what lies ahead.

But Mexico has set patterns in motion and exposed patterns at work a very long time. In my life, Mexico is the beginning of an end that will take ten years to complete. Because time is restless, it curls and simmers beneath the surface of things. The currents my parents kicked up in their border crossings are on the move, awakened causeways that twitch in the night. They carve their way back to Wyoming, tides on the rise. They are the Mexica of lost time.

4

Edge

Maybe my family has always lived on the edge of a precipice.

Lost at the back of the back of the barren beyond, where the untutored teeter on the brink of oblivion and only the natives know how to live. Debris slides down a decaying steep slope, route lost and gone.

The slide that began for my parents in Mexico wavered then settled for a time back in Wyoming. My beautiful mother planted beautiful gardens, nurtured pets, built ponds for wild things we brought home from the prairie, created dozens of messy projects for us on our dining room table, cooked fabulous meals, made most of our clothes, involved herself in politics, put her sizable will behind joy and grace and goodness and plenty. When I was very young, before we moved to Mexico, she spent hours drawing with me when my older sister and brother were in school. On our return from Mexico her resentments grew — for the failures of Mexico, for abandonments, for eruptions in our blanket of security; for our father, who traveled now much of the time — resentments that hovered beneath everything. And within her a cavernous fury began to take hold.

Deeper patterns yet, bigger than all of us, were also finding form. We agree to a lot of things for love. I came to this life for love. I came to the world in love. But there was sorrow as I made my passage through, knowing what I could not hold onto and would soon forget, what would slip from me for unseen years. That the world keeps turning, arching through pathways that look and feel nothing like love. Yet our beloveds are with us always, near and waiting. I loved my mother, my father, my sister and brothers. I chose them for love. But life would test that love again and again.

As my parents fell from love of themselves, so they fell from the love of the world.

At the end of my grade school years, my mother went to work for the first time. Whispered tension spread through our house like ice, crackling the edges of things.

She quit taking us to get groceries with her because we asked for things she couldn't buy. My last year of grade school the school principal refused to let my little brother and me eat lunch in the gym with the bus kids. She didn't think mothers should go to work. She didn't want us eating lunch at school at all. Around this time, my father failed financially.

We moved away from our childhood neighborhood when I started junior high, into a rental house across from the high school. When our television broke, my father said, *Let's not fix it. We'll read in the evenings instead.* For months he read Kipling aloud to us every night. Then he suddenly had the television repaired, though my sister and I begged him not to do it. He laughed and swore he'd keep reading us stories aloud in the evenings, but didn't. After that I quit watching television. I read and did small art projects instead. And I wove a thread between my parents, sister and brothers before bed each night, kissing them one by one, saying, *I love you. I love you.* They hardly noticed in the glare of the TV screen. But I knew. It was the only thing that could save us. I wove that thread again and again.

One night I woke with a start in the dark, snuggled deep in my blankets, then jumped as loud voices cut down the hall from our living room. It was my parents and two others. The voices muffled. I lay electric, rigid on my bed.

Suddenly my mother cried out, upset then sobbing. My father's voice rose over hers.

And another voice sang out, "Hit `er again, Al, hit `er again!"

And then several voices clanged together and everything went spooky silent. I lay taut in my bed then finally crept out to the hall to peek around the corner. Bright lights shone at the far end. Adult voices rumbled and fell. A door closed. I crept back to bed, straining to hear the voice of my mother. There was nothing. I finally fell back to sleep.

When I woke in the morning, the jolting sounds in the night were faded, ghosting away.

I dressed and walked into the kitchen for breakfast. My parents were standing near the stove. My brothers and sister pulled cereal boxes out of a cupboard. I started to smile as mom turned around, a question playing on my lips. It strangled to silence.

My mother's face was covered with thick makeup. She never wore thick makeup. Beneath it dark blue smudges spread around one eye and across the side of her face. Her haunted look froze us all in our tracks.

"Mom, what —?" I started forward.

She turned, gathering her things to leave for work.

"Look," dad said, "your mother got hysterical last night. I had to slap her to bring her to her senses. She's ok."

We all scattered out of the house. Wearing snow boots, carrying shoes balanced on top of my books, I lost one of my brand new penny loafers on the way to school. They were the nicest shoes my father had ever bought me. I never found it, hard as I tried.

That lost shoe connected to a growing litany of mixed messages, creating a whirlwind of bewilderment. I couldn't tell for sure who anyone was anymore. No one ever spoke again of that violent episode between my parents. My mother's bruises healed in a tense place inside of me. Her humiliation changed faces. New masks were donned. Then my sister tackled me during a particularly twitchy argument and split my head open, blood everywhere. I had to get stitches. I had just started my periods and they seemed endless, my parents concerned that the injury was causing problems. Mortified by everything, all the blood seemed familial.

Surface and substrate contorted, tectonic plates on the rise.

I felt like we were all dodging unnamed bullets zinging along the margins of our lives. Our father upped the ante by baiting us at meals around the dinner table. My mother lost patience with his antics more often. The rippling effects of our Mesoamerican foray were coiling tighter. The dark hand had a stranglehold on my family by now.

Yet we were oblivious. And time twisted again. Just when I would have been able to walk across the street for high school we moved to a newer, much nicer house an hour walk away. The drudgery of the long walk home from school pounded the changing course of our lives further into substrate. My parents seemed happier. I disappeared into my own changing life.

But there were always arguments with our father around the dinner table, and they took on a different hue. Hot debates between my sister and him left me scrambled — it was hard to keep up, how could they have so many opinions, where did they get them? I just wished they'd stop.

One night, dad went off on a bigoted spin, forbidding our friendships with black kids at school. I rose from the table furious and lucid, to beat back his arguments, fast and sharp. My father had finally hit on something that mattered to me, at a depth that left me breathless. For once I knew exactly where I stood. Everyone gaped as I challenged every point dad made. As I was leaving the room, too angry to finish my meal, our parents looked each other in the eye and bemoaned their great failure to plant prejudiced views in their children, wondering out loud how this could have happened. The shock I felt was as great as their own — that they had such intentions and that their intentions had missed us was relief beyond words. I wasn't sure what was more stunning, the full admission of their hidden racism, or their common alliance in the face of it.

This hit the raw edge of an ancient secret. First marker, that moment with my father, and another current began to rise. Its depths laced through fragile old history. I had no grasp yet of what this meant at a conscious level. But the blunt exchange with my father had pressed something to the forefront that I cared radically about: bigotry based on the color of skin.

At the threshold of turning seventeen, in the oblivion that was my late teens, I didn't really see the poisonous years of my parents' lives together nor could I parse these new revelations into whole cloth. The uneven ground of most of my conscious childhood seemed normal to me. I assumed I was secure. Were my siblings as blind as me? I can't say. I see now that we'd each been living separate endurance strategies for so long that denial was an affliction. At the end of my sixteenth year I'd never considered that there might be an end to us, not to my family. Whatever change lay ahead, it lay in our natural and individual paths out of the house, my siblings and me. For ten years after our return from Mexico a delicate equilibrium held. And then the scales tipped, shredding our lives in the unhinged aftermath of a moment.

Christmas night 1968 burst into red-hot flames belching chaos. Our father hurled coffee mugs, a gift that morning from our mother, against the brick fireplace by evening, and our parents took each other apart. Desperate and against my father's raging orders, I called our grandmother. My sister and I were terrified to leave the room for fear of what they'd do to each other. When our grandmother walked through the door with our uncle, he forced our parents apart then gathered us all in the living room.

"You two have done enough damage," harsh and cold he skinned our parents every time they tried to open their mouths with another barbed jab. "It's up to the kids now. They can choose who they want to live with."

The weight of his words was crippling.

Choose? What — between our parents? What was he talking about? I trembled as we stood facing them.

"Their mother won't be able to do it!" dad snarled. "She won't be able to keep it together."

What was he talking about? Our mother was the one who had always been there. Our father was half-vacancy, coming and going, rarely involved except for provoked arguments at the dinner table. *Choose?* I couldn't stand to look at my parents. Of course I would choose our mother.

Her face was twisted, a bitter crazed light in her eyes.

It would take a long, long time for me to digest my mother's expression. I looked to my siblings. No one spoke.

I wanted to sink through the floor and disappear. In a strained voice, I finally blurted, "Mother!" and shuddered. Then turned, the words like razors beneath my skin, "Dad, you're hardly ever here. Mom's the one who always is." My siblings' murmurs turned to dull haze around me as their choices echoed mine.

From the worthless sorry horror, the shambles of it all, there was little to nothing left to hold onto.

Not long after that Christmas unraveling, my family pulled further apart. My brother Tom was headed for Viet Nam. He'd decided against fleeing over the border into Canada, though we'd talked it over dozens of times. I wanted him to go, to be safe there. But in an unexpected shift he volunteered for the draft. Why wait for his number to come up, he reasoned, the inevitable fact of it skewed his every waking hour. He told me before he told anyone else. Panicked, I couldn't get him to change his mind.

By the time he astounded everyone with this news, the die was already cast. My older sister, home for the holidays when all the chaos hit, had gone back to college. So they both avoided the battleground that became a daily fling of heavy artillery and uncertain maneuvers that checkered and sank the last weeks of our parents' time under the same roof. It was left to my younger brother and me to endure the up close and personal of all the malice and change. We juggled the agony together, wondering uncertain but hopeful how things might arc to the good. Mostly we trembled in our boots.

And so my family came undone.

The split was finally complete. Our father moved out. Our mother seemed slurred, blurred most of the time. I was trying to keep up with my own life when I realized how much she was drinking, how heavily she'd been drinking for quite some time, how much it had become a way of life. The desperate calls I made to my grandmother on the days and nights of our mother's sodden disarray were endless and wearing. Grandma always came — if I called. The confused part of my brain kept trying to make sense of the rat poison that our mother's party-girl transformation deposited into the bloodstream of our days, and then to simply survive it. This was not new to the aftermath of the divorce, but it escalated. Loathing turned to humiliation-by-association. It was far worse once we became a lonesome threesome. Around the corner here, down the hallway there, one could never tell what might spring out or be lying in a soggy heap.

One morning, my mother begged me from her bed in the throes of a particularly bad hangover, never *ever* to leave her. This clung to me like a ball and chain.

"Tell me you love me. Tell me. Tell me again," she said. Her words choked me, transfixed.

Bewilderment spun any semblance of calm into a muddy, wrung-out mess. Oh how we needed calm, a resting point. But calm never came. What I really wanted was to bolt. I was a solid seventeen by then. A permanent accessory, that ball and chain. It dragged with me everywhere, fueled by a pounding need. Run and just keep running. Somewhere, just about anywhere.

I could see no way to pull my mother free, and there seemed no way clear for myself.

I staggered through the days in growing confusion, violated by my mother's swinging miasma. Where had this woman come from? My younger brother was rarely around, half relief and half concern. I wanted to keep him as free from our mother's chaos as I could. Why couldn't I help her? The impossible struggle to tell my mother I loved her in the midst of her gruesome downswings was like a garrote brought tight around my throat. Who was this woman? I didn't know her. I didn't know her at all.

One day she got a phone call from one of her newfound friends and rushed out of the house. Alarm shot through me. I followed and asked where she was going. She turned and looked so disturbed that I asked if I should go with her. A strange look came over her face. With a cold, hard stare she suddenly snapped, "Sure! Come on!"

We drove to the house of another friend a few blocks away. The front door was standing open. We walked in. On the carpet lay a little dog, turds trailing behind. A sickening smell wafted through the rooms.

"Suicide," my mother said, turning to me. "Hose from his car to the house."

I gagged, reaching out to comfort her. She walked away down a hall to a bedroom. I stayed where I was. When she came out she finished talking to other people who had begun streaming through the house, then we drove home, my hand on her arm. She barely noticed.

"Yeah. Makes sense to me," she mused with a knowing smile, pulling her arm away.

My mind circled around the implications. What had happened to that man? What was happening to my mother?

———

The violence of my parents' unhappiness had swallowed them whole, my brother and I caught in a whorl of unfathomable forces, clueless to how far it could go. All our mother's dreams and ambitions, the artist she longed to be, the beauty and love that once filled our home were funneling down the long necks of glass bottles, regurgitated in a bottomless pit of skewed dreams, our father slipping further out of sight.

5

Sock Hop

The violence that had found my parents and circled around us began to move in closer.

Time surged ahead. One Saturday night I went to a high school sock hop to listen to Cherry Lace, a favored local band. It was a beginning of sorts for me. A taste of what one would generally call a future. The kind we all took for granted, revolving with sparkle and promise. Even then. Even by then. I certainly still did. Feel that. A future with a golden kind of feel, maybe even splendor and glory in some greater or lesser mix — a future that was, well, interesting. And it was there, all right. A future. It just wouldn't resemble what I had in mind.

That evening at the dance things were simple. The music was good. The crowd was dense. I needed to use the restroom. So did a friend. We went in. As I was finishing up in my stall I heard a flurry of voices, my friend Cindy's included, then flinched to an unmistakable thud, someone hitting the floor. Outside the flimsy door was the bleat of Cindy's voice, in pain. I wasn't a tough girl. I didn't know anything about this kind of scene. Shy, uncertain, wanting to avoid whatever was out there, I forced myself to shoot back the little bolt and step warily out of the stall.

And there was Cindy, lying at the feet of three sniggering girls. Bleeding. Whatever it was that kicked in, whatever it is that kicks in every time I'm caught in tight quarters, took hold and kicked in then. I walked over and pulled Cindy up off the floor. Half-carrying her to the row of white porcelain sinks lining one wall, I started to rinse blood and wash fear from the startling shock of her face. The three girls who'd done the damage stayed close at my back, hovering, barking, yammering.

Quiet, I talked them down, dried what looked to be serious bruising as I maneuvered Cindy toward the door — the three so wired they talked over each other. On a breath I pushed Cindy out of the bathroom, then turned to face the girls, feeling oddly relaxed.

Tense exchange jumped between us. I'd go so far as to call it respectful. They fired the questions. I answered, keeping my voice even.

"Hey, bitch, what you doin' jumpin' in the middle here?" one girl spat.

"She's my friend. She's hurt. Why'd you hurt her?"

"She's a cunt. That's all." The biggest girl laughed, jeering.

Questions hurled about individuals and groups from our school and other groups around town. The girls almost fell over each other in their zeal.

By instinct I knew what they were about, could spot the land mines strung out inside their far-ranging inquisition and avoid them. They were trying to figure out where my loyalties lay. It wasn't that hard. Move around the obstacles, get out the door soon enough. For maybe five minutes, easy does it.

A shift in tone and it seemed like they might just decide to like me, in an edgy sort of a way. Girls from outside the bathroom gathered then crowded the door, a curious flock like startled gulls. Belligerent questions rose and fell. The threesome played a little humor into the strained atmosphere.

"Hey, ba-bee, how'd ya' get so tall?" the smallest girl prodded.

"Eating my spinach, ya' know," I answered, smooth and quick. I seemed to be holding my own. I knew I was holding my own. Moving targets. Exit any minute on good terms. I didn't think much beyond the dagger of each hurled question.

"Who you spend your weekends with, the whiteys downtown?" the middle girl pressed.

"Mostly with my whitey family, I guess," I shot back.

It would be a long time before I understood the ease I felt with these girls. Subterranean currents were filtering, flowing beneath us, a meandering river that watered long roots.

It was then that a strange thing happened. I was dancing the conga line of their questions, deft and rapid as they came. A sudden shift this time to the names of Hispanic kids who shared the halls at our school. The girls themselves were black. They had pushed me on bikers, pushed me on nerds, pushed me on soshes and the never-ending stratosphere of every other group we might know or name in common.

There was something just under the surface they were trying to get at. I didn't know what it was. I really didn't care. I just knew I wanted to avoid it.

When they came to "spics, what about the spics, how about those stupid spics" all the humor left me. A hot ember-stoked fire shot up through my core. It felt like a claim staked in some unholy war they were recruiting for.

I stared as the fire rose in me. *This was too far.*

Impatient, they turned suddenly vile, "Spics! Spics! You know. Spics!"

Blind rage banked inside me.

"Spics!" the biggest girl spat.

And something snapped. I flung back hot and disparaging — not about spics, no, not about Mexicans, no, not Hispanics. It aimed at the three of them.

"You sick fucking chicks!" Fast. Just like that.

Locked on my face, stunned, they stared. Then wrath broke out, guttural it raked my hairline and all hell cut loose. I went down on the connection of three hard punches. Fists on long arms kept coming, pummeling my body to the floor. There was pain, agonizing pain, but it became distant not long after I hit the floor. I found myself watching from some high corner of the bathroom after the first punch caught me in the face. No fight back. None. Not another word on my part. I just went down. As I watched, the three moved in a knot to kick my prostrate body where it lay curled on the cracked linoleum tile. Six feet swung vicious repetition. There were impact blows. There was my curled form. And not one move on my part to fight, it never occurred to me to strike back. A sudden rifled gasp of warning, and the girls at the door scattered. My three attackers stalked out cursing and laughing. For a moment, there was no one but me. I must have come down off the ceiling. Because now the linoleum was not a view from above, it was a close-in whoozy state.

I heaved up to sit as a voice boomed through the door. The thin, strained face of the building manager churned insults at me through flapping lips. Disheveled and bleeding, I watched his alarm screw up in the doorframe, flinched as he tossed acid vitriol onto the pain etching down my face and limbs.

"You! You! Get out of here. You're a troublemaker! Troublemaker! You could get this place closed down! Get out! Get out!!" he shrieked and disappeared.

Incomprehension turned to magma-hot rage inside of me. *This wasn't my fault!*

Two boys I knew from school hustled through the door, grabbed me by the arms and pulled me to my feet. A known duo, brothers sexy, tough and troublemakers in their own right, they were getting me out of the building. By direction or by choice, they were taking me home. As we cleared the bathroom door and pushed out into the open room, shining glee burned our way from the faces of the three assaulting girls in the midst of their group of friends. They all laughed and pointed. Fireworks exploded in my blood.

"Fucking bitches!" I screamed. The boys dropped my arms and stepped back.

I ran out the front door and down the steps, a mass of girls and their boyfriends at my back. They caught me at the bottom, threw me up against a chain link fence, and an avalanche of fists launched again. I thought I was going to die. Two cops cruised by in a patrol car. Their slow-motion faces chiseled in a forward stare. The scene was a din. They didn't even turn to look. They did nothing at all to end the sorry slaughter. It was the boys with the girls who finally pulled them off me with stark warning.

"Get out of here! This is trouble! Leave her alone. You better run!"

The two boys from the bathroom were by my side in an instant. Grabbing and half carrying me to their car, they poured me in. I listened to them gloat about the battle. At my house they helped me out of the car then disappeared.

My grandmother was at the front door when I got there. Shocked, confused, she tried to make sense of my wired story, the blood, the mess of me. My mother was nowhere to be found, off drinking somewhere for the weekend with a boyfriend. I found out much later that the boyfriend was married, the father of one of my classmates. On this night, though, I didn't wait to find anything out. Leaving my poor grandma standing alone in the pool of yellow porch light, I raced on foot across town for the home of the friend I'd pulled from the beating.

When I got to Cindy's house, adrenaline was wearing down. It seemed like her nose might be broken. Maybe mine, too. She was bruised but seemed otherwise ok. Her mother refused to take her to the hospital. I felt helpless and called my dad.

In the outwash I spent that night at my father's apartment. His girlfriend from California was a nurse and gave me a sedative, even as my father worked me into a kind of tight frenzy over details of the night. The arguments we'd had at the dinner table suddenly boiled down to this: The girls who had hurt me were black. I couldn't see his glee about this. I was too caught up in the injustice of what they'd done. Exhausted, overcharged, I finally said I'd go to the police. We pressed assault and battery charges early the next morning, first thing under my father's thrilled watch.

The charges opened a floodgate of vindictive whiplash. There were ongoing threats and humiliation at school. And there was my mother's fury at being forced to carry forward the weight of the decision made by my father and me. Once the court charges were filed, my father left town. Typical. It would take a long time for me to understand how much he had abandoned us over the years when the going got tough, how much he had abandoned our mother when we were in Mexico. But the fact that my mother was out partying when all this came down, out of reach and care when my grandmother tried to find her, never seemed to cross my mother's mind at all. So continued many recurring disconnects in our lives.

Pathetic. I hadn't been doing anything wrong. I was just at a dance. I stood up for a friend. Even after the agony of court dates and the effort of getting witnesses out of school again and again, my mom was more than willing to throw me to the dogs of easy injustice, rather than see the case through. She wanted me to agree to shared probation, though my "punishment" would be less severe and of shorter duration than the three assaulting girls. I flat out refused. Stalking from the courthouse and out into life with my mother barking at my heels, deep disillusionment with justice in all forms took hold in me then.

But much later, the vivid heat the racial slurs had roused in me — spat out by the girls in the bathroom — would give me pause. It was like the heat I felt the night of the argument with my father at the dinner table. The force of my reactions was immediate each time, fierce and utterly clear. I didn't understand the ways the rage of the girls got tangled up in me. I shudder to think of what would have occurred, if my father had become more involved. But more, this was not a single moment on a seemingly random night. My father and those girls were pieces of a puzzle with a much larger pattern.

Both moments had opened a quick pass of an open gate in time, and knots tangled deeper, strange forces moving in close. Another subliminal marker, this etched to a growing circle of questions into pain so old and sharp I could not touch it — not yet.

Between this and other times lay currents I felt, but could not see or understand. The immediacy of the changes I faced at home took over my attention — and there would be more coming on the heels of it. Ages-old history lay buried under new history layering on, hints of a time and a place that flickered and burned, where the color of skin could make or break you. It was too soon to unwind history's weave, a long time gone. Woven to these strands were other strands, multiple filaments converging. And Mexico tied to them all.

Within the bedlam of overwhelm, my gift had become my burden.

6

Beach

Mexico turns in my thoughts. I'm four years old. Mommy is taking us riding on a beach south of the border. My heart is thumping. Horses! We pull up at a beach and get out of the car.

Horses line up along a rope looking sleepy. A man stands up from the sand and walks to us. I can barely hold still. We all walk to the line of horses. The man looks each of us over. He looks at mommy and starts pointing. Tommy and Colleen get up on different horses. Mommy's helper, Sharon, gets up on a palomino right next to me. My lips start to pucker. When mommy lifts me to the back of the horse behind Sharon, I start to cry. *No. I want my own horse.* But mommy says, "Look you get to ride the best-looking horse they have. A palomino."

Happy, unhappy I wrap my arms around Sharon's waist. Mommy walks away to another horse. The palomino suddenly stands on its back legs to snort and scream. I slide down its big butt then get flicked off and land hard in cactus. I can't breathe. Hands grab and yank me from the cactus. I can't breathe. Mommy's hands circle my back. I can barely breathe.

Over and over her words are breathing and snapping on me. *You have to get back on a horse now, you have to get back on a horse. Don't let this scare you, Cathi. You have to get back on a horse. Don't let this scare you. Don't be afraid. Get back on the horse. Now.*

I nod as soon as I can breathe. Something fierce fills me up like hot flame. I stand and wipe away tears. Cactus pricks are pulled from my jeans.

There's another man on a big black horse that runs around on the sand in front of the pounding ocean. *Caballero*, my mother smiles this word. The caballero and fidgety black horse come in close.

Mommy lifts me to the saddle in front of the man, eyes shining, and beams from the sand below. Brown hands take my shoulders and I look up. Dark eyes sparkle under a brim of straw. Fire. We look each other over. I twitch uneasy, settled face forward. My hands are pressed to a tight fold around the saddle horn. Mommy hurries away to another horse. The black horse begins to move. We are the leaders at the front of the line. I puff up a little. Everyone else falls in behind.

We ride along the beach. It glistens. Waves hiss and roar. A little wind strokes us. Rocky outcrops jut straight up out of the ocean. There are lots of them, tiny mountains under the sea. Seagulls squeal and poop all over them. The sky is blue blue blue white clouds foamy ocean. I sink in the saddle legs dangling, split wide.

The caballero cries out. Sharp spurs clink, kick into the sides of the horse. The black horse leaps. My arms wrench. We lunge across sand. I hold the saddle horn tight. Arms pull and yank and I slide and slip down the side of the horse. A cry catches in my throat. The caballero pulls me back to center. The horse stretches out, and we're flying. Spurs strike into heaving black sides. I wince and cry out.

The horse leaps in a blur of speed. Wind burns to tears. I try to stay up on the slippery stiff saddle, nightmare of changing motion. I slide down. The caballero snatches me back to center.

Faster the horse stretches beneath us, flashes of muscled lightning. The caballero laughs loud, laughs long. Words jumble up in his laughter. Strange words, they echo. I don`t understand them. But then I do understand, I know them. Through fear and pain I know what he's saying.

He laughs harder, harsher, howling, *little one, little one, oh brave little one,* he singsongs across spitting sand. His words spear and illuminate.

My family falls away lost. Good-bye forever, tears streaming.

But anger burns sharp. *Stop!* I cry. *No!* Sobs constrict in my throat. And the caballero lets me go.

For a moment I am the surging and buckling beneath us. Massive. Shining. Fierce. I don't need to hold on. In perfect rhythm with horse, wind and wave we ride on. Forever beach shines before us.

My disappeared family stretches behind, distant on sparkling sand. Face wet, thrill pulling, I feel it. *Lost. We are all lost.*

Hooves come pounding behind. Inside the pounding hooves a voice screams. It is my mother, furious viper. My name blows away on the wind.

———

My mother will give me many things. She will take many things away. Rider and beach, broken moment in time, do I feel guidance then or forewarning?

Foreboding strums in my cells that day. It will quiver a very long time. Pluck and the thrumming began. The strings of my life, what came after Mexico, all unwind to this moment. It was the new beginning — the demarcation. A cusp. All that long time gone a pattern formed when there would be no turning back.

7

Brad

"Tell me about your childhood," the man said in our interview. "What was it like for you when you were young?" His search for participants to attend the first-ever session of a project to begin in Montana in June encompasses me, holding me rapt.

A deep breath, and I name a close-held treasure: "Well, my family lived in Mexico when I was young."

Complexities curl inside me, sparked by my words and a sorrow that has no name. Within that sorrow lays mystery. It causes me to shiver in sunlight where we sit on a bench outside my school.

"Oh," his eyes brighten and I look straight into them, feel his pulse quicken. "You lived in Mexico? What was your favorite thing about Mexico?"

"Freedom," I say without pause, "my favorite thing about living in Mexico was freedom," and a plumb rod shoots straight to my core. I feel how the word freedom becomes exactly what he wants to hear. I know then that I'll be going to the program.

Captured by my own answer, I watch as it captures him.

I want to turn that answer over, see what lies under, inside it. How the sorrow within it has flipped on his face to such joy. Desire for the strange new program rifles the surface between us, and my loaded deck of memories torpedoes back into darkness.

It is summer 1969. Still smarting from the beating and courtroom experiences, unnerved with the changing ground beneath my family's feet, I fly north for an environmental awareness program in Montana.

Grief, guilt and fear over my agonizing five-minute farewell with my older brother in the airport just as I was leaving fuse with my excitement. Home for leave from boot camp, my brother will ship out for Viet Nam in two weeks. I have no idea when I'll see him again. This has made my choice to leave for the program excruciating. But I'm desperate for change, for new possibility. The ache for my brother sinks into overwhelm, as the banshees that are home recede, and my plane flies on.

I'm about to hit a minefield of new thinking that will bowl me over and spit me back out five-plus weeks later, long after my brother has left. The morning after my arrival, hardly knowing the names of my 25-plus new acquaintances, we're all sorted into encounter groups. Sixteen of us split into two groups. Everyone else is staff. In our encounter groups we're directed to confront one another. Relentlessly. I hold so much inside that is frightening and tightly packed, and here I am with people who poke, prod and pry. There are some kids who know how this works. Most don't. We're encouraged to hammer each other past private feelings and ideas, to press with excruciating personal observation and questions, both in the encounter groups and increasingly in our daily lives. This will be a center post of our time together. I'm a deeply private person. There is no privacy. Getting to know you. Encounter groups. I thought I was coming to band geese and do forest growth studies. I've never even heard of encounter groups. As an inexperienced small-town girl packing a heady weight of confusion already, I'm staggered. What horror is this? Ambivalence is frowned upon. Several of the kids are as hip as they come, from Berkeley and other parts of California. Begin the unlacing.

Almost from the beginning I fall completely and deeply in love for the first time. I hardly know it in the spinning pace of our days. He is an Indian boy, Brad, from one of the Montana reservations, the last of his family, all the rest killed in a single-car accident the year before. The day we meet in the midst of the wildly turning new group at the moment of my arrival, he gathers my hands into his, looks directly into my eyes and fully unnerves me. This may be the first time I've ever felt completely seen. As the weeks play out and in a constant tailspin, I balance the heat of new attraction and the opening of my heart for the first time beside currents of unending disturbance, novelty and provocation. Vague and threatening realities wait for me at home. Alongside this I carry deep fear for my older brother, who is courting Viet Nam. I rarely mention these things to anyone. The rest is what it is, its own kind of unnerving. New love. New everything.

The frightening ugliness of the beating a few months before is oddly heightened then left hanging within this powerful new prism and its overwhelming lens. In our first encounter groups, one young black woman from California looks a remarkable duplicate to one of the girls who beat me so badly. My first sensation, when I sit next to her in our circle on the floor, is of fists flying into my face — unsettling at best, worse as I describe her effects on me and why. She becomes one of my closest friends in the coming weeks.

Adapting to the constant onslaught of newness and strangeness, being stripped bare of natural boundaries and defenses, navigating the trepidation and excitement of everything coming at us in an avalanche of the unexpected almost daily, life is a writhing, living serpent of transformation. And then there is this boy-man. This beautiful, beautiful boy-man with his huge, flashing white smile and eyes half-hidden half the time by a shock of long, dark, thick hair, I love him. It is as simple as that. And at a level I can't name aloud or even fully know, I believe we are meant for each other.

As a whole we're all from backgrounds as diverse as our numbers. The most unusual is a homeless street kid from New York. On the other end is a preppy kid from a wealthy eastern family. One other girl from my home-town and then we're everything in between: black, white, reservation kids, small-town kids, rural kids, city kids, middleclass kids, upper middle class, wealthy and poor. It's the late sixties and the "environmental" is to be self-motivated discovery, a cabin with biology lab, tools and a photographic dark room, as well as several acres of untamed land and a pond. We are smack in the middle of wild country in an extremely conservative neck of the woods. Group time ranges past encountering one another with fervent vigor, from which I never stop flinching, to food and resource awareness; environmental issues discussion and action plans; morality lessons per our individual decisions and in regard to responsibility for the group; time management; live trapping; and wilderness backpacking with several kids who know little to nothing about anything outside urban life. We confront the Missoula Hoerner-Waldorf paper pulp mill leadership on everything from their abysmal track record on air quality and acid rain to employee management practices. And in time our very open coed living in a great log bunkhouse where there are no doors on the bathroom stalls, the showers are completely open and undivided and everyone, female and male, sleeps together in one big open room, layer and condense into a single long road trip west.

We drive to Portland, where we interview alcoholics and drug addicts on skid row. From there we travel on to sensitivity training in Seattle, which breaks down our natural boundaries further and often feels as much like massive group-gropes as anything else. We're introduced to a young man who grew up in all-black neighborhoods, though he's white. Some of us talk civil rights in private homes with him and at a couple of rallies, riveting and deeply moving experiences for me. I want more of it. All the deep aversion to the contradictory bigotry of my father begins to find first handholds, new possibility.

Our adult leaders peel away here and there when the process they put us through becomes too emotionally tough for them. The psychologist counselor from New York, Penny, leaves the program early when her own "buttons" get pushed too far. For me the experiences are startling. Disturbing. Shocking. And they are also dazzling. I will carry much that I learn through the endless summer weeks out into the world with ardor and passionate intent.

When the parting comes for us all at the close of the program, to be thrown back changed into the worlds from which we've come, Brad grasps and holds my hands between his, much as he did the first day we met. And this time tender knowledge looks deep into my eyes and gives me his farewell. Reserved and blushing I hang on wordless, bookend to our first meeting.

That final lingering separation haunts me. I go home scared and elated, made new, a heady mix. Though Brad stays on in Montana, he travels home with me in my heart. I'm transfixed between making plans for some indistinct future with him, having no idea how to go about it, and a weighty overwhelm that clings to every plan, every letter composed in my mind, every thought turned his way. Somewhere a ghost I can neither name nor see disturbs at the edges of everything. Unflinching within this mix remains certainty. I believe we are meant for each other.

My mother and younger brother have moved to a different house in my absence. Though it's disorienting, I feel relieved. The appalling change is done. We pick up with a life we can maybe make the best of. Things seem ok, and entirely more interesting post-Montana. My mother is furious with unfolding stories of my time there, so I move between keeping them to myself and throwing out selective bits here and there. At last an edgy truce takes hold between us.

We begin to talk about our life as a threesome. Under the unspoken influences of my Montana experience, we make agreements on how to meet one another's needs and expectations, work on a plan for shared responsibility. Mom lays out her ideas about how much independence we should have, and we negotiate on hours when we have to be home, on chores around the house and how we can each contribute to keep things running smoothly. For the first time we all feel like friends working together to make life better. She goes out less for a while. I feel her sorrow and loneliness in a palpable way. Once, on the way out the door to spend an evening with friends, I ask her if she wants to come with me. For a tense moment I think she'll accept, grab her jacket and follow me out the door. But she doesn't. I feel perplexed relief.

One morning a few weeks after leaving the Falls Creek Project in Montana, our mother at work and me grinning as I watch my younger brother's best friend, Jim, struggle through the last giant pancake of an all-you-can-eat breakfast, the telephone rings. It's Jake, an area rancher on the Board of the Falls Creek Project. Feeling nervy, happy and fine I joke Jake past first greetings. He slips quickly to the purpose of his call. In flat, indifferent tones he gives me his news. Brad is dead. Hit and killed by a night driver, on the side of a Montana highway, hitchhiking home from the program.

As the news hits full steam, I collapse against a wall, gasping into devastation that expands from every direction. Hard to grasp the finite edges of what Jake is still saying, one casual statement falls into my reeling brain. The news is three weeks old — and past. Jake hasn't had time to call. This indecent single fact takes me down in a plummet I can't stop. He seems puzzled by the stark silence punctuated with an occasional choke from my end of the line. No words. No words can claw out of the opening chasm. It is implosion that ricochets off Jake's indifferent, "I didn't think you'd care," that takes me out in complete annihilation.

The phone misses its cradle on a last agonized swing. Flinging myself through the door of my bedroom, I somehow make it to my bed. My brother and his friend stand in pale fright at the doorway. When I finally choke out what's happened, I swear my brother to secrecy. He must not, must not, tell our mother. I feel certain I'm dying. And I am. As the first cudgel of bewildered, bawling agony passes, one thought finally spears through: I have to get to the house of my friend from the program, six blocks away. Before Jake's second call can reach her. In case a snippet of conscience moves him to try. Jake's calloused delivery burns blistering at the edges of lacerations so great they'll bleed on for the rest of my life as I know it. I don't know that fragments of myself, shattered on impact, are spinning off into the ethers. But then I wouldn't have cared.

I can't know that in time I will find Brad, or that he'll find me. Dreams at first, but later there will be more. It will be a long, long time before anything like happiness or well-being returns to me. I manage a face to wear in the presence of adult duplicity. The pain, the loss, the degradation of Jake's thoughtlessness — the emotional separation I feel from my mother — all create a no man's land with a tiniest inlet. From that hidden place I come and go. As pain goes deep, then deeper, in hiding and isolation, Brad lost and gone, I too in some way go missing. In that strange lost place my heart quavers. I begin to lose sight of the light. Along a seismographic undertow I journey now, alone through darkest dark.

8

Bathtub

My mother begins to slip, she begins to slide. Soon after Brad's death, the plummet at home starts in earnest, disarray into rapid descent.

One night she comes home near-crawling toward a long soak in the bathtub, a nightmare of endless proportion. Water runs full blast, pounding from the faucet behind the closed bathroom door. I sit on the edge of my bed, not ten feet away, twitching with anticipation, listening for the water to turn from blast to trickle to drip to silence on the other side of that door. And when it doesn't, it doesn't, I press against the door going into slow panic, calling crying then yelling the name of the person who's supposed to come, always come when you need her.

"Mom! MOM! *PLEASE, MOM!*" But there is nothing but silence, beneath the pound of the running water.

I force the door. It jams less than two inches in. Terrified I slam it again. Desperate to reach her in time, needing to reach her in time, I slam and slam that door.

But it is my mother's head the door slams against. She is not in the bathtub at all. Passed out on the floor behind the door her smudged cries at last halt me cold. "Stop it, stop it, you're hurting me!"

Sobs choke horror as I stutter and gasp, "Are you ok, ok?" Fear and relief slice against my pressing need to get her out in time.

Out in time for what? I never know exactly. Chaos vibrates on the close edge of everything. I back to the edge of my bed and stare at the firmly closed door. My mother's wordless voice smears behind it, hazed pain to anger and back.

I cry out, "Turn off the water, Mom. Turn off the water!" And the water slowly slops to a standstill. Time slips and moves along.

The between times begin then. Maybe two months pass, maybe less. But she begins to be more present, clearer in herself. The echo of my father's splintering mugs against brick push somewhere to the back of our days, festering in dark recess. Water drips into the cracks of unanswered questions and damns all assumptions. Needing only one half-credit to graduate from high school, I gird courage into action with a request for early release, so I can attend the local community college. The high school principal doesn't even consider. He turns me down flat, with a smirk. (I wonder now what might have transpired, if he had used some imagination. Maybe he just didn't care.) My parents' restless fury is a long cataleptic spiral in my blood by then. I resent the principal's callow attitude, the chafing confinement it means. All the narrow thinking surrounding me curdles hope to a hard seed. Held to those simpering school halls, I'm filled with contempt. Boredom caps the rest. I vow to do no more than gain the single half-credit I need to graduate from high school. Let the rest fall where it may.

There's something pressing I need to get on with. If no one will help me do it, fuck `em, I'll just turn my back and walk.

———

Strong memory bends and wavers. Time slides in and out of itself.

I'm a child, very young. I wake in the night to stillness. It's before the nightmare phantoms begin. Before fear gnashes along all borders. My awakeness is different from that. The house lies silent around me. Darkness floats textural and restless. Inside darkness winds a long string of feeling. It moves through our hallway. It reaches my room. Comes to rest on my body. Inside the feeling, fear tangles. It does not belong to me. Agitation permeates the house. It runs loose then returns to my awakeness. There it pauses. The feeling cowers before its fear. Grain of the darkness is palpable. I feel sorrow, anguish for the feeling. I trace it back to my mother. The feeling connects to her heart. This feeling of fear is her loneliness. Inside it stacks fear upon fear. Another. And another. And another. The feeling ties a long thread. The line of its trace is to the future. There it makes itself fact. The thread moves on to old age. It settles, far, far away in the years ahead. Becomes a shape. Makes a claiming. Owns my mother.

A landslide begins in earnest.

9

Halloween

Was it my mother's fear that fed the demons that drove her, fear of aloneness, of loneliness born of a lonely childhood? Was it Mexico?

Life makes long chains of staggered events, and history fills with knowledge.

My mother's keys lay within the knots of her history, tangled inside her, unresolved. All she needed to know, to become decent out of indecency, was tied up in those knots. Stopping to listen, to unravel the tangle, that's where my mother's peace lay — and within that lay our redemption. But to the day she died, forgiveness eluded my mother. At the end, though, I believe she was able to receive it.

In 1970 my mother was far, far from such thought. Forgiveness was not on her calendar. It held no weight in her mind. My mother did not pause to look back, not long enough. And out of the past, her hauntings bore down. From the fruit of those hauntings, our fate was born.

In its bloom, I was caught unaware.

It seemed like violence was emerging out of nowhere, bleeding into the fabric of my life. Why was this happening? All I could do was try to stay ahead of it and claim a life for myself.

In the fall my mother remarried for the first time. It was on Halloween, and the heart of the world skipped a beat. She had known the man, a tool pusher on a local oil rig, for a total of thirty days. My younger brother and I learned all of this after the fact. We hardly knew him before the fact. He was nothing like our father, but then he was nothing like anything we had ever seen to that point. Then my cat died of a malady I should have been able to treat. But in the numb spiraling that was my reality by then, I somehow screwed up. From this point on, our mother's downward corkscrew escalated, pulling my brother and me with her.

Her new man was beyond scary. Carl. He was younger than our mom by a couple of years. When he smiled, something uncanny glinted behind his eyes. He was taut and wiry, seemed always on the verge of a leap or threat. He started out smooth talking us all, said he understood the role of a mother with her kids and had no intention of interfering. Soon after they married, that personal philosophy went out the window quick. He had an opinion on everything and did not like his opinions treated as anything but ironclad rule. Respect, he called it. Disrespect is how we experienced him with each passing day. A kind of electric energy seemed always about to erupt from under his skin. Just being in his presence made me edgy. This grew to a kind of odd anticipation, a sharp sense of disaster that as yet had no outward form. But it was present, hinting and pushing through every room all the time. On the surface I stayed light, moved light, skirted the edge of my mother's schoolgirl crush and the overt sexual infatuation that took over our house. It was creepy to be around. There were always coy notes left on mirrors and cabinet doors, sticky with innuendo. Carl smiled a lot, but it didn't exactly feel friendly, more like a predator's waiting game.

At Thanksgiving they told us we wouldn't be spending the holiday as we always had, with relatives and family. Instead, he was inviting his drill crew, their wives and girlfriends for dinner. My brother and I were shocked, disappointed and uneasy. There was less and less solid ground for us to stand on. Our opinions held no weight whatsoever. When his friends arrived for the holiday, everyone gathered in the abysmal setting of our basement where it was dark, close and hardly festive. A couple of ugly tables had been pulled together and though mom had made an effort at holiday cheer, it was so unlike our normal celebrations that everything felt small, cheap, cramped and repulsive by comparison. There was nothing about the table, the people, the mood or even the meal that felt remotely like Thanksgiving. My brother and I were trapped in some surreal reality that was burgeoning out of the ethers, taking over our lives.

All the guests, eight of them, arrived with bottles of hard liquor and descended into the basement. Everyone started pouring stiff drinks, gawking at us, laughing amongst themselves along one side of the room. There was little in the form of actual conversation and little attempt to it. Carl went off in sporadic intervals of egotistical babble, meaningless self-promoting tirades, swaggering where he stood. Mom ran up and down the steep narrow stairway from basement to kitchen, nervously bringing food to the table, spewing odd niceties at the group that were awkward at best. Then she'd disappear again. She wouldn't let me help her. I had never seen her like this before. My mother had immense natural grace and social skills. They were nonexistent that day. Feet shuffled. Ice cubes clinked. Nervous titters sparked here and there. Up and down the stairs mom ran. I finally broke out of an immobile trance, distressed and confused. I was desperate to break out of the room, breathe fresh air. I started up the stairs after my mother. But at a bark from her new husband, mom shooed me back down into the gloom, the alarming near-silence of our awkward guests. My brother was doing his best to break the ice but it seemed unyielding. The next time mom scurried back down to place a dish on the table, Carl pulled her suddenly to his side. She giggled. Then he grabbed me, pulled me down hard on his lap with one arm cinched around my waist and leered at the men across the room. They leered back at him.

"Whaddaya think of my new stepdaughter? She's a keeper, huh?" his oily voice cooed, slippery hands holding me fast.

Shock and humiliation ran acid through my veins. My mother turned away, nearly running back up the stairs and leaving me there on Carl's lap, skin crawling. How could she? Confusion consumed me. My brother took a step forward, face contorted and nearly hissing. The other men clustered a few feet away, smirked and laughed low and knowing. The women mostly turned their faces away, but a couple took drags on their cigarettes, eyes hard on my face. I thought I'd vomit. I stood up, knees almost buckling and left the room to follow my mom upstairs. *This man was not my stepfather! He was no relation to me at all!* Revulsion twisted as I climbed the steps. Mom shoved a dish into my hands and pushed me back down the stairwell, following close on my heels. The rest of the evening was a nauseous blur.

From that moment forward, Carl rocketed hot to cold, spiky and unpredictable hour to hour, day to day and grew worse week to week, month to month. He whined to our mother like a child, and she forever placated him. With us he was clipped, easily insulted and quicker to anger. Creepy as they were, his smiles became less frequent, replaced by black moods. A sense of violence emanated from him and felt like it was overtaking the house. I couldn't have named it then, but I was like a wild animal, listening for the pounce that would come out of nowhere any moment. Ready to leap, run, I had no idea where.

Our mother worked full time and was rarely home until after 5:30, though a couple of times I was surprised to find her at the house, looking strange and half embarrassed when I arrived home after school. Yet that was rare. She started asking me to call and check in with her whenever I got home.

Something dark was overtaking us all.

The sense of threat in the house got so bad that by the time I got home after school each day, I would be shaking uncontrollably. I'd grasp the door handle, uncertain if Carl was inside or not — and if he was, I wondered where exactly. A nerve-wracking search never led to any sense of safety, never any way to relax. If he was there, locating him helped but only slightly. If he wasn't I couldn't trust it or be sure when he'd turn up. Often enough, I simply dumped my books inside the door and left faster than I arrived. My brother was rarely at the house until evenings when mom came home. On weekends, when mom and Carl were out on the town, my brother and I could settle in for a while. But when they returned, they were invariably drunk and that brought new twists into play. It became bitingly clear that being female would always be a pawn in the game of Carl's lethal intentions and, being male, my brother a minute away from fists and other confusions that seemed ready to punch, rip or tear out of Carl any moment. The man had not yet hurt us physically, beyond constant threats and mockery, but the feeling of violence was there, always there, sulking and shirking, hissing at every turn. For me, I lived with the feeling that his pant fly was unzipped, at the ready, every minute, all the time.

I managed to figure out ways to circumvent him, mostly. But my brother never really did. My brother was kind, generous, smart and incredibly funny. He had some of the best natural social skills I'd ever seen. He loved people. But he could barely manage to interact reasonably with Carl, easily hooked by Carl's endless provocations. So he stayed away. A lot. I avoided being alone in the house and beyond that had an instinct for the man's ways and just what his snapping point was. I thought that my relative success with this was mine alone. But later, as I looked back, I could see that there may have been something else, some warning or threat laid down to Carl by my mother. But that's a big maybe. Many years later she would tell me that she thought he had probably raped me at some point. In that moment, I sat speechless — aghast and staring at my mother's mild candor and its implications, withering in the shock of her raw transparency. Disarray would rise again, so long after the fact, on the spin of my mother's bland confessions.

But whatever it was that kept things checked, it did not hold over time. Everything began to fray. Malice was the expanding undercurrent of our every day, danger the ricochet tone. We were also young. We were sometimes righteous and full of ourselves. We had no reference for this kind of man. In the dance of power, we sometimes provoked, through the sheer innocence of behaving normally. And so peril ululated. It ululated anyway, no matter what. In a final frightful betrayal, swift and dreadful by our mother, their threats joined to turn violent. They came home dragging drunk one afternoon and ordered us to sit down for a family conference.

"We have a plan." Carl said, weaving, slurring and holding hands with our mother where they sat in front of us, a sloppy smirk on his face. "We see that you've got lots of problems, young man, and you're just naturally headed for trouble. We're gonna clip that in the bud, just take care of it now. We're gonna send you to the Rawlins State Boys Penitentiary. That'll take care of it, quick."

My brother and I stared, looked at each other, and for a moment the ludicrousness seemed almost laughable.

"What are you talking about?" my brother asked with a broken smile. "You can't be serious. Rawlins isn't a boarding school. And I haven't been in any trouble to warrant sending me there."

"This is nuts!" I added in disbelief. "You can't do that! It isn't even legal!"

"Oh, yes, we can," Carl drawled, voice rising. "I've looked into it. You're headed for trouble, it's clear, and we're going to take care of it now, before it gets out of hand!"

"You can't do this, you can't!" I could barely catch my breath. "Mom, he hasn't done anything wrong, what are you thinking?"

She looked at us with the most brazen hateful expression I have ever seen. And there it was, that look I'd seen on her face, the Christmas night our parents came undone; that look that had said everything. She didn't want us then. She didn't want us now. She didn't want us at all. She looked at Carl, her mouth transforming into a lopsided almost drooling grin. "Well, yes, we can. It's time. It's the right thing," and she wiggled closer to him. "You'll see. It'll work out. We'll come visit you. It'll set things straight."

"Oh, my god," my brother's voice broke, "you're serious. You can't be serious."

Staggered, we stared at them. This couldn't be happening. We struggled to find a reasonable tone. Carl snapped. "This is not up for discussion. This is exactly what we're going to do!" he bellowed.

"You're out of your mind, mom. How can you even think of going along with this?" I shot back.

My brother's voice rose, bleak pleas giving way to anger. "You're crazy. I'll call dad! He'll never let this happen!"

Carl leapt from the couch. Mother stumbled to her feet. Bedlam unleashed. I faced mom off as I heard my brother yell. "You sorry son of a bitch. Who do you think you are? You can't get away with this!" Carl was in his face, the two of them screaming at one another. The wiry muscled form of Carl leaned into my brother, terrifying.

"Mom! What's wrong with you? We're your kids!" I cried out.

"My kids? My kids? You're all just a bunch of useless trash, every one of you!"

My heart split into a thousand needles. Before she could take another verbal swing at any one of us, I broke in, yelling in her face, backing into the kitchen as she stalked me with belligerent dagger-like focus.

"You don't know what you're saying, mom! You're wrong, and you know it!"

But she was spewing profanities, verbally taking her children apart one by one. "You stupid girl! You goddamned stupid ignorant girl!" she jeered.

I screamed at her, "Wake up! Get some sense! This is insane!" The venom in her face yawned, lancing like snakebite.

"You and your brother are losers!" she hissed. "Losers! You can't do anything right! And Tom! Tom's just a worthless no good … "

I blasted in so fast the walls shook. "Don't you dare say one mean thing about Tom! Don't you dare! He's in Viet Nam, for god's sake. He's not even here to defend himself!"

She spat, "Tom! Tom's a … " I slapped her hard across the face. She slapped me back. I turned and ran out the back door, slamming it hard behind me. Glass shattered as I leapt then fell to the driveway.

I turned to see jagged glass shards knifing up from the door frame, and behind them my mother gloated. Her legs were cut and bleeding from the shattered glass of the door. Hate distorted her face with a kind of crazed satisfaction. The hideousness of the violence between us — her venom and betrayal, slapping each other, the blood on my mother's legs — crumpled me into a sobbing ball on the concrete driveway. Silent blank faces of the neighborhood houses gaped around me, spooling a glare of exposure. I curled in on myself, longing to disappear.

Sounds of my brother and Carl inside the house slapped me back to my feet. I ran for the front door.

My younger brother was caught in the midst of a near-brawl. Carl screamed in his face. I somehow pulled him from the savagery, just before blows rained down.

We spent the night walking the streets.

And so, there we were. Lost children.

We had no money and nowhere to go. When we finally returned to the house it was as though nothing had happened. There seemed a temporary truce. Calls to our father were vague. Sometime soon after, I caught my wings and flew. Leaving home was part relief, part terror, but I was fueled by unflinching rage and outlandish optimism — and some searing idea about freedom. This fulfilled my mother's intentions. But I could not get my brother to come with me.

So there I was, flung out on my own into wild abandon.

The stories we tell ourselves to survive, to make sense of an unreasonable world, to cover our tracks, to find a place of calm, to heal, to put ourselves to sleep — these stories drive us. Yet inside our stories are the real stories.

My mother told herself many stories to cover her tracks. I would tell myself many more to survive my history. The heartbreak of Brad, the girls who beat me up, my mother's betrayals, the strange vicious man my mother led into our home, parts of my childhood in Mexico — all became demons of a past that began to drive me. And out of them I wove an internal landscape, stories to keep the demons at bay. These stories would whirl inside me. Whirl and whirl. Until I reached an edge. Once I had stepped back from its endless pitch, I would want to know the truth of my life, my story. Not what I had told myself to survive, but the truth, or as close to it as I could get.

This would be the moment of becoming the seeker. This would become the point of taking up power. By claiming my story, I would claim myself. Only then could the past be complete. Only then would the demons abate.

But that was still a long time ahead.

My mother didn't reach her still point in time. She didn't try to make sense of her stories. She didn't try to take her past apart. Her life was a train wreck that consumed every track in all directions out of our house. As she raced toward destruction, she pushed us off one cliff, leapt off another, and we all plunged.

10

Freedom

Managing through some fluke combination of luck and a friend from high school, I found a basement apartment beneath the home of an elderly woman. On the heels of that, or was it just before, a job came. Kismet.

My flight from home wasn't pretty. But there was a feeling of relief in my forward momentum, a flavor of escape mixed up in the baffling morass of my first muddled independence. Fright and thrill worked as dual engines to get me out of my mother's house in a final flash, propelling me forward. And for a while, it seemed like I was heading somewhere. It seemed like enough.

I didn't understand how broken I was.

Supporting myself was a depressing affair. Work at a dry cleaners, pressing men's shirts on a mangle amidst the steam and vapors of a heavy-drinking, but fairly kind boss. In my survival sprint I couldn't have pulled apart the quagmire of what had led to what, and how I had come to be where I was. I could only ply enough threads of possibility together to make a patchwork cloth, just whole enough to make do. A job in the public eye would have been unbearable. At least this was off the streets, out of sight. I paid my first month's rent and the deposit on my apartment in increments, with the second month and third. My boss must have been desperate to hire me, transparent inside his lecture-like interview. I was attempting to hold up the weight of the world but barely knew it. I think he might have had a clue. The collision of the past was dancing with a luck I was somehow determined to find.

I staggered through the last months of high school, graduating only on the success of earlier years. Caught in the moment, I would not question how I arrived at that crossroads.

The narrow bridge I hovered upon, where one heart might have conceived an opening for another, glints from the past. A simple act of imagination could have changed the course of many things. As it was, I was lucky to grab my diploma from the smoke and ashes of my life and graduate with the rest of my class. Vacuous emptiness had by this time tarnished the shine of normal hopes. In the confusion, I had the heightened sense that the confines any school offered held only endless monotony, unimaginative tracks. I wanted a life that was vibrant, filled with meaning. These complicated feelings drove me to turn down two small scholarships and instead claim a dream of real-life quests, where interesting things actually happened.

About three months into the exorcism that my bewildered new life intended, I was on a fast track to leave the past behind. Ideas about freedom were kicking, bucking and rising to the bit. I met a woman, her two sons and her artist boyfriend at a new community center. I bonded with the little guys over games with pebbles on the sidewalk. I was still half-kid myself. From that beginning, we all became friends. The woman and her boyfriend were older than me by several years. They seemed very hip, savvy to the world and intriguing to me. Though I liked having my own place, I was lost and lonelier than I could have allowed. Within a month of meeting the couple and two kids, I gave up my apartment and moved in with them to live communally. A short time after, I quit my job with a vague idea about travel. The travel idea pulled hard, from a deep place I could barely articulate, let alone attach to any sure thing. My planned bicycle trip through Europe after graduation was a long gone vision. For one, the close friend I hoped to travel with was given luggage instead of a bike from her parents for graduation and got pregnant instead. And then there was the reality from which I'd just extricated my still-inflamed life. But the promise of something wheeled around my imagination with quickening pulse. I didn't have a car, didn't drive and wasn't interested. I bicycled everywhere. This made transportation for any long trip kind of an issue. But I had cash from my job burning a hole in my pocket. I was ready.

In the meantime, I pitched in to help with the kids in our little extended family. I paid for their school supplies and clothes from my savings, whipped together homemade granola and yogurt, read stories, made up games, sang songs at bedtime or any old time and baked bread. Every week I sent a fresh loaf off to my younger brother, who to my great relief had moved to California to live with our dad and finish high school. One time I got the bread into its wrapper and out in the mail, still warm from the oven. It arrived on their doorstep as a fuzzy green growing thing. We both found this hilarious. I continued a penchant for making outrageous clothes, started making cloth toys for the boys, put in a vegetable garden and learned to crochet afghans when we all sat around drinking tea in the evenings to discuss tarot, past lives and the turning of the karmic wheel. The mother, twelve years my senior, drew in other characters much older than myself — poets, writers, artists, philosophers and musicians, who gathered at the tiny rundown house and held court. Wide-eyed, ill at ease, fascinated and trying very hard to be cool, I moved through this atmosphere with uncertainty, feeling I may have struck gold but having no idea how to fully belong. Anywhere.

In truth, I was wobbling on a crumbling edge.

Nineteen and with money holding from my brief work career, four months post-graduation, I got a strong sense with an almost desperate edge to find a new and worthy winter coat. I wanted a down jacket. I knew I needed a down jacket. This knowledge drove me. I had no idea why, or where to find one. My search became a bust.

Too shy to ask for help, too proud to seek out my sister, who would have known but lived far away, I finally gave up searching the local stores and wandered into Sears Roebuck to flip lazily through the racks. In a short time I was standing outside on the corner, a bag tucked under one arm. The bag held a kingfisher blue car coat. Its thin quilted lining was a far cry from the function I sensed I needed but a great stride toward cool that would have to do. The natural tendency to err on the side of fashion seemed lodged in my bones, passed down from my milliner great-grandmother to my handsome silver-streaked grandmother and on through my mother. No less could be said of my paternal feminine line. So with that sassy package tucked under one arm, I walked smack into two people I sort of knew from high school.

I was in a soaring mood by then. It was good to see Cora. She was glad to see me. I hardly knew Will, but we weren't total strangers. Cora began to gush about the plan they'd hatched to hitchhike to San Francisco. *Hitchhike. San Francisco.* I was mesmerized. The Haight. Shades of the Summer of Love. Woodstock. Riffs of Richie Haven. Strains of Joni Mitchell. *If You're Going to San Francisco* wafted off the sidewalk. Spellbound, a colliding echo ran through the center of my brain, a lit-up collage of old dreams, longing and envy. Will was on to describing the fast pace of the trip. There and back in five days, cheap and backpacks filled with whatever they had in the cupboard; visit some of Cora's San Fran friends; get on back home fast. I quivered with exhilaration and desire. Cora was onto this quick. She asked if I wanted to come. Did I! They'd leave in a few days. This slowed Will down some, but I barely caught the change as I rushed to say yes. I mean, think about it. So we all agreed. They'd call soon. We went our separate ways.

Back at the communal house, my friends weren't exactly keen on losing my help for most of a week, though they could see the possibilities. We all knew it was inevitable sometime. I wanted to test my wings on the road. Another invitation, extended by a friend of theirs, had been stewing in our conversations for weeks, but I knew I wouldn't go with the guy. He gave me the creeps. Cora called the next day. I was on with them for sure if I wanted it. I wanted it. Less than one week to blast off.

We took off in Will's car on a late September morning, feeling full of light and promise. We drove to Salt Lake City, spent the night with cousins of Cora's and left the next day for California. Will and Cora's families thought we were driving all the way. My mother barely noticed when I got the urge to call and let her know I was going. We parked Will's car on a side street, in a deserted-looking neighborhood on the western edge of the city. Then we clambered onto the interstate with our thumbs hooked and ready. Nobody knew except my housemates, some four hundred miles away.

By then Cora and I were in fine form. The thrill became hilarity, and madly rhymed poems took wing into nonsensical song, as we stood then frolicked along the roadside. Punctuating wild games of stones skipped across the highway's centerline, we laughed ourselves sick. Will sulked on the shoulder of the road. From the moment we stepped out of his car and into our hitching journey he was obsessed with time and a looming deadline to return to his job. Rides seemed scarce. I was one too many. He couldn't have been more obvious about it. Cora and I were utterly confident and unconcerned. I teased Will, humored him, assuaged his touchy ego in dozens of ways and then finally left him alone. Cora and I laughed and laughed then turned philosophical, debating wide-ranging ideas about life on planet Earth. We danced and smiled and sang along the side of the road, thumbs quick and ready.

Standing at the side of that long highway with destiny smoking, the edge of the Great Salt Lake felt like a mythical gateway to me. My father was a land man, an oil lease broker who traveled incessantly throughout my childhood. Of all the places he spoke of, two seemed woven from the fiber of fable and mystery: the storied Great Salt Lake and Canada, separate and heady imagined landscapes. The mythological breathed all around us in vast expanse that day. Life felt ripe. It was my first taste of presence along those saline Salt Lake margins. The city hung on the edge, a kind of mirage. The bed of the ancient sea was the real thing. It whispered brackish scent and subsoil nature. I'd stepped into inscrutability to which I belonged and from which I had sprung. There was nothing in Will's attitude or the shape of the world along that roadline that could shake me from conviction, from the mysterious cloak of belonging to something I couldn't quite name. I was stepping fully into my own story and I knew it. Words and knowledge do not necessarily link. There was nothing to say. There was everything to be. Daimon.

Cars whizzed by. Will became restless, disconsolate. He raged a little. Cora and I hunkered down for the wait but never lost confidence, steadfast and often giddy. His negative bent on everything grew. We naturally deflected, grew more philosophical, kept to ourselves. And out of the wash of city haze a Cadillac sped past. Slowed down. Pulled over. Backed up. Will sauntered alongside. Solo driver. Open seats. The man rolled down his window. He nodded at Will. The ride was ours. We gathered our packs. Big western hat and fancy suit sat at the wheel. Going to Reno. We piled into the big boat of a car.

The reek of booze was thickening smog, as he gave us one simple instruction. He could get us a long way. We would take turns keeping him awake. Then he applied all of his weight to the gas. We shot off. Past ninety then on over a hundred, I held my breath over the next fifty miles. He kept that pace all the way across Nevada. We kept our end of the deal. At the driver's insistence, I was in the front seat for the first round. I found myself tongue-tied half the time but kept him driving by the rant of his dissatisfactions with my paltry stories. At the first pee break Cora took my place. Will came in third, talking a blue streak.

For his part the driver was a proverbial piece of work. We learned more about quick-draw weddings and divorce in Nevada than I would ever care to know. He left us abruptly on the side of the road at the eastern edge of Reno, where he veered to an exit he decided would be his. We barely got our gear out of his car before he was scorching off in a blaze of vapors. Looking around in relief, free of the hours of inebriated rollercoaster-platitudes, we clustered at a crescent in the middle of a speedway, with cars whipping by and cutting in close, too close. We'd gotten pretty far on the first day. With the tense slow start behind us, we all felt confidence now. Reno looked big and blazing. We cringed in the fast pace of traffic rocketing everywhere no way to cross it, but then our luck came.

A single guy pulled over, signaled us into the back of his pickup and dropped us off on the western edge of the city. From there it was a hay truck piled high with ranch hands, and we toppled in with our gear. They took us some miles west past Reno, leaving us at the edge of a dirt road just off the interstate. As they trundled away, I had the distinct impression we were far too interesting to the ranch hands dangling their legs over the back bumper. A couple of them seemed to be memorizing Cora and me. There wasn't much traffic. It was near dusk. Rides looked slim to impossible and felt like a bad idea. An unshakable conviction drove me to insist that we move away from the drop-off point, as far as possible while we could still see, eat a light supper, no cooking, no lights and seclude ourselves out of sight. We found a spot that seemed obscure, swiped away prints from our trail and not long after dark settled into sleeping bags burrowed among high sage. And sure enough the choice was right, because later we heard a group of men drive up to where we were dropped off, roust around then figure we must be gone. It was an edgy but otherwise uneventful night. The next day was easy. We got as far as Vallejo, California, by afternoon but then were stumped. Fancy new cars flashed by, filled with staring people. No sidewalks. No rides. There we stood.

———

A crossroads had formed by the end of my late teens and all directions were dangerous. By the time I stood along that old freeway, harsh patterns had fully set. The past picked up steam. Threads of old lives were converging, breathing fire beneath the soil of the ordinary.

11

San Francisco

Time filters. It's 1971 and I'm young with my friends, Vallejo at last behind us.

Next to me Cora can barely sit still as the red car drives up a winding road toward her friend Vega's house, perched on the edge of a hillside in a suburb of San Francisco. Will is silent on the opposite side of the car. Vega's younger brother is at the wheel, his friend in the passenger seat. They jive to Frank Zappa. The Great Salt Lake, a vague mutter now behind us, falls back from the living sea I can smell along the western horizon.

I feel shell-shocked, the novelty of our journey buried in a landslide of urban mass, freeways, endless noise and traffic. I long for solitude, quiet. The coughing, choking smother of asphalt coating seeds, soils, stones, roots and history clench in my gut. My long-held dream, to be part of the scene of the Bay Area, falters. Maybe I don't belong here after all. The idea is shattering.

Immersion in the cool groove of this place is sidelined. I feel like a mismatch to this more-than-hip domain. The Haight, the Panhandle, the echo of the radical free, immersion in the easy of street scenes, the Filmore, some scent, maybe, of North Beach — they all shred away. I get it fast, man. These realities are past, already in decay. I wince as they smoke through me.

What's here is something else. There's simple elegance in the upscale design of Vega's house, she and her brother solo, their parents off somewhere for the weekend. We get out of the car to walk inside. I hold back in the entryway, on the outside edge of our milling group. I feel like a hick, shaken to discover how much I don't fit in. Old dreams about what we were moving toward shake out, dog-eared realities, rough in the here and now. My tarnished ideas feel abrupt and bruising, as we all stand and stare.

Cora doesn't notice. A joy bird, she's a tumble of reclaiming old ties. Introductions circle and fall away. The two boys who answered our call for the ride from Vallejo wander around in a meandering hubbub. They speak Zappa but they speak it as natives, first born. My Zappa wrings flat on original ground.

Cora and her old friend, Vega, catch up as fast as they can. I stand frozen to the middle of the room then snap away to a wall of windows. Green, green, green cascades along a steep descending slope. Familiar Zappa lyrics bandy about like popcorn as Vega's stoned brother and his friend giggle, tossing around plans for our single night in the city. We have this night, this one night only. In the morning our trek will reverse, carry us back across Nevada again, to where we began miles and rides and eons ago.

I know this time means everything to Cora. It's why we've come. But I can barely breathe. Something shifts, whispering at the edge of hearing. Unnerved, I turn back to the group to find Vega walking toward me, confident in the easy swirl of her short dress, slim tanned legs, the swing of her straight brunette hair. "Hey, isn't this great, what do you think of the Hills, the Bay, California?" she smiles.

I blink, stammer, "I, uh, I can't stop feeling, uh, what's below all this asphalt." Vega looks stunned, and I gasp at my words as I continue. "The soil feels like it's, it's suffocating. Buried alive beneath all this concrete." The pillage of place and the stink of urban sprawl pour in. Abrupt silence blares as my blunt tirade quivers against basic courtesy. I feel haunted. Why?

I know this place. Beneath all the asphalt and noise. I know it *before*. I know it beyond what exists here now. *How is that possible?*

"Uh, sorry," I stammer. They all stare. Vega stands wide-eyed.

Suddenly the two stoned boys pop forward. They've got a plan, man. Everyone turns. Anxious relief and laughter spill out at their shuck and jive. I flinch, thankful, stand squinting at all of them. It hurts me, this place, being in this place. But seeing the startled eyes of our hostess, I feel another kind of agony. It's the place, not them, that hurts. Trying to decipher one thing from another here is a draining, baffling strain.

Vega's brother smiles through a jazz of nonsensical lingo, twists into glee as it riots and uproots everyone's confusion. "Where d'ya wanna go, man? C'mon! Whaddaya wanna see?"

"The ocean," I'm stunned as my words fly out and flop into the middle of the group. Cora shoots a scathing look my way. I cringe. Vega turns toward me, eyebrows raised, a slight smile.

Cora, testy about the few precious hours ahead, turns away to face the group. Will hangs back, the watchman. I stutter, "S-sorry, sorry, it's just, I used to live near the ocean. I, uh, I've never been back, not since I was a kid in Mexico. Hard to believe." My voice drops low. "It doesn't matter, let's do whatever you want, Cora, this is your time." I shrug and step further away from the group, more confused than ever.

Vega looks sharp at Cora then smiles. Cora ignores her. Ideas fly wild.

And then there's an abrupt circling back. "You know, I'd like that, too," Cora says as she looks at me, smiling. "The ocean, I mean. That'd be great. It doesn't really matter where we go. I just wanna be together, wherever. Let's go into San Francisco, then we can find a beach!"

We look at each other. I nod, "You sure?"

She grins, nods back, ice breaks. Everyone laughs. We dispense without any real effort for dinner. Why waste precious time? Snacks appear out of nowhere, cabinet doors flap, and the fridge becomes a revolving door. Milk cartons and juice jugs pass around in communal inhale. We mill from kitchen counter to front door, spill dancing from the house. I finally feel connected in some loose way as we Zappa to the driveway.

Piling into the small red car, we peel out and down the steep driveway past linking byways that head off in sharp inclines every which way. Thick potions of unfinished sentences and half questions fly through the car, tintinnabulations of a riotous mood. In this crush of newness and mirth we're each overlapping high notes. Images whirl past the windows. Whizz and buzz of insects are a rushing quicksilver that pulses and fades into evening light darkening. Soon we're merging into city traffic.

The two boys laugh all the time now, a kind of rib-clenching stagger of glee, words a stumbling twist and tumble out of stoned delirious minds. We careen through dusk into darkness that flees, out beyond glare of lights and glowing catatonic air. Air so thick I feel like I'm drowning. Somewhere we cross an invisible threshold, leave suburban, enter into full-on urban. Blaring cityscape looms. Artificial, impossible massive buildings condense, jutting up everywhere.

We cruise through and past downtown, into a no-zone — no lights no city no nothing — and then it's dark, full dark. The lights that blast from cityscape behind us don't cut the black intensity. Air takes on a wild scent. Shapes shift and change out beyond the car's flowing motion. Ocean surf roars, pulsing. Suddenly we launch as the car lifts in a running leap off pavement. Some new line is crossed clean, asphalt to open sand. Utter dark. We land, still rolling in a sacrilege of oil and metal, mechanical turnings hard on a beach. Sand grabs tires, and we whiplash to an abrupt stop.

I recoil then nearly gag in a reeling collision of opposing worlds. Urban. Wild. From relaxed joy to dismay, feelings of desecration rip through my senses. The wild beach careens in my cells.

Outside the car the ancient ocean sprawls away into darkness.

Everyone else in the car is squealing. Doors fly open. My friends pour onto the beach and laughter erupts.

Wild danger edges around the playfulness. They don't see it. They don't feel it.

For me, still in the car, an otherness expands with every breath. It's like nothing I've experienced before. Some numinous reality heaves, eviscerated by spinning rubber and steel wheels holding court on sand. My mind staggers, struggling to hold together. Whatever this is, I'm nothing, spare light at a crossroads. I reach for the door. But I can't leave the car. I cannot. As my friends move away toward the ocean, wild forces pour in and claim me.

Night, full night hisses and sucks against our intrusion. I shudder as untamed energies erupt. Undeniable power breaks open. Resistance is insanity closing in. I sit dormant at the middle of the backseat. Whatever this is, I can't fight it.

I hear and feel the shared revelry of my friends. They twirl away with the waves. I envy them, their freedom as it escalates, and I'm held at the cusp of some crossing. The ocean of my childhood is here. Yet I melt away at the center of this backseat. My friends return for me. I try to laugh, and for the briefest moment the wild bonds that hold me soften. But that is all. I cannot move. I shake my head.

"Just, uh, gimme a minute, I'll, uh, I'll come out in a while. I just need a minute," I say and they withdraw nodding. *Yeah, man.*

A prescient foreboding unwinds. Within the deafening pound of the waves I can't find any beginning point. Where I end, where I begin, not with my friends, not without them. I can't find anywhere that I am. The battering of waves is close, so close it wrenches and coos in my blood. Overtaken and caught between worlds, raw power ancient beyond meaning vies for every fiber of what I am. Pulled in the primeval undertow I hunker within colliding rhythms, slide prone on the seat like a slippery dissolving thing. I'm there and then not there at all.

Ancient prescience expands. Sand, surf and roar. Antiquity turns and answers. And in that instant I know one thing and one thing only — I dare not move, I cannot move, some border I must not cross.

I feel the claiming sea, a rite that tears against the glare of urban threshold hard up against wild domain. Dragged, caught between, I feel stretched to breaking. Opposing forces vie for something I do not know that I have. I slip from seat to floor as inexorable demands drill bones, pry mind, and my body lies, a slim line, artifact along thresholds of extremes.

Attempting to raise my head to the old tongue of the pounding breakers, each thunderous approach of surf strikes dread, despair, indecipherable caution. Grip of an impossible meeting tears what was once me apart in the stretch and batter of immensity. And searing awareness bursts past strain. *Let go. Be what this is or nothing at all.* Lacerations bare and raw as the earth herself carve and pare. *Let go, surrender or nothing at all.*

Origin, single pearl of enormity, is this wild skin pressed against the urban brink. And I am nothing. Gone.

What speaks is braille and code written on sand. City snarls metal, concrete, stench and whine, snatches DNA of sinew nerve and chance. My body flinches, electrified taunt, strange cousin. Divergent opposites speak through tongues of blood, vine, leaf and mystery. Fire ignites. Dictate of steely constructs belch mass. Nuclei expand, contract, stress capacity. All convulse, tutelage on a certain kind of war. Breaking apart, the dissembling goes on forever. And then the old ocean heaves, casting me wretched on distant shores.

In a single breach I am gone and back, bleached by stark tumult. I rise to my knees in the car, trembling. Beach and pounding surf settle into perfect ordered form around me. The liquid ocean body swells. City lights glare and dim. Stars sparkle in near-distance. Bent by ruthless brutality, I drag back onto the seat to gather the shaken fact of myself into one place. I can't find my breath. Pounding feet jolt the sand, echo through chassis and frame. Upright and panting I dash tears from my eyes. A deluge of laughter, sand and sea spray fling through open doors. My friends tumble in. Their life force piles in around me.

Group voice, one word, vibrates, "Ok?"

Shaky, glad, so glad for warmth and change and question, I murmur on the last whisper of a sob, *"Ok."*

"Ok," they echo. "Ok."

Motor roars to life. Chatter freewheels out open windows. We lurch, forward motion toward lights that careen ahead in all directions. Leaving the beach we enter the urban domain.

I don't know what has happened to me. But I'm glad to be with my friends as the car runs through city streets, my nerves ratcheting toward calm. We stop again and again at places Cora most wants to see. In the crazy ride through cavalcades of buildings where people wander rare and random, I feel both warm and lonely as I watch them. But I lean toward them, not away. Lean toward fish market, explosive lights and converging streets with my shattered, reformed mind.

I have no marker, no touchstone, no guidance for what has occurred. But all these things lie buried within me. In time I will unearth them.

The mush of hours condense into dozens of topples out of and back into the car, and then again we are on the steep, winding climb to the house where our evening adventure began. I smile at the house, its perch over green descending slopes. We fall out of the car, amble through the door and splinter off. The two boys wander away along hallways to further oblivion. Feeling more normal but in heightened distraction I move to the all-glass divide of the wraparound windows. The night presses insistent, unremitting vigor.

Vega is kind, offers many rooms with many beds for sleep. But in particular she offers to make up a simple palette on cushions along the extended window seat, and I'm grateful. Will settles in somewhere, I don't know. I'm relieved to have his morose nature at a distance, away from the shell shock of my own. All I can manage, all I want to manage, is quiet. And sleep. What has happened to me in the car on the beach in the wild dark? I don't know. But finally there is respite from the day and the unnerving night, which I cannot name even to myself. I pray then to exhaustion.

Sleep, though, takes not the slightest turn in my direction. I would beg if it would make any difference, but there's no suit to make. There's only the day night run together, unraveling in tissue, traveling outside thought. Staccato blips and spurts, word images that layer. Flash in fade out. Nothing sticks. In the night shine that ephemers on ceiling and surface, time peels off me and falls away. Murmurs giggle and float — Vega and Cora. I sigh into these friends cuddled in somewhere, sharing longed for time. Stillness settles more closely, relaxing the cocooning dark. Curiosity finds no footing in my restless transferring mind. Light from star or lamp or moon iridesce across wall and windowpane. I do not sleep. I lie in the dark light. There is nothing.

And then there is something.

Immense cliffs tower above vast, flat sea. Land and water stand barren, breathless. Water laps. There is no life. None. Nothing stirs beyond the lunar swell. And then a tall slender form appears, walking along the shoreline, long coat, hair cascading.

Spit of land extends into sea, narrow, narrowing. The lone figure walks the length. Primordial origins breathe visceral potency. Epochs whisper the beginning of everything that will come that has been that will be – and pulse nothing. No breath no flight no fin. Soundless weight. The beginning. The end. Ancient penetrates, life without life. The figure stands at the edge of the shore utterly alone. Forever water. Mineral stone nothing, great vacancy of the endless.

Nothingness swells and blows spare. Antiquity beyond reckoning awakes. The prehistoric exhales. Dinosaurs will walk here, whisper, hint of time porous yet absolute. Other creatures stir, unformed. A breath sifts where nothing breathes. Not sea. Not land. No air. Vast saline body, infinity of land is the weight of what is held and not held. Leaf hints but is not. The lone figure stands amid the lifeless. Out of time, out of mind, eternal void infuses, stains.

Transference unleashes from my cells.

I fade into restless sleep. Dawn glimmers in a room held by green foliage. First light is breaking. Air hangs heavy. Streaming filigrees of water bead then trail along the glass. My eyes flicker. Wisps of fog lift, float and sail the green canopy outside. I watch the slow change, dark to light. Hold it against terrible knowledge pinning my limbs. Mind smothers in cloying weight. Voices, cheery in the low-light kitchen, shuffle and clink. Suck and drag, I pull myself slowly upright.

I'm still in my clothes. As the blanket falls away, I try to shake shame and sorrow into its overlapping fold. Find some greeting that can meet the morning joy chattering just a blink beyond me. But I can't reach it, not here, not now. Hissing shadows press from every side. I don't know what they want, these shadows, how to match words of this morning world to their dark aspiration. A shudder on the early air, caught in the gap and I feel sad, sad. My friends will feel this as attitude. How strange, strange, bigger than all of us, I drag the thing as I rise, decline coffee, decline tea, decline everything. I'm just trying to breathe and keep breathing. I want to fall back into heaviness, to discover its catch and release.

But this is the time for movement.

Will is hurried. We can't delay. Walking through webs before ghosts, I bat phantoms at every step. Until finally there's simply a bowl of oatmeal, a second of granola and the common-sense mustering of the pressing needs of the day. Travel. It's all I can do to keep from drowning in forces reaching out from the dream.

We gather at last beside the red car. Vega watches me closely, asks if I might be sick. Tentative, like, *Is there anything I can do?* I thank her and shake my head dumbly. I have no answers. I can't explain. I don't know. She nods, we all climb in, and she drives us the steep winding descent below the house, a very short distance beyond and pulls over on a leafy shoulder near the roaring zoom of the freeway.

"This is the best and easiest place to catch a ride without getting hassled," she says as we all step from the car. "Remember, you can't put your thumb out on the actual freeway. You've gotta start from places like this, catch a ride from someone about to get on." She turns to Cora and they embrace. "I'm glad you came." She smiles and turns to Will. "Take care of her." She laughs and they exchange a hug. "Call me if you need anything. I think you know the way."

In front of me Vega pauses, looks deep into my eyes. I look back, steady. The sorrow in her gaze has a body, a voice but stands silent. We embrace, and she lingers for an extra hug, then steps away and nods looking shaken. As she turns, she reaches out to squeeze Cora's arm then swings into her car and drives off, so quick it seems she was never there at all. I can feel it then. A die is cast. And with that, something shifts. I can breathe. It's time.

We shuffle our packs and sling them up on our shoulders, step across the road and put our thumbs out to the oncoming traffic that will split moments later into some who'll go our way and some who won't. True to Vega's word, we have a ride in less than five minutes. Back to Vallejo, where we linger briefly to see another of Cora's friends. And then on, beyond the beyond, we've crossed it once before.

———

It's 1956, and I'm four years old. We've come to a place in Mexico my daddy has wanted to find. Ensenada. We stay in a motel on a beach where water and sand curve. My mother takes Tommy, Colleen and me out into crashing waves. We hold hands. Hold on, mommy says. Hold on. Tight, she cries. When the waves crash us we can't hold on, we can't hold tight at all. The water pulls me under and under. I don't think I'll ever come up. I can't breathe. But then I am up. I'm on top of the water, it's throwing me around. I'm choking. Water settles to shallow, and I'm sitting on sand. We're all in shallow water, sitting on sand. Mommy's eyes are huge, full of startle and light. We laugh and laugh. We gather shells, little crabs and sand dollars. We put them in dishes of water in the motel room. The water can't come from the sink, mommy says. It has to come from the sea. We stare at our booty then all go back out on the beach.

Mommy doesn't stay. She goes back inside. We see large lumps all along the curving beach and run to investigate. The first one is a seal. It's very still. It stinks. It's dead. A strange, ugly creature pushes out of the flesh of its neck and burrows back in. Tommy and Colleen think this is the neatest thing they've ever seen. They get closer to look. I can't stand it. The smell. The ugly. I back up. I feel sad. I don't understand them. I wander down the beach. All the other lumps, strung out like beads, they're seals. So many. Now I know it. They're all seals. They're all dead. They make my heart hurt. I don't want to see them. I turn and run back, past my brother and sister ogling the first dead seal, the sickening burrowing creature. They're singing. "The worms go in, the worms go out … " They snicker at me. I run back to the room. All the dishes of water, the crabs and the shells smell putrid, like rotting.

Later we will ride a beach into distance. I'll be carried away on a horse plunging beneath me. My family will return to Wyoming. In that streamlined freedom that childhood holds, I'll become horse and gallop through summer hours, summer days in a race across time and what's left of my childhood.

And later, in dark winter basements and cool summer basements hidden away,

I'll become storyteller, entrancing my friends with tales of extraordinary circumstance. Something will unleash with each telling.

Life will turn again, archaeology laying down its strata, and a larger story will erode out of days and nights where wing beats of unseen promise glide out of nevermore.

12

Looking Back

Jung would describe some of my experiences of 1971 — the waking visions, the channels between times — as instances of a soul's code erupting into consciousness. Such powerful experiences are prescient. They foretell the individual's path as she approaches a particular trial and a threshold of death. At such junctures there are no guarantees. I would not consider this viewpoint of Jung's for another thirty-seven years. But long before that I would begin to understand that an inner metronome was guiding me, preparing me for what was to come. And that night it was a date set in time on the Nevada desert.

It is 2004. I work on a ranch in northwestern Wyoming. I'm leaving my job here soon. The unknown breathes before me as late summer gathers toward fall. Worn concerns turn on current concerns, decisions that have to be made. Within them old history gathers. I sit at my desk and feel all of these things, anniversaries and seasons and change.

Looking out onto the world past desk and window frame, the countless details of a room mildly chaotic, I fall out of myself into the wild world beyond. Old cottonwood snags pull my eye, perch for fledgling osprey. They nest in a storm-topped fir nearby. The babes are growing, changing, leaving, like ripened fruit abundant everywhere now. Flower heads droop, scatter inner wealth, as pine cones smack, bounce and burst on the forest floor beyond. Daily winds shake loose the old, brittle maturity of this plant world and send it flying. Osprey adolescents scream and cry as parents wheel overhead, keening. Babes are growing, changing, leaving — falling into vast sky, rich soil — overflow of teeming life. Seeds.

As sunlight glows in blanched, full midday glory, grasses bow with the glisten of future generations. I'm as ripe as these fruits, ready to feed, seed new ventures. The ancient forest heaves, creaks out of sight beyond, old portal keyed to some inner mystery. My heart swells within log walls as I turn toward the call of that old wonder, moving within its shadowed reverie even as I sit at my desk listening. The lush green that has carried this summer burst into verdant form out of rain-laden days and nights is turning. Browns and golds are coming in everywhere now, though less-dry and more tawny because rains continue to come. The lush youth of all this world must ripen, cannot be held back in only greens, that first fast flare that has fascinated all these summer days until now.

Memory flickers, moves through light and shadow, pulls toward a ripening I can't name.

I look to the twin aspen that flash along the outer wall of the facing cabin. I see how they hold the light wind and the fast light and the ever presence of all day in their shafts of vivid-white shadow. Something in me cleaves to these changes, like bark paper peeling back and away. Transitional skin. Words unfold worlds at seed depths. Story seeks form. I follow a flow that is really not word at all but conduit, river channel, estuaries of response. My blood courses seams and folds.

Seeds find their soil, split open. Impossible and merciless, memory gathers speed — slow start of a runway train.

There is a shift to exhale and a settling. There is the season. There is the room. There is a flirt of memory. And then there is the sudden slip of a different late summer into fall, a tumble toward early winter, another time of change. Yearning, like now — but not like now. It breathes into the room and enters my heart whispering there. Sighs cross thresholds, though sun still shines and seeds hang heavy. Warm winds rustle along the cusp of cabin walls. Currents pull deep and hard. I'm uncertain if I can find my way among the changing terrain.

The coming season is a season of weight. I remember how it was, how it is, how I enter the season of falling leaves hopeful as a child welcoming change. But this is the season of old errors, missteps and the grinding of the wheel. Patterns haunt, seek settling ground. A thousand reasons speak to resist at all cost, close the senses, bar the heart and hold all memory at bay, left to eddy in the backwaters of decay. Yet I loosen my grip, slip into the current, ignore the old gnaw of confusion and shame, twisted isolation. Raw pain lives here, has the power to send me back reeling. But I approach this time with tenderness. Once-tough machismo singes, dissolving, a useless melting husk. Hollow, it floats.

It is hard to cut through the thick skin of the past. Cut below first layer is sharp, breathless agony. I don't linger. Cut mercifully, one layer and with each return, another. But even gentle peeling becomes locomotive tonnage hurtling down a deserted night track, full throttle.

No brakes. Sheer and white-hot in my blood panic races to catch that train. Stop it. Change its course, anything but the unholy distance ahead. But nothing can stop that train. Nothing. Its course was set too long ago. I wither with the knowledge.

Time splits and breaks on the violence of memory, finds its moment, catches fire.

Like an eagle from her eyrie I see in the distance three people on a late afternoon turning bitter. Wind up, storm coming in. Two young women and a man pull warm gear from backpacks thrown off along a California roadside, where routes meet to carry those who care to go across Nevada. It's barely October. An early winter storm breaks fast, midday dimming to premature dusk. One young woman looks back over her shoulder to warm neon lights that blink from a crossroads behind them.

She imagines the comfort of an innkeeper's welcome, the coming night spent inside lighted rooms. A tasty meal and a phone call home. But then she remembers three things together: Home is not a place but a nightmare; they are all basically broke; and Will refuses to delay getting back across three states and half of Wyoming before Monday morning dawns. Still, magnetic chance throbs in that neon. It pulses and pulls, bigger and more important than these facts — something to be believed. She digs a kingfisher blue coat from the depths of her backpack and pulls it on. Bizarrely stylish in the hard-rimmed place, its thin, quilted lining is barely warm against a freezing blast that lashes sudden and harsh across the bleak highway.

Caught unaware, all three hurry to pull on every last bit of gear they have and close up their packs. The other two stand close, talking as they wrench pack straps tight in the growing gale. Kingfisher blue can't hear them above the screech of the wind and steps closer. The warm room idea hovers in her thoughts, feeling impossible yet insistent. Neon hums high lament, like a Rosetta Stone nearly lost. As she steps close to her friends she hears Will, going on again about his job, his need to make it back to Wyoming fast, his urgency weighing above all else.

She listens, feeling frustration with his blind agenda. It's taken long for her to break free from the darkness that's shrouded her all through the night into morning and half this day. It whispers now again at the edge of his words, like tides hissing on ancient sand.

A white van passes, slows and pulls to the side of the road ahead, unnoticed.

The three button jackets, search pockets for hats gloves bandanas — anything that might mean warmth. Kingfisher blue presses her hands to chilled ears. Words form in her mind that might punch through Will's belligerence, words that push and shove up her throat.

This point connects to I-80, their route and the long haul across Nevada. Her thoughts rest on the small amount of money in her pocket, the neon sign, the freezing wind and the storm that's hurtling down on them. She wonders what the others might have, guessing at the cost of a room. Their packs are still full of food — solid, enough.

She leans in to speak. Will yanks on a pair of thin gloves as her voice staggers to him and sleet slashes out of nowhere, ripping at their hair and clothing. Eyelashes freeze tears that spring unheeded. They grimace, duck down then shout to be heard. Will casts slit-eyed resistance as she flings her arm back toward the neon blurring behind them, struggling to speak through the blast.

He cuts her off. "Look, forget it, my job," he almost snarls as he throws a glance at the clouds massing, severe. Low, dark and fast-moving they overtake all light and sound. He shakes off their threat, glaring, "Cat, you just don't get it," he hisses, but another sound bites through the wind.

A horn, bleep, bleep, bleep and someone hollers. All three turn toward brake lights flashing ahead, a white van, a hand waving from an open door. The three look at each other, startled. Will whoops, hollers and leans down to grab his pack. He pulls at Cora as he turns to run toward the van. Cora hesitates, looks at Cat but then follows Will in synchronized motion. Both yell, exuberant, amazed at the timing and this good luck. Luck like the Greyhound bus that picked them up earlier in the day, the driver who told them to be silent before driving them to this point where heading north becomes heading east, a ride sent from heaven. Cat shakes her head feeling luck lies in a different direction, and casts her eyes back toward lights, phone and shelter. Her friends race on ahead. Their forward momentum pulls counterweight until she, too, is stumbling behind them, imagining the luxury of such a ride.

My mind staggers in backward momentum. Iron horse careens full speed ahead, bearing down on the late day dawning. Hot iron burns tracks shears distance, scalds memory. Horror unravels in my gut, held secret forever. I cry out to stop these travelers. Stop their approach. Pull them from terror and the savagery that's coming. But like hapless victims tied to the rails yet still in motion, they run on as the van door squeals open. Locomotive whistle splits through time, foretells the coming of unrelenting mass. Tears meet freezing rain, alive in the ice dream. These three do not feel a train. They do not hear a train. They do not see a train. Only one hesitates and then she, too, is caught. Train-whistle screams. There is no train. There is only memory, the night and the storm, the press of time and a ride waits.

Reaching the van Will slides the side door wide, a hollow dissonant thrum. Cora crowds up behind him. Cat sallies up behind Cora and sachets, waiting, as something inside her coils and catches, insistent. A sound? A voice? Faint, like a high-pitched keen. She looks around, blinking. Neon at the crossroads fades, distorting. Cat's interior urgency presses. Wind freezes a mighty gust, and she trembles, longing for shelter.

Trailing words stream over her head, blowing out of the van into the storm: "Going east, Salt Lake? Sure, we're goin' that way. Hop in."

Will and Cora clamber in together. Cat follows, climbing aboard. Ghost whistle screams as winds howl through a night not yet born.

The shelter of the van brings instant relief. For a moment warmth and quiet fall like a balm. But the hollow interior rings, a cluttered, dirty, hard-used wreck. There are no seats behind the driver and two passengers, no luxury at all. Cloying metal fills Cat's nostrils with the smell of oil, rust and used tools. The two passengers crowd on the single front passenger seat. Respite from the storm blurs Cat's repugnance, and her barely articulated dread. Strangers and questions twine as her backpack scrapes to the floor. No answers, and the van rolls into motion. The ghost train reels. Steel wheels cut ribbons of my heart.

The driver looks back. Blue eyes bore as Cat shifts her pack, casting around for clear space. Will and Cora settle shoulder-close nearby. The blue eyes blaze, animate a beat then go flat. The driver turns back, breaks the idling forward roll and puts the van in full gear, pulling onto the road heading east.

The three do not see, and I pity them. The man in the passenger seat speaks over his shoulder with only the sparest of glances, his focus locked on a woman who shares his seat. Carnage is near. It is the carnage of lost hope. Hot iron cleaves straight through my body. Weight rips against accelerating silent wail, echo ragged through time. Begging praying groveling for a change of course to the sharp snap of time, tears whirl to nothing.

In a cabin far, far away senses rove among summer's verdant blush going fey. No memory. Time is a meadow. These children, so long ago and far away, grown though they are, we share a skin. It reaches for me now.

Part II

Love's the only engine of survival...

Leonard Cohen

13

The Ruins of Time

Set to head east along I-80, I take in the new ride with curiosity. At nineteen, still clasped in the thrill of adventure, deep down I long for home.

Feelings of relief to be out of the storm mix with unease. But the quiet in the van transmits relative calm. We settle into what we can make of it. The chipped walls of the van match the rusted mechanical debris crowding the floor, everything hard-used. We shove and shift to make room for our packs. In the driver's seat a round-headed man, close-cropped blonde hair, medium build, is oddly silent. He ignores us and shifts the van into gear. This plagues me as I lean back against my pack. He hasn't answered even one of our questions. Once, before accelerating onto the road, he turns wordless, eyes a shocking blue.

Across from him, in the single passenger seat, a slender guy with long, thin hair caught in a ponytail seems really cool and friendlier. I don't know why I think this, he's so totally caught up with a totally hip chick sharing the seat with him. But I like his look — worn, tan, corduroy sport jacket over T-shirt, faded jeans and western boots. I can barely see her, but her long, dark hair sways into view, flowing skirt skimming the floor beneath their seat. They're pressed together tight and awkward on the narrow seat, and he just keeps murmuring and whispering to her. They must be really in love. His head bobs like punctuation, a bald spot glinting when we pass under overhead lights. Those lights are on way too early. It should still be daylight out there. We're lucky to be out of the storm.

Cora and Will are a bit further back, cozy and close. I nod at them as I loosen my pack straps. No one's talking, makes me nervous. Seems kinda peculiar. Everyone else who's given us a ride has been curious, looking for conversation — we've been the entertainment — but not today. The Greyhound bus driver who picked us up earlier swore us to silence, kept her eye peeled on us in the rearview mirror the whole ride, and the only things she had to say were, *I'm breaking the rules to do this,* when we got on and, *Be careful,* as she left us off at the exit, where these guys picked us up. We were kind of swelled up and full of ourselves in the empty extravagance of all those bus seats. But now these three, we might as well not be here. There's this funny vibe I can't put my finger on.

The driver flicks a glance back our way. "Where'd you say you're going?" he asks.

We're a chorus, "Salt Lake City!" and the shell of the van rings like a gong.

The driver pins us with a brief look and those wild eyes flash. "Cool. Great. We can, uh, get you, uh, partway there." He glances back. "I'm on a break from my job, just killing time, giving hitchhikers rides until I have to get back." Then he clams up, and he's all gone again, focused ahead. Lights flicker to nothing, and darkness overtakes the windshield.

The tension up front is like a g-force. All three are older than us. But she's younger than the two dudes. I sink into the silence and imagine being so hip. Exudes from that couple. A lover's spat, it must be. He's sure appeasing. Every time she sparks at Ponytail (my new name for him) he just leans in and murmurs stuff in her ear. She's curt. He placates. She pulls away. He moves closer. Every now and then I get a glimpse of her face and, whoa, she is beautiful. He's not great-looking but he's interesting, cool. I can see the attraction. Her skirt is amazing.

I want to belong to this fellowship of the road. I try to cover my inexperience, like this trip isn't my first time hitching. Ponytail is kind, in a sidetracked sort of way, so I pepper him with questions about food on the road. And so am I, distracted I mean, as he coddles us both, really, the woman too angry to speak and me too nervous to shut up. He tells us about a park where we can spend the night in the next town. But there's something that's curling around, a sniper, some unspoken vixen of dissent. I'm sympathetic to both sides of their puzzle. The miles peel away beneath us, my friends almost as quiet as the driver.

The heat in the van builds. I grow sleepy, tired but jangled. Strained attempts to create a warmer atmosphere fall away. Finally silence is fine, and I settle against my pack and doze.

All at once lights, town lights, glow and glare ahead. I jump as we barrel down an off ramp quicker than questions can form. The driver asks Ponytail with a certainty that doesn't require an answer, "This is it, end of the line, where you want to be, right? Right? Where your friends are, the house you wanted to get to, who'll be so glad to see you?" It's like they're talking in code.

Ponytail is exhilarated. "Yeah. Yeah! Oh, yeah. It is. Sure. Yep. This is it. Thanks for remembering, yeah, thanks, thanks," he says, and the driver swings an easy left into Lovelock and pulls over across from an old white house with a high porch.

Ponytail can't seem to get the door open fast enough. The van has not quite stopped, and he's reaching across the woman to grasp the door handle. "Thank you, thanks, thanks for the ride," and he's pushing the woman out of the van ahead of him as though they share a single body.

Nerves on edge, I call out for directions to the park. Ponytail waves east and calls back, "It's at the far edge of town, easy, you'll find it." The woman struggles against him as they cross the street.

We watch from the back, look at each other, at our packs and swallow. This change feels too fast. The small town is dark, seems already buttoned down for the night. Since our plan is to stay in the park, Cora and I climb out, take our packs as Will passes them to us.

"Hey," the driver suddenly turns from the disappearing couple, "Look, sorry. I'll take you on to the other edge of town, the park. It's no big deal. It's cold. It'll be easier for you. Just a little further. I don't mind. Get back in."

We look at each other, but Will has our packs back inside the van without a word. I shudder, feeling murky, and uncertainty ignites. A riot takes hold in my mind. Getting back in the van puts off the inevitable. The lure of a few more warm minutes out of the cold swirls, an eccentric pulse. Will grabs Cora and pulls her in.

"Hey, thanks, that'd be great," he enthuses. I hesitate then climb in behind Cora. Will slides the door closed.

A vortex picks up inside me, no settling point. Why? The park? The town? The weather? My emotions start to whirl. All spin a rampage through my mind. Will and Cora seem decisive, settling again on the floor. But I'm up on my knees with my hands on the back of the passenger seat. The van moves along the night street. No one speaks. I grasp for some clear point through a mass of conflicted feelings. The night reels and images topple through my mind. Another block and I feel caught in a vise. I jump at the driver's voice.

"Hey! You know, I was just calculating in my head. I think I was wrong. I think I still got extra time to kill." He looks back at us, smiling.

Apprehension shoots through me. My hands quiver. Slightest pause and he looks in the rearview mirror into the back of the van. Streetlights illuminate outside. "Park's just ahead, must be. But I bet I could take you to the next town, Winnemucca, maybe, let me think." His voice changes and alarm sizzles up my spine. "Yeah. I'm sure of it.

I could do it and still get back on time. It's late, lousy weather, strange place. I don't mind taking you a bit further. Whaddaya think?"

Panic hits like a punch in my gut. His words spill out wrong, all wrong, too fast. My mind stumbles, circling. Something inside me sits up, watchful, clear. I know at once what we need to do. We need to talk alone, just me, Cora and Will. Stunned, breathless I scrabble for words I can say out loud, stacking up words I want to say later once we're out of this van. I turn to my friends. I speak with my eyes. *Wait. We should wait. Talk first.*

But Will's face is lit. He totally ignores me. Words shoot out of his mouth, "Really? Really? You'd do that? You don't mind?" He looks at the driver like he's God descended from the mountain. I shudder.

"Will," my voice flows, very quiet past the constriction in my throat, "Cora. I think we should talk. First. Together. About our, uh, plans."

"Wha'?" Will asks, staring at me as Cora's eyes bore into mine.

The driver rattles on, "Naw, I don't mind. Why not? Why should I get back early? Don't wanna get back late, neither, but work's work, it'll be there. Yeah. It'll be tight, but I can do it. Don't need to sleep, really, I can just drive straight through if I need to."

"Uh," mind racing, I struggle to speak, still looking at my friends, "We, uh, we need to talk it over, I think, first."

"Oh," the driver changes his tone, very understanding, "sure, sure, `course you do, `course, go ahead, sort it out, not offended."

"I, I think we need to, to have some time to think this over," I stumble, little more to say in front of this guy. I just want to get out of the van and talk to my friends.

"Hey," the driver speaks out. "Hey, sure, talk about it. See what you think."

I shiver. This limbo place, the unknown park, the town, the night all jostle confusion. Nothing feels right. But staying in the park, yanked away so quick and replaced with this new choice, it's knocked something loose that shimmies through my core. I turn to Cora again. She looks surprised. "Look," I manage, "I think we should all talk first," and my voice drops, "alone. Before we decide." I try to get my breath.

I try to catch Cora's eyes but she's set on the van floor. I can imagine what she thinks, my weirdness last night in San Francisco. My tangled feelings won't settle. I feel desperate. *We just need to talk alone. I don't know why. I don't know what other choices we have. But there's gotta be a cheap motel in this town somewhere. It's not that big. We could walk to one, I bet.* Will jabbers with the driver about distances.

"This is so cool that you'd do this," Will enthuses as Cora joins in.

I open my mouth and close it, chasing the web of their eagerness and suddenly know. I'm not going to get them alone. They look at me but turn back to the driver. *The park and its trees and strangers, cops probably, uncertain these figments rattle and dissolve in my mind.* I can't attach to any certainty. Danger oozes through every choice. My friends don't seem to suffer. What's wrong with me? This freakin' day and a half seems endless.

Will quips, "That'd be fantastic, a ride to the next town, really fantastic. This is so cool."

The driver sparkles a smile, "Well, whaddaya think? Shall we do it?" but the van is already accelerating. I shake my head. I pull at a pack strap. *Shouldn't we be stopping before we leave this town?* Thoughts of the park feel threatening. Staying in the van feels wrong. *What should we do?* I turn again to my friends, but they're leaning into falling words, a soft torrent over the driver's lips. No words fall from mine. Nothing. "Well, here we go then," he smiles, and the van picks up speed.

The spinning in my mind slows and goes dormant. I sink to the floor. I lean against my pack feeling squeamish. I haven't been carsick for years.

The driver chatters on about the Army, about coming back to the States, uncertain what to do after being in the military. The saga builds and grabs hold. He gives no pause for questions or comments. Finding a boat job and the real heart of his boss, the driving intensity for perfection — sounds like a complicated guy. Peeling paint off boats, the sweaty grunt of it, the ever-changing stream of other guys who can't cut it. His own restlessness, the satisfaction of the work, the love and hate of it, his lack of ambition, all tumble and bounce through the shell of the van, a mesmerizing litany, detail somehow vacant and feckless. A steady never-ending river, it seems. Will looks ecstatic. Pale blue eyes meet vivid blue eyes in the rearview mirror, mutual admiration.

My confusion rises again, then spins to a halt, goes underground.

Unwinding into the miles ahead, I listen with little other thought as the driver's nonstop narrative somehow soothes. This must be how he stays awake, endless talking. He's turning out to be a nice guy. Never would have guessed it at the beginning, shows you never know. Seems like this ride is the best thing after all, good that we've skipped the park, that must have been what was really bothering me. Bet that was a losing scene. This guy is kind of funny. I laugh at a joke about his dorky good-guy jerk boss. Cora and Will chuckle along. We share a smile, tension gone. They seem happy. It looks like Will's going to get back to his job on time. I'm glad for him. Cora's snuggled up against him smiling. I'm glad that they're glad. The floor's cold but I lean against my pack shivering only a little, thinking about friends at home, not so far away now.

"Hey!" The driver looks over his shoulder. "It's kinda lonely up here. Why don't one of you come up and take the passenger seat," he flashes a quick smile and waves a hand forward. I hesitate. Neither Cora nor Will move. "Someone oughtta have the comfort, it's still a longish drive. C'mon up, enjoy it." I look at Cora, and she shakes her head. Will nods at the passenger seat pointing the way.

I hesitate then stand up slowly, bend to climb over the engine case between the seats and slide onto the passenger seat, feeling embarrassed but kind of pleased. The driver glances over at me, smiles briefly and continues on about work and no play at a boatyard somewhere in southern California. Friendly. So friendly. I'm glad to be off the cold floor.

He stays with his course, endless talking. I'm tired, drowsy, imagine maybe we'll all be friends, keep in touch when we go our separate ways, maybe letters, clever perspectives on life to shoot back and forth once we get home. He turns up the heat. The van grows intensely warm. I start to peel off my blue coat. All at once I feel exposed and extremely self-conscious, unnerving how close he is in his seat. He doesn't miss a beat, goes on rambling, skipping around always circling back to boats and docks, peeling paint and cranky bosses. The heat is making me groggy. I want to ask him to turn it down. He's in a T-shirt so maybe this is his comfort zone. Cora and Will are quiet behind us. I struggle against the heat that brings on an overwhelming urge to sleep.

He winds down a fast-moving stream of babble. "Hey, no worries if you need to sleep, do it. I'm a good night driver. It'll be ok. Sack out. I like the quiet of the night and the road to think, you don't have to entertain me. Bet you're really tired. I'll have time to catch a few winks before I turn around. Relax, nod a little if you want."

I don't want. But it's hard not to. It's so hot. My eyes are heavy. I nod and startle awake, nod and startle, fight the urge to sleep, really sleep, I'm exhausted. I try to imagine us all being friends. Maybe it'll happen, staying in touch. How cool would that be? I chase these thoughts, but my eyelids droop, head heavy. The miles spin away beneath wheels that sound like singing, a high whistle call somewhere out along dark margins. The old sea from last night hisses, waves flirting edges of my mind.

Ocean lap, roar, crash and lap, roar and break over ancient, sandy seabed. On fumes of prehistoric life we cross Nevada. Our arrival in San Francisco, the hip voices of Cora's friends sputter as fish market stink wavers on glare of night city lights. Ocean repels, boats rock, no, it's a van — we're in a van, a van traveling east. Only yesterday, no, no it was last night no it was yesterday when we crossed this same ocean floor going west. Hiding out, fleeing hay trucks, now we've tricked them going back, back to the Great Salt Lake. They've missed us, missed us. And the sea is roaring, crashing, waves hiss and pull in undertow along the surface of dream.

Deep consciousness of time opens a window, then opens window upon window upon era upon interval upon season. Where was the split in my family when one thing became the other? Thresholds, crossroads and then we are where we are.

In the ruins of the past lie many things. The soil of time turns. The old becomes now. Were my parents' decisions all the way back to Mexico a beat in the fabric of now?

Along the ancient seabed deeper patterns echo, imprints of other lives, footprints tracking through time... each of us brings our own history... we each bring our history ourselves...

Little more than a girl in reaction, in a white van I doze and dream.

And the van flings down an off-ramp. Racing descent yanks me from realms of sunlight and shadow. I sit up electric, shuddering through muscle and bone. I grasp for the door, feel Cora and Will as they quicken behind me.

"Wh-what're we doing?" I stammer, alarm bell rioting inside me. Flashing white lines and black pavement consume beneath speeding tires. I turn to our driver. "Wh-what, wh-why're we getting off the highway? What're we doing here?"

The temperature in the van has dropped from suffocating heat to freezing. The driver's voice croons, a slight edge wavering through his words. "Somethin's wrong with the engine," and we rocket toward a stop sign that pops out of darkness, red-white, red-white, "I dunno, kind of missed and staggered back there, lost speed, need to check it out," he stares ahead. My mind snaps into focus as we jangle at last to a stop.

Questions from Cora and Will shoot from behind us, "Whaddaya mean, what, what could be wrong?"

"Needs oil or somethin', forgot to check, prob'ly no big deal. Or could be worse, somethin' with the engine," the driver says, shrugging.

I imagine trying to find help out here if we need it, push panic down. He flips on the interior lights, reaching for the latch of the engine case between our seats. He pauses to look out the windows. There are no lights outside within view.

A host of fears flood. I hope that he's some kind of mechanic. What if he doesn't know how to fix this? No help here, and repair shops must be how far away?

He shrugs again and says, "I'm just gonna take a look." Rubbernecking to look around beyond the windshield, he settles, flips the casing latch and lifts the cover. Will and Cora push up close from behind. He drops the cover. I start as it smacks closed. "I think we better get off this ramp, outta the middle of the exit," and he accelerates past the stop sign in a left-hand arc, drives through the underpass and pulls over on the shoulder of a narrow road. He flips the ignition off and twists again toward the engine casing. Pulling up the cover he peers down into a mess of metal, wires and grease. "Don't know what it needs, somethin', it can be kinda cranky."

I stare down, willing apprentice, but have no idea what connects to where or how. Questions stream, "Whaddaya think? Think it's the oil? Have ya' got some? Think it's serious? See anything?" I peer deeper into the oily space. He tinkers briefly, withdraws his hand to wipe it on his pant leg as I continue to look at the preposterous puzzle of parts and wires. "Think maybe it's just hot? Needs to cool down? Maybe we can get to town, somebody can take a look. It's not so far, right?" He doesn't answer and I prattle on, "Think you should check the, uh, the, uh, spark plugs or something like that?"

"Cat," Will's voice pops.

Study in earnest, I've no idea what all these parts are except the oil dipstick."You gonna check the oil? Or what's that?" I ask, pointing past the dipstick, hopeful.

Cora's voice pounds in behind Will's, "Cat!" I wonder if maybe he's got any tools and what he'll start with, how far we are from a garage.

"Cat!" Will barks. Hearing him, not hearing him I flounder on what it will take to get us out of here.

Will's flat tone slaps against my concentration. "Look up!" he snaps. I wait for the driver to make a move, adjust something, but he does nothing.

Wavering over the curious mess of the engine and lost in tumbling ideas, my eyes rise smiling to the driver's as Will says softly, "He's got a gun," and I'm looking straight down the barrel.

Whirligig thoughts smash against cold metal. I freeze.

Behind the gun sits a man I've never seen before, his face chiseled ice. Blue eyes bore, laser focus. I've never seen anything so cold. The man's unflinching focus is savage, voracious. Pleasure gleams in those eyes. Dumbfounded by the gun, horror plummets.

I shrink back. The axe of his face goes harder still and the iceman barks, "You two back there, take the rope from under my seat and, girl, tie up your boyfriend tight, hands behind his back. It better be good. Try anything else and you will be very, very sorry. Do it! Now!"

I hear them scrambling behind me. Panic takes over all thought as he stares into my face. "Take off your clothes!"

Stubborn fury burns fierce inside me. I stare back and don't move. "Now!" He waves the gun, punching it at me.

I turn away slow, face forward. Rigid steel fills in down my spine. Disbelief jolts to staunch resistance. Staring into blackness beyond the windshield the glare of interior lights exposes us to the night. We're visible in high relief to anyone watching. I wonder who's out there. I shrink into myself as shuffling low voices behind me stagger across my racing thoughts. *This road. How late is it?*

"Shut Up!" whipping around to the back the driver curses Cora and Will. "You don't need any words for that!" then rips back at me, "You! Do it! Undress!"

Steely I sense to the door handle on my right, eyes locked ahead, ignoring him. The door pulls like a magnet. How fast I can get it open, get out? "Get `em off!" He waves the gun.

I will not, he will not, I will not.

He looks back behind the seats quick and hissing, "You, girl, I'm comin' back there. You better have him done right." I barely hear. Resistance coils every fiber of my being. I lean slightly to my right. He ratchets back to me, growling. "You're not going to feel very good if you don't start peeling those clothes!"

I lean over, untie one shoe. My muscles are bunched and ready to bolt. His focus shifts to the back for a split second. "It better be tight and it better be strong when I get back there or you'll pay!" he says. My hands shake as I lean to the door. He turns back spitting, "Get `em off!"

A light goes on in my head. If I make it out the door there's nowhere to go, freezing desolation.

"You, too, back there! Peel off your clothes! Fast! I'm comin' back there!" the gunman hisses at Cora.

The bolt in my body, ready in every muscle, locks unfazed. My hand is a split second from the door. The gunman's eyes train to my movements, iceberg time. His next threat lashes back to Cora and Will, but his eyes stay on me. I despise him forever as one shoe peels to a sock and I start on the laces of the other, slow then slower. Poised for a race into the night, into the freezing empty night, I tremble. His focus splits to the back of the van. My hand measures the distance to the door. He barks, the gun jolts, and I remove the other shoe. Layer by layer shirt then jeans fall to the floor. Impossible cold ferrets along bare skin, my mind grasps for what lies outside beyond the door.

When there are no more layers he climbs out of his seat and into the back of the van. He checks Will's ropes and binds Cora's hands. I hear little of it. At the ready, I shiver. I reach for the door handle.

And an explosive thought stops my hand cold. If I make it out, my friends will still be here, in the van with the man and the gun.

My hand drops. Dread washes through me. I stare into endless darkness.

The past lunges hard on our heels.

14

So He Did

The van is racing along a hardscrabble road, the driver an unbearable presence. Horrific certainty paralyzes my mind, my body numb with the ache of his violation. Shivering in the terrible cold with only shirt and coat now for cover, I can't tell where the freeze of the night ends and terror begins. Disgust heaves just out of range, buried between bewilderment and pain. Lost in dumb agony my resistance, even more useless when Cora's turn came and he raped her too, is a shade falling somewhere behind. Sight and sound of her only moments ago reverberate on litanies of helplessness. My only choice was the decency to turn away. As the van pulls over and the engine dies, these feelings cling in a leaden shudder that perambulates against rising panic.

What futile defiance remains in me melts away. Cora's soft mewing riddles the silence, barely breaking through a blanket of despair. In the yawning shock dust settles around tires and what's left of our lives. Burdened clouds open and rain patters the windshield. There's no doubt at all about what comes next. It's only a matter of how.

We sit staring ahead, the driver and me. I can't see or know much more of Will and Cora. Blue coat pulled tight around my chill mocks against the cold. Shaking so hard I can't hold still on the seat, I lean away from the voice of the man in the seat across from me. He muses as though comrade in arms, words just out of hearing. Bullets along the threshold of a full-blown unraveling, his words fray the icy interior, cuff the naked moment and pass on. Some strange careless tranquility sits dead center in his self-created world, and begins a slow turn again toward rising agitation.

"Ya' know, in `Nam I had a bunch of buddies" he says, stopping a moment to consider. "Went through boot camp together. Real close."

He digs at a fingernail. "All of `em killed people over there, everyone of `em killed at least one, some more. `Cept me." His hands drop to his lap. He stares out the windshield. "They gave me hell every day about that." He turns in his seat to face me and scans the back of the van. "Every day, all the time, I heard about it. Still do. Even when they don't say nothin', I feel how they think and they're sayin' it." He shifts again. Silence presses against the windows. Shaking hard, cold to the bone, I nearly shiver off my seat. As his words penetrate the gloom I grab for the armrest, sickening plunge in my core.

"Now I would like to know," the driver stares across to me and into the back, holding for one second, two, like a born storyteller capturing his audience, spellbound we're already clear on the closing line, "I would like to know. What's it like to kill somebody?" His eyes steady and harden. I look away. "I think I just wanna find out. What it's like ta' watch somebody die."

Dread, no end point now, locks in and shatters the paralytic freeze. Struggling to breathe, hang on as thoughts chase circling faster and faster, I barely manage to stay upright. *No return then. There will be no return.*

The driver sits up and looks out the window, almost languid. "Okay. This's a nice place," he says, and abruptly rockets forward in his seat, shouting. "Get out! Now! Everyone!" knife words splintering.

My hand shoots to the door handle but stalls. "C-c-c-c-can I p-p-p-p-lease p-p-put on m-my c-c-c-c-clothes," I dare to look at him sideways. He gapes and I go on, "It's s-s-s-so c-c-c-c-cold," quavering, resistance ignites the slightest tick of warmth inside me. I fight to control my trembling against the burning shove of his stare.

His eyes bite, hover, then wing away, "Nah! I like to look at yer legs," and his door flies open. He leaps out with a nasty, trailing grin. I sit very still. As his door slams shut a guttural command rips through the van, "Get out! Out! You think this is bad? You ain't seen nothin' yet."

Unmoving uncaring frozen, it is dumb terror that rattles my door open. I slip to the stony-cold ground. And already he's there, jerking the sliding backdoor free, the squeal clawing the night. He yanks Cora then Will from the van, hands bound. They stumble and he shoves them forward, motioning me in behind. "Move it!" His voice cuts and I lurch, barely staying upright.

A few strides in the dense darkness, and we hover at the lip of a shallow ravine. A snarl thrusts Will then Cora scrambling over the edge. I crouch, straining to see, sidestep and stagger in a crumbling slide along rock and weedy soil onto a rutted path. We trip along uneven ground, and my legs suddenly buckle at the sight of the glint of water ahead. Its vast, dark murk and sparkle paralyze my heart. Deadened senses electrify, reel, a flood of visions engulf me.

Images of bloated bodies discovered floating, my mother and sister receiving the gruesome news, their shock agony disbelief. All comes in a torrent. Overcome, the sure thought of death cloaks the vision, their horror … the incomprehension of horror. I take a single uneven step. Lashing grief takes hold somewhere in the days ahead and it isn't mine it isn't mine, the pain of my family seethes along endless night.

Sudden revelation catapults from the terror of our march. The clean upsweep of a hill lifts clear from vaporous gloom. In its dark silhouette I find an answer to the ghastly scene waiting ahead to claim us along the shoreline. I grasp onto the desperate promise of the hill line as we drop to the beach below. Nothing has changed. The death march is unchanged. But now there is this chance and it claims me entirely, a last twist on the final turn of our fate.

In some racing moment he'll shoot us. Leave us. Bodies in the water, I know it as certain as I know anything. The one thing left here at the end of the world is this. *Can I get him to shoot me, not on the beach but up on the top of the hill, away from the water?* Clambering thoughts crowd forward. Feverish to plead my case I trip and nearly fall as we reach the sand. The gunman shoves past to stand glowering before us. And I see my error with lightning shock. *If I ask him to shoot me on the hill, he won't do it. Floating bodies in water will be certain.* A plague of alarm for my sister and mother scrambles against this certainty.

"Get in line!" The snarl wrenches me from depraved reverie. I topple in next to Cora. A flick of his wrist here, a wave of the gun there and we face him, a lineup. Covered picnic tables hulk, strange dream between us and the water. The thought of families coming to this place quivers against the nightmare, the joy of children at play. Water laps faintly beyond.

I'll run. Nerves shatter against bitter air. My muscles bunch in the dark. A sprint, the agony of effort collects for a full spring forward. Something struggles to come whole in my mind as the gun waves in front of us

The man's searing voice drives a battalion, old demons driving him. "You!" Sharp motion toward Will, "Get over there!" Laugh of derision. He punches the gun at Cora, slow to move, until it pushes sharp in her face. She steps with sluggish resistant and stands before Will.

I hang in frantic suspension, separate from Cora, Will, the gunman, mind whirling up the slope to my left. Adrenaline pounds the way. *I probably won't make it to the top. But if I get far enough he'll leave me where I lie.* Then it won't matter.

"You!" He barks. Cora and Will are both standing stones on the sand. "Get over there! Your turn!" My eyes snap, flee from hill to the wicked glee of the madman and the glinting barrel of the gun. I stagger slowly to stand next to Will. Tears freeze stubborn denial. Everything about this night is a question, and the answer is always the same. A hyena voice screams behind me.

I hang my head, fight panic and wait in the glowering dark for a bullet or his next command. Will looms against the sky. I recount the angle of the slope at my back, how fast can I run?

The sneering hiss and crack of the gunman's tirade flounders into angry boredom. I move slightly closer to Cora. He belches profanities across the curving waterline. Some new fury about the Army snakes to a mounting taunt.

"Well, they'll find out, they'll find out! I'm one of `em!" he wails just short of a shriek, old fiends driving him.

Endless fear sucks everything but the hill from my senses. I hold that rise like a failing lifeline, gauge timing through riveting terror. He raves. My temples pound toward the moment speed can burst out of me — will I make it any distance at all? *Will it be enough?* Fright rips against the drop of his voice as he moves closer, rifling the gun from Will to Cora to me. My muscles bunch.

And pandemonium breaks open, an explosion of arms and legs. Will, Cora and the gunman hurl in a knot, howling across churning sand. They lurch and career into me, fighting over the gun. I jerk back, almost fall and launch forward fast on their heels. Around the clench of their reeling forms I circle and circle. Giant blur, single body, they twist left, right, forward and back. Cora's voice fires from the middle.

"Cat! Cat! Take the gun! Take it!"

I scrabble to keep up with their roiling mass. In a ferocious twirl they change directions. I twist to follow, running blind in helpless dismay.

Cora and Will cry out together, "Get the gun! Cat! Get the gun!" Voices pierce from the rotating blur, but there is nothing. I circle back in a corkscrew. Tight hurtling mass, they spin and I see no gun, there is no gun.

Will grunts, "Cat, take it, take it, take the gun!" I race toward the moment, but it's gone.

Inside mayhem they are locked. Outside the circling outburst I'm lost. Twisting with their twist, circling with their circle I'm lost. There is no gun. There is darkness and muddle and crisscrossing sand. I race, frantic. Voices call out. *Take the gun.* But I can't. I can't. I don't see it.

And then sudden certainty catches in me. *I don't want the gun. I can't see the gun. But I don't want the gun.* As the three turn and tangle I orbit them, dismay spinning with me. I'm searching inside chaos for a clue.

Crack! A flash rockets from their midst. I stumble back then forward again. Straining, I stay with the fury of their pitch. *Crack!* A flare pierces upward fleeing the packed center.

And they split apart. Their spiraling forms break across open sand like debris settling around me. Will and Cora stagger then stand upright. A thin streak of blood angles along Cora's right ear. She crosses in front of me.

They don't have the gun. The man has the gun.

Cora leans close, presses something into my palm. The gunman is shrieking. My fingers close and flee to my coat pocket. The man dances frenzied before us, gun waving madly, a crazy disembodied thing.

Rage flames from his howling mouth. "You fucking assholes! Who — d'you think — you are! Who the fuck — d' you think — you are! I'm the man! I'm the man! You're gonna to die for this, you fucks, you are going to die!" His swollen face belches past words. A space. A breath. And then the torrent hurls more abuse.

Within the burn of his bitter tirade, certainty shifts. *Why hasn't he shot us?* I stand very, very awake. Paralyzing fear is gone, missing in action. Terror remains but no longer owns me. The leer of the water no longer claims me. They siphon off hill and the race to the top. Riveted to the gunman's voice rather than his words I listen as his rant winds down. My body still trembles on impact. But another certainty rises. As it penetrates, some element of the night wavers and falls away. The tiniest flicker of light grows inside me. *We have a chance.* The gunman wails on.

"Of course, you bastards, you had to try it! Of course you did! I'da done the same! Have to, you had to — I respect that, I … I …! Dammit! Goddammit! You fucks, I'd try!" He stabs with the gun, a cylindrical blur through darkness. "You've done it! Doesn't matter! You're gonna die, die, an ugly little death," and he herds us to a place on the sand in front of the picnic tables. Ordering us apart he steps away. I shudder. Some monstrous atrocity erupts as he stalks the sand.

Waving the gun, lurching in wrath, he chomps back and forth before us, "Get down! Get down on y'er knees, on y'er knees," he says, shoving the gun at Will, then Cora then me and we drop to the sand. "Dig! Dig! You're gonna take care of this job yourselves! *Get y'er graves ready! It's time!*"

Ghost families gather and fill the tables, blind to what will lie here but close on discovery. We will be the hideous treasure filling the beach. Trembling we dig. Digging we move closer together. I feel the press of Cora, Will beside her. Our hands skim, overlap and scoop sand. Particles hiss in tiny avalanche. The hole grows wide but not deep. It's as though we ponder in our dread waiting for the final punctuation, exhausted at the dull, wicked edge. Grief fills my chest. Sorrow sloughs against our sweeping motion, *wide but never deep, wide but never deep,* wordless chant alive, endless and unswerving. Cora whispers, but I can't hear what she's saying. A mask of calm hovers, inside me, inside the chaos.

Yammering stretches the gunman's voice to breaking, forces effort, drives his demand. I dig. But I do not hold to his words. I hear something that blooms inside his furious agitation. Angst tremors. I stop, head low, and look around. He paces. Will digs just past Cora who digs to my right. Stricken within the dull glow of night, the gunman's profile is etched on the pitch-black sky. Nowhere, going nowhere, we dig, waiting for the last sharp crack that will end the night.

But the crazed voice climbs in sudden distraction, drops, rises again, and a new command pitches through the dark. "That's it! Get up! That's it!!"

Tugging to our feet we face him. Shallow grave spreads at our backs. But no backward tumble of one, two, three flares out. It's an explosion of words that rocks the darkness. "Line up! We're headin' back to the van! Move! Move! Move it!"

In a shift to the same order that carried us down the ravine we cross to the upward climb. Strange stillness follows us. Sharp alarm ricochets along stones, shushes through dry brush, snaps open in my heart. My mind bursts to stunning awareness. *He still hasn't shot us. We do have a chance.* As we heave to the top of the ravine the man pushes past to the van. The side door yanks open. He grabs a handful of rope. "Get in!" he spits, pointing me to the passenger seat. I open the door and climb in. He binds Cora and Will, shoves them inside, and their door slams.

The warmth of the van, hardly warmth at all, mocks at the deep chill in my bones. I hear the scream of the sliding door, the scrape of entry and the gunman, spooky genie, jumps into the seat across from me as though it's all one motion. Cold, aching I curl into my seat.

He fumes like a whining child. For a moment I close my eyes. But something in me fights against this. I force myself upright in my seat. I see him reach for the back of his neck as he starts the engine and flips on the heat. Wrath splits in an open howl. He jerks his hand in front of his face, frenzy detonating. "*Blood!* There's blood! You assholes! *You hurt me!*" shrieking howls and a hideous twist rampage through his body as he thrashes snarling toward the back of the van. I close my hand around the tiny oblong knife in my right coat pocket. I know what's next. He will search. When he does worse things are going to come quick. He screams and screams. I pull the knife free of my pocket and drop my hand into the space between the seat and door as he menaces Cora and Will.

"You hurt me, you motherfuckers! There's more than one cut! You stabbed me, *stabbed me!!!*" leaning into the back, wincing, shaking his bloody fingers he whimpers and roars. His words hack, "You stabbed me, you stabbed me, you fuckers! Who's got it? Who's got the knife?"

Scrambling behind my seat, barely audible, Cora's voice spews, "Don't, don't have nothin', I, I think I, I must have scratched you, when we were struggling over the gun, see, my fingernail's broken, see," her voice wavers and drops away.

Will mumbles, "Nothin'. Nothin'. Didn't do nothin', don't have nothin'."

Hurling invectives, jumping in his seat the man screams like a cornered lynx. Rigid in my seat I listen as his anguish drops to sullen accusation, "Yeah. Right. *You hurt me!*" One hand worries at his neck as he wrenches back around to face the front of the van.

"Maybe, uh, m-maybe it was an accident," I breathe.

He turns on me, looks at the blood on his fingers. We sit as he peers at his hand.

"Do you need something, a cloth or tissue or something?" I barely whisper.

"No! No, don't need nothin'!" his says as his hands drop to his seat, and he stares past the windshield into darkness. The tiny knife glides loose from my hand. It clatters to the floor beneath my seat. I stop breathing.

"*What the fuck was that?*" the gunman whips around to the back.

Will and Cora's words stumble over each other, "Dunno, foot hit something, dunno."

I flinch, scrunch in my seat and wait for a blow. Immense agitation coils through the gunman then it, too, dwindles away. He slumps back around in his seat, rubs his neck and stares ahead. I turn in my seat and do the same. The timbre of night swells on a moving tempo.

Beyond windows hollow orphans of light flicker, stars twinkling through cloud. They seem to shiver then disappear across distant sky. The weight of us all stacked with no answers wavers away from the turning planets out there. I don't find myself in the stars or planets or the desert beyond. I don't find myself anywhere. There is only silence, and this waiting, the desolation, the pain and shivering isolation.

His awful voice growls from an abyss, "One of you girls, get up here. I don't care who."

Turning in his seat, he leans against the door at his back. An easy turn of his head takes in Cora then Will then me. His eyes bore through the darkness. I don't look at him. I hold to vacant thoughts. I don't care what he does. I'm not going to let him rape me again. My will feels like iron.

"Hustle, one of you! You won't like it if I have to choose!" Refusal rises in my blood on waves of disgust. I let it come, despising him. Hate for what he's already done, hate for what he is, hate for what he intends to do. I seem to have passed a point of no return. I don't care anymore. I can refuse him and not care. I turn my head and stare out my window.

"Take yer pick. Either one of you, doesn't matter. But it is going to be one. Hurry up!" His cold voice bounces on the metal shell of the van.

Disdain sneers through me. I shiver only slightly.

Almost indiscernible, I hear Cora weeping. Muffled sobs stifle, circle, return, following a life of their own. "Ya haven't got all night! One or both, *move it!*" As his words wrench across the van, halfway to me a granite wall of revulsion stops them cold.

Cora's sobs break like a quiet fracture.

I hate this man. He's nothing. *Cora's my friend.* I can't bear her pain anymore.

With loathing I turn to face him.

———

The girls in the bathroom in high school, all their rage, this man and his bogeymen playing out on us, my mother and her second husband, what drives them? How have I fallen onto this path of horrors? What am I doing here? In the years ahead I will take these experiences apart, the past that drove me, the past that drives hate, the past that drives malice and cruelty. But on this night I'm trapped in the whirl of a madman's chaos.

That man and his demons preyed on us. Feral, old demons preyed on him. How do we lay it all down? Where? When? How? In the parade of many lives, where is peace, the path to completion?

Fate or karma are neither punishment nor reward, neither judgment nor blame. Time, karma and fate are not rigid. They are flexible. They are circumstance, cause and effect; fluid, fluent and ever-changing. Each of us in our ignorance strives toward intelligence, each in our time resolution.

My friends and I hovered all those years ago on the floor of a vast ancient seabed. Mountain. Basin. Range. Within layered geography our stories sang. Mine was one. I could catch it or not. Resolve it or not. Move beyond it — or return to come again.

15

Desert Voices

The gunman at last is distant from me and dulled. Indifference to his violation hangs vacant inside me. I long only for warmth. The world is shattering, shattered. I hunch into whatever extra cover I can find in my upturned, fake fleece collar.

"Can I put on m-my clothes? P-p-please. It's s-s-so c-c cold." Unbearable shivering forms the question, barely audible plea that boomerangs through silence. As my words tumble and mute I pull my coat closer.

Scant memory whispers to the day I found this coat; to the conviction that I needed a warm winter jacket; to the same day when I met Cora and Will; the day of their invitation that led us all here. It whispers to the months, not far past, when my mother's enchantment with Carl carved out this path of my first independence. I barely notice the brush of these thoughts as they flatten and stifle.

There's just this. I'm so cold. Thin, quilted lining fails to resolve the mystery of body heat. The tremble and clench of deep chill excruciates. The ugliness of the night stagnates and whines. The sound of Cora weeping close to silence somewhere whittles at something I can't quite see. It crowds in through freeze and utter despair, something that rings just at the edge of hearing. Whatever else I've saved Cora from, we're still here.

Abruptly, as though out of nowhere, the gunman's voice lifts, "Yeah. Sure. Why not? Get dressed."

I shrug off furtive meanings that twine around his gesture, grateful at whatever cost, and turn away. As I face the side window I ignore everything but the layers of clothes pulling on. Shifting in my seat I lean over to tie my shoes, dart a quick glance at the gunman. Hatred, revulsion and fear flash just about past caring. Yet an odd, tenuous certainty filters, spun in whirling webs of doubt — he still hasn't shot us, we have a chance.

Nostalgic, the gunman's voice combs through chilly air. "When I was in 'Nam I knew a lot of guys that, uh, that didn't go home. Maybe they were stupid, maybe I was lucky, it was a hellhole, draft just took us any which way," and as agitation jumps in his voice, he barks, "But me, I enlisted! Enlisted!!"

In the plummet to silence an incandescent echo flurries around his declaration. When his voice reappears it's turned around, dropped low and ambling, "A lot of 'em didn't care much about anything, most days."

Letters scattered across eternity and held in a private box at home melt into my heart. Tommy's words from his years in Viet Nam make their way into a thousand colliding thoughts, teeming. My own voice rises, tentative but deliberate, "My brother's in Viet Nam – or he was. He'll be getting out soon."

Blue eyes pierce and pin me to my seat. His voice startles and deepens, "What? What'd you say?" Dark clouds pulse outside the windows.

"Uh, my older brother, he's been in 'Nam. Just getting out, at least I think, I hope he is." A chord drops low in my belly, tightens a notch and releases, carrying me I don't know where. My voice takes up again like a thing with a will of its own. "I worry about him, all the time. He sends me letters. Some of them are terrible. I know it's bad for him. Bad. He got strung out on heroin for awhile." Every fiber of my being keens to this.

"Yeah?" The blue eyes stay fastened on my face, his body crouched in the dim sharp coil of the night.

I nod back at him. "Yeah."

Blue eyes ferret away. There's a sigh from somewhere. He leans back in his seat. "That's bad," he rasps and then some convergence of past and future claims him. Claims me. After a few minutes I turn toward him slightly, the night dragging static charge.

Sorrow too deep to name lugs a question across my lips: "How, how long w-were you th-there?"

His hand lifts, waves and drops. "Doesn't matter," he says as he grips the steering wheel with a ferocity that makes me wince.

Past the facts of the night, past the unknown future, curiosity falls and catches on the closing ring of his words and I falter, "Well, yeah, my brother didn't want to go, he was in college, dropped out, couldn't stand waiting for his number to come up so, so he enlisted. I didn't, I didn't want him to go b-but he said, he said it was inevitable, felt like he couldn't get on with his life. So he ... he volunteered for the draft." My brother's last letter hangs in my thoughts, and I'm not in this place anymore.

And then I am and the blue-eyed man still sits in the seat across from me. "He ... he's a pretty gentle guy, not really a fighter, my brother. If he were on the front lines he, well, it'd be awful if he, I don't think he ..." and I'm lost again, gone.

"Yeah?" Blue eyes turn, facing me. "How old is he?"

I startle at his question and shiver, "Twenty–one, about, he's almost twenty-one." My brother. Twenty-one. "I really miss him. I, uh, he's, uh, gonna be home, soon, I hope." A piercing ache stabs through my heart.

"I knew a lot of guys that did that. Volunteered for the draft I mean. Hated it. Not all of 'em. But a lot, maybe most of 'em did." He ponders a minute and looks directly at me. "Do you write back to him, yer brother?"

His question reaches me through plunging space. I think of my brother's letters, the ache and care of all those lost thoughts pouring in words across paper. The yearning. What he said about my last letter to him. "Yeah. Yeah," I breathe, "I write to him all the time." A soft, heavy stone sits on my heart, pressing. "But I wish, I wish I could talk to him."

Time cracks. Leaves of memory float down in the shushing darkness. They settle, and there's nothing again in the silence. Only silence. And pain.

Our captor's voice rises, percolates along a stream that disjoins, breaks and rejoins. He talks and fidgets until a steady flow builds, a coursing meander, certain, uncertain. Precise and attentive I listen, every sense awake, alive.

He's back again to his work on the boats, personalities of the changing crew and funny quirks of the short-timers who, "just don't get it. Every boat's got its own way, you know, its own feel, the way it sits and moves through water. When you change somethin' or fix somethin' you gotta work it into the way the boat is, into the way it already is. Y' know?"

This time I'm right there with him. "Yeah. No. I mean, I don't know boats, but my dad had one, we used it at the lake, a reservoir really. He loved it. Me, I ride a bike, almost everywhere, and with my bike, I fix it and tune it myself, it's kinda the same thing."

We parry around about boats and bikes and work and then he takes the lead again, "Whaddaya do, y' got other brothers?"

I shift in my seat. "Yeah. One. He's younger," I say. "Our parents got divorced, our older sister and brother were gone by then. But we, well, we weren't and it was, uh, not so good, until we both got outta there." I clear my throat. "I worry about him too, all the time. I moved out early, before I graduated from high school and got a job, an apartment. He wouldn't come with me. Now he's moved out too, gone to live with our dad in California. I worry about them both, together, my dad and my brother, about how they're doing … about how lonely they must be."

The distance I feel with my father vibrates. The quick bite I feel thinking of him, of them alone, it's a lost feeling. I don't know why I think of my dad this way. Lost. But now it's both of them, my younger brother and my dad, lost together.

The driver muses, "That's, yeah, tough, that's sure, yeah," he shakes his head, "Being in 'Nam was a way to feel far away, from everybody." He sort of rocks in his seat and picks up the thread again, "tough, sure," and then it's another tack, roving between job and Army. He talks on.

I listen very, very awake. Rapt to his voice, I'm locked below words to a current running fast between us. I read that water, clear channel, treacherous rapid and each mystery snag. What claims me is not just what he's saying, but the sound inside his words, the flow, the way words run through and out of thought, link and separate. A dirge, a lament, an echo and in the rhythm the words cycle, pass and return, my body a shaman's flute. Where truth lists and sways through sound, I bend toward it, water witch. There's doubt, certainty, insistence. Moments build, gather on the surface, sustaining as his words stretch and grow.

Like Sunday dinner, like salvation, I bend to the rumor of home in the dip and the fade and the rise of his voice, a quiet, ephemeral thing. It's there, I feel it, in my answers that strain to speak true, only true, always true from my own returning cascade. I'm careful, not too careful, it's a feeling where clear passage opens, where whitewater pounds in a sweep to every side. Concentration claims the whole map.

My fear and revulsion step back. Fall away. They are dangerous in this navigation, this fast-moving water. He's here. I'm here. We're both in this river. There's little more than this listening. Telling. Listening. The river's course is my brother, this man, Viet Nam and our stories converge and slip down separate tributaries only to meet again and again. Words hum and mutter, a steady run. Until the natural course cycles back to drop us on the beach of the night in the van at the center of the facts. Four of us sit alone in the darkness. Silence, only silence, and words run aground.

In the density of night, still night, forever night, I breathe in my friends and the hover of waiting. I know nothing, feel everything, listening, listening, I'm a finely tuned bow, and silence holds the notes. Currents pulse and drop below ground where I float. Waves lap, I'm treading toward shore.

The driver's voice beads crossing from far away. Immersed in its cadence, I turn. Palpable but like mist, change hangs on new swells. Something keens deep inside of me, dowsing the new course, finding nucleus in the next pace of his thought.

"So, huh. I'm not sure what to do here," he looks back at Cora and Will then glances at me. Holding a moment, two, he sighs into the central question, a heavy hanging canopy that cloaks us, "I'd like to let you go."

Cora and Will surge forward, desperation gathering hope. "But there're obvious problems with that," he goes on. "There're cops and there's what's happened. And there's me."

All of us taste the strength of these things. Compressing his lips, he hesitates. We fall toward his next words like stars from the heavens. But he doesn't speak. He sits in his seat looking out on the night. When he turns again toward the center point between us I'm rapt to his every nuance, his movement, to his words, not what they'll say, but how they'll sound. He shrugs his shoulders.

"I could take you with me, south of the border to Mexico."

Skin crawls and I shudder. I feel time surge and twist, a serpent on the move.

He goes on, "But that seems, uh, pretty complicated. Seems maybe impossible." He looks down at his hands, out the windshield. His eyes turn to rove between all of us.

Will and Cora crowd forward, crammed up against the engine casing. He looks at his hands again. "No matter what, there'd have to be promises."

"Sure. Of course! Sure!" Breathless, the two shove up until the casing creaks, "Yeah. Sure!" Biting lips, almost panting, their voices rise and toss, one over the top of the other, heads nodding with vigor. "Of course, yeah, whatever you say." A pause, the strain to hold it, and their voices tumble again, "We could, you know, travel with you. And ... and then, uh, you could let us go near ... near the border or, or somewhere like that."

I watch the driver, uneasy, calculated play across his face, in the pensive weave of his next words. "Yeah. Sure. Sounds good. But the border is a long way from here." He picks at a fingernail. "What about things like, uh, using bathrooms? What about gas, pretty hard to keep you guys tied up, hidden all the time. It's a long way to *Mexico*."

I shudder once more. The clear point in his words, the watershed between us, grows murky. I shudder again and start to speak.

But Cora pushes upright on her knees, breaking in over me, voice bright and snaking, "We could work it out. We could lay low, stay in the van. We'd do whatever you say. We can keep quiet, keep a promise." Will nods like a bobble-headed doll on a dashboard. Their eagerness jars hard against something sharp inside me, a nerve ending stabbed and left raw.

The driver looks at them, leans into their enthusiasm. "Uh huh, but what about food and all that basic stuff?" he asks. "You couldn't just lie in the van for hundreds and hundreds of miles." A picture forms in my mind, the three of us lying bound in the van, and it gyrates against a side current that's forming. A string stretched taut that whines out of tune. Something curves through time that should not be called forward.

"Oh," say Will and Cora, both up on their knees now leaning over the engine casing, both talking at once. "No! No! We could do it! We *could* work it out! We'd promise to stay hidden, not cause any trouble. You could bring food to the van, there'd be ways, we wouldn't need much."

Anxiety and hope grate beneath their words and lash crosscurrent in the spaces between. A chord tightens, strident, and I nearly gasp. The driver cuts in, "Yeah, and that would be expensive, food for what, days at least, a week, a couple of weeks? You'd get tired and want to get attention, find cops. It'd be really hard to keep all of you hidden all the time. You wouldn't be able to just lay in the back, not moving day after day."

Cora jumps, "Well, no! We'd promise not to try anything, we'd just, you know, ride along and, and ..." racing and pleading, her voice promises, promises, stretches and stretches so thin. ...

Squealing across nerves the shrill ring of false tone cries discordant beneath her words, beneath Will's words, beneath the debate flying between them. *We need to get back to speaking the truth. Nothing else can save us. I know it. It's the only way to break this spell.* The bowstring inside me strains impossible tension. Dragged in the wake of their desperate lies I suddenly see it, feel it — gaping rifts cut by the howl of each false promise, holes torn by every false claim. *We cannot beg him. We cannot lie to him. We cannot lie to ourselves. We have to speak truth. We have to meet this man speaking truth, only truth.*

The driver tips forward, smiling in Will's face. I see it forming, a cat and mouse game. The driver nods, nods. Like delirious children they all nod as the screech of phony promise clashes against this strange idea of a traveling troupe to Mexico. Anything they say, anything they'll say, anything to convince the lie, convince him. Their desperate sham hangs us out over a sheer edge, and they're oblivious. I feel the ropes unraveling.

Our captor transforms again. He's enjoying himself. Their shared goal spins like a top, fast but at the edge of teeter.

Cora and Will leap forward, hubbubs of reassurance: "No! Oh! NO! You wouldn't have to worry, not at *all*, we'd promise not to talk to *anyone*, we'd promise not to go for help, we would *promise* to stay out of sight. NO, you wouldn't have to worry at all. Hey, and you'd tie us up, anyway. You, you, you could *trust* us! *You could trust us!* We wouldn't cause trouble. We wouldn't talk to *anyone!!"* On a communal breath they exhale false certainty, "It'd be ok. We'd just ride along and get to the *border.* We can get there. And then you can just let us go!"

Panic crawls, constricting my heart. Coercion flashing through every word spells our doom. Truth isn't here, it isn't inside these words, not the sound of them not what they say — not his, not theirs. As clarity pops I feel the tuning string inside me bend to the point of breaking.

The clutter of a new impossible plan plasters across their open mouths, falling over Will's loose lips. "Look," he sniffs, takes a breath.

"We ..." Cora plunges in.

"Yeah?" Our abductor leans to the hub of their desire.

"NO!" my voice sheers, snapping through tumult. Echoes launch through the metal fittings of the van.

All three faces stun in my direction.

Clawing up my throat, words leap to gain ground from Cora and Will. "NO!" I bite out again. "Stop it! *Stop it!* You all know this won't work! It's impossible! You know we can't make this work!"

As the force of my words hit, fixing in the stares of three sets of eyes locked on mine, blank incomprehension flips quickly. Slicing fury from Will, confusion from Cora. The gunman's eyes drop, daggers cutting between us. But I latch onto their eyes, one by one by one, unswerving.

I want most to clap my hands over my ears against the next harangue the next sham, a new attack for my impudence. But in the upset momentum, deceit suspends for one moment, avalanche on the brink of burying us. One more false promise, and there will be no chance against what will come.

Menace smolders in Will's eyes. Disgust curls his lip. Cora's eyes narrow to slits. Our abductor watches us closely. From face to face his attention travels until his eyes fasten on mine. "We can't make this work," I say. "You all know it. There has to be another way."

Will's mouth opens, closes and smothers. The driver watches me. Cora drops to her haunches, lips slammed in dismay. Hushed momentum festers. We all stare into the breach. Sitting very straight I wait braced but utterly clear. The driver leans back, slow against his door and the window, the night, the pressing night. Arms cross over his chest. His eyes rivet from my face to the dazed, bewildered slump of Cora, Will deflating, and back to my face again. The burst of their collective bubble reverberates in the silence.

Vivid blue eyes watch me unflinching. His gaze shifts only briefly as first Cora then Will lowers back to the floor. Boot eyelets squeal against metal. I, too, sit back in my seat. Clarity dangles. A sense of great risk hovers inside the vacancy. Something new has entered between us. The truth that has ruptured to the forefront locks in my core. For the first time through this awful night I feel absolutely no fear.

The driver speaks, "If I just let you go, you'd go to the police. I need time to get to the border and across." His words settle like a monk's habit around us. The night crushes emptiness beyond the windows and metal shell of the van.

He turns to face forward, holds both hands clasped at the center of the steering wheel. His chest heaves questions that drop and float in a welt of indecision. "If I was to let you go," his head rises and he looks across and then over his shoulder as he turns sideways again in his seat, "You'd have to promise not to go to the cops," leaning forward, forearms on his knees and hands clasped, his voice and eyes rise together, "promise not to report me to any authorities at all." And then it's as though he's stepped away, leaving his words to spin between us, eyes piercing each one of us in turn.

I sit with utter certainty. There is one possible path toward daylight and this is it. I know I'll make this promise and make it absolute. Otherwise there is no point. "Yes," my answer comes plain and immediate. "Yes. I promise. If you let us go, I promise not to go to the police."

From the back there's nothing, complete stillness. As we breathe I don't think but listen, from a balance beam of simplest clarity. It's not just up to me. Out of nowhere Cora's voice rises, a murmur pitching forward on a wave. It rings decisive, true. "Yes. Yes. I promise. I won't go to the police."

In slow-motion repeat Will's voice sputters along her trail. "Ok. Yeah. I promise. No police."

Our captor makes no answer. His hands drop to his lap. Turning away to face forward again, his head falls back against his seat. I turn to face the front, too. We are all silhouettes in the gloom. Shoving my hands deep into coat pockets I slump into worn upholstery. Ease lifts and settles, as though straight out of Earth herself. Exhaustion wells up. A spaciousness widens in my core, drifts in the opening between unknowns, and I let the weariness come. The bitter sky, where stars wheel as clouds surge, darkens.

The breathing of my friends joins the breathing of our captor to fuse with a larger breath the desert is taking. Vast feelings of wonder at the enormity of this lost place of the world cross between one breath and two and fill me with utter surrender. Everything is as it will be.

A swell moves up through my throat. Startle to a tiniest sound rises to smallest trickle and teases across my lips. My voice low and vulnerable breaks into song.

"Oh, the sisters of mercy, they are not departed or gone. They were waiting for me when I thought that I just can't go on. They taught me their comforts and later they brought me their song. Oh, I hope you run into them, you who've been traveling so long."

Barely past whisper, my shy, tight voice grows in the shadowy dim. Songs ply and nothing stops them, every song I've ever known. One after another and the narrow pipe of my voice expands, flounders in low, airy lament. I think of Brad.

"I loved you in the morning, your kisses deep and warm, your hair upon the pillow like a sleepy golden storm. Yes, many loved before us. I know that we are not new. In city and in forest they smiled like me and you. But now it's come to distances and each of us must try. Your eyes are soft with sorrow. Hey, that's no way to say good-bye."

The songs pour and take up a life of their own. Ripening they spill arboreal across dry desert air.

> Like a bird on the wire,
> Like a drunk in a midnight choir
> I have tried in my way to be free...

> ...Suzanne takes you down to her place near the river,
> You can hear the boats go by
> You can spend the night beside her
> And you know that she's half crazy
> But that's why you want to be there
> And she feeds you tea and oranges that come all the way from China,
> And just when you want to tell her that you have no love to give her,
> She gets you on her wavelength
> And she let's the river answer...

> ... Like a worm on a hook
> Like a knight in some old-fashioned book
> I have saved all my ribbons for thee. ...

An endless current and I feel the life that's been mine, give it over, feel my sister, my brothers, my grandmother, my father, my mother, my friends. I feel the earth pulse beneath me. Sorrow and joy become one and the same. All songs pour out of me, childhood to the woman I now am.

And my mother's voice rings clear in the night, clear in the heavens, clear through the dark van, how she sang to me as a child, "Somewhere over the rainbow, blue birds fly. Birds fly over the rainbow, why then, oh why can't I? Someday you'll wish upon a star and wake up where the clouds are far behind you. Where troubles melt like lemon drops, away above the chimney tops, and that's where you'll find me…"

Songs come full circle, my voice winds away.

> Oh, the Sisters of Mercy, they are not departed or gone.
> They were waiting for you when you thought that you just can't go on.
> And they brought you their comforts and later they brought you their song.
> I hope you run into them, you who've been traveling so long.

It's all a melting, life emptying unstaunched. Longing and contrition spark and flee, all things release.

There's only emptiness. As the last word of the last stanza of the last note falls from lips and memory, velvet darkness quivers around me. Within the silence there is no fear, no terror, no confusion. There is no hope, no concern. Evaporated to only stillness and the four of us sit within it, there is nothing. Dark and light pillage the sky. Wrapped in warmth, vibrating, I long only for sleep.

A glimmer expands inside of me. The night and the desert and the old pain suffuse into joyous bliss. Ecstasy swells to encompass every particle of who or what I am or was or thought or might have been. The facts of the night disperse. Indifferent to where we've been, glistening on air that hovers in sleepy completion, I drop into utter repose. Ease prickles into expansion, supple along scalp, spiraling down spine through every limb. I dissolve into atoms, inside outside streaming.

We will live. We will die. It doesn't matter. No claim, no hold. Letting go, there's the night. There's nothing. Whatever comes will come. It is sleep that finds me.

16

The Way Home

"Move it! Get y'r gear!"

Shocked out of sleep I snap forward at the stark zero warmth of our captor gathering himself. I do not recognize him.

With brutal force he barks once more, "Move it! Get your gear! Out! Get out of the van!"

Scraping and scrabbling sounds grate behind my seat. I look around in confusion, trying to locate my pack. Our captor's gaze sweeps through the van, not looking directly at any of us. His chiseled features crack on a third precise order, harsher yet. *"Get out! Out!"*

And he launches from the driver's door, a torpedo pushing the night on muscled breath. I catapult out my own door into darkness. Stumbling to the ground, heart racing, I find him abruptly beside me, the rapid stiff shell of his body heaving the sliding door free. He yanks Cora then Will then our packs from the gaping maw of the van and frees their hands. We all stagger into a loose circle. His head flicks a swift and wordless command and we clamber to pull on our packs.

For a brief moment there's a veneer of normalcy, gear prepped, straps checked, fitted, belts buckled into place. Gathered again in a circle, we turn to face him — and find ourselves facing the gun.

All eyes rivet to its sparkling menace. Each motion in military precision, he beads its threat on each of our faces. "I'm lettin' ya go. Remember y'r promise."

His face is set as hard as the first moment he pulled the gun on me, a thousand lifetimes ago. We all stare for a beat. I don't know him. I know him. I don't know him.

Surrender still permeates my cells with expansive bliss. At this moment it winnows on the caustic clash of our captor's armed front and arcs like a revelation. I tilt across the small space between us. "Thank you," I say, "thank you," and enfold him in quick embrace. I pull away and words tumble, unbidden. "I love you," I say, a brief smile ghosting through my euphoria, untouched by his violence, unfazed by this strange man. His eyes flicker and startle.

We take hold of our pack straps and all stare for the length of one breath.

"Run!" he snarls.

And we are leaping to the desert shadow as the gun rakes across bitter night, acid haunting our backs. "Run! And don't look back," he yells behind us. "If you do I'll shoot every one of you!"

We race, deer in flight from the man and the van and the gun.

Running parallel to Will and Cora we pitch through rabbitbrush over rock and fear as headlights arc wide behind us. They swing across our racing forms.

Panic seizes me as I see my friends' packs slipping low on their backs. I cry out, an echo into eternity. "No! *NOOO!*" Running breathless I stumble, pull upright. "Leave your packs on, *leave them on!!* Don't let them drop, *they're our only protection!!*" In the looming quagmire of shadows I trip, catch myself before hitting ground. On the rise, next stride and I yell again, panting, *"Don't take them off, leave your packs on,"* and in a glance see their packs shift back up as we fly across the night spectrum.

The headlights slow, stop and we're captured, all three of us in full spotlight as we run. *He's gonna do it,* I think, body clenched within the brilliant reach of those beams. *He's gonna shoot us after all.* But I don't slow. I leap sage and rock and we are still three racing, his sharp menace a torment at our backs. No word, no signal, but we separate, the curse of light prying apart our flight. We spread, running into darkness away from terror that burns through each suck of freezing night air.

And the lights begin a slow arc again, pan across our backs and the whicker of gravel grinds beneath rubber. Light passes away from us. I flounder in the sudden black pitch and turn.

The van completes a half-circle rotation, pauses. No light no sound to reveal us. I hover under the weight of the clouds. Pebbles grind beneath boot soles to my right as they scramble to stop. I cringe and look to Cora and Will. Gravel squeals again beneath tires racing. In the dim I see Will then Cora half-turn to the sound, and watch the white van surge onto the road and disappear. We stand separate and dumb, blind with relief as dread holds us. I listen with every cell in my body.

When there is no more sound we all rush together. Cora and I leap in the air in dizzy abandon, cry out.

"How'd you do it, Cat, how'd you do that?" Cora grabs me, and we wheel around.

Will is scathing, bringing us back to Earth. "We can't be sure he's gone."

Somebody's voice breaks the spell, I don't know whose: "We've gotta get back to the interstate. It's our only choice."

Cora's face swings upward to take in the sky. It feels like the edge of a flood, hovering tumult about to wrench open.

Giddy and shell-shocked, we choose the direction we think will carry us back to the interstate, the same direction the van went. Falling in together we attempt a steady gait. Every step is hard. Each movement lashes at jarring memory. We each wage a separate battle to face forward, step out and keep going. I feel like I'm sliding along a dark surface, slippery one moment, sticky the next, steps jolt no matter how much care I put in placing my feet.

We speak at lowest levels. The world feels ethereal, crowding around us. We struggle to plan from little-known detail. It's hard to say what's worse, silence or the sound of our voices breaking it.

There was an exit ramp. We know that; we came off it. What else? A phone. We need a phone, maybe more than anything. We can't grasp barest points beyond that. We could be hours walking. Pressing together, we break apart, too much distance is unbearable, too close, a tangle. But forward we go in wincing, zigzag motion. The lonely expanse of desert and sky scare us to silence. We could all shoot off in different directions because of our distracted, fearful thoughts and hardly notice, but for a word here and there.

I don't know how long we walk. But out of nowhere an archaic ruin stuns immediately in front of us. We careen, veer away and stare. No memory and wrong turn hiss through jangled nerves. Where did this looming impossible mass come from? Locked in bizarre wonder and awestruck I gawk, unable to make any sense of it. Will and Cora turn and stagger, turn back and stop to grapple with soul-sinking dismay. As though time itself has split, we stand lost in confusion. I feel caught in the wreck of an ageless tempo.

And all at once, Will cries out. The span ahead settles into known form. Dazed we approach the freeway overpass and walk under it to the other side, bemused. A stop sign stands at the end of the off-ramp in octagonal triumph. For a brief moment we hover at this place of beginnings and endings. Shudders course through me, and I veer away from the salient marker, pass it by.

Flinching in the darkness, fear rippling off our backs we find no white van in sight. There is no one here, no one at all. We gaze across wide expanse to a massive upslope. There is nothing else that stands out in the darkness.

And then we see a square white building. It vibrates out of the gloom. We step forward. Archaic standing stones materialize between the building and us. My mind twists to place them. And they too, settle into known form: gas pumps and a station. The night breaks open on waves of saving grace. We rush toward the shelter and the promise of a phone. Scrabble of boots hit concrete, and intaglio caution rakes through me. Will slows at the first set of pumps. He reaches his arms out to catch Cora and me mid-stride then presses us back.

"You should wait here," he mumbles. "It's better if I go ahead and knock on the door. Then we'll know something. If anyone's here it`ll probably be guys. I'll check it out." He looks at Cora. She nods and we take one step back to wait by the pumps. Will strides to the door.

His knuckles rap on the hard surface. Silence. He raps again. A rustling sound scrapes from inside. Gruff voice strikes from the other side of the door. "Who's there? Whaddaya want? Go away!"

Will clears his throat and calls back, "Hey, look, sorry, I know it's late but I'm with some friends out here. There're three of us. We need help."

"Can't help you. Go away!"

"Yeah. Look, we just need a phone. We've had a little trouble. It's really cold. Please." Will ducks his head and leans on the doorjamb, one arm raised.

"Can't help you. No phone here, just buildin' this place, no phone. Go on, get away, we're not openin' the door!"

"Look, please! I've got women out here and they're hurt, it's cold. We just need to get inside until morning, we won't bother you." Belligerence laces Will's voice.

Alarm rises in me, and I take a step forward watching the changing tension of his stance.

Anger turns to a holler behind the station door. "Get the hell away from that door! There is no phone! There's no help! There's nothin'! You're not comin' in here! Get away!"

Will lurches and pounds on the door. "You gotta help us!" he yells. "Come on! There're women out here, hurt. You've gotta help!" Will's unhinged stupidity wrenches inside me. A whine like a saw blade picks up in my core. I turn and push Cora away from the pumps, shove her hard away from the station, point off to the desert beyond.

"Run!" I hiss, *"Run! Fast! Get away from here!"*

And I'm sprinting toward Will as he strikes the door with both fists. A growl erupts inside the building. "Don't gotta do nothin'," curses fly behind the door, "You better get outta here." I hear scrambling and other voices. "Not opening that door, fella! Unless it's to come after you, get the hell outta here! We got guns!"

"Will! No!" I yell. "*NO!*" he leans into the door, demented, hands girding to fists. Fury and disgust pulse through me, but I run for him. "Will! Come on! Give it up! Get the fuck away from there!" Cold rage takes hold in me as he pummels harder on the door. *Can't he see it? Can't he feel what's coming? How can he be so stupid?* I grab his wrists and pull back before his fist hits the door again. I'm yanked half-way off my feet. He wheels around. I grab one of his arms and pull hard. Grappling against his size and the rage beginning to pour from his mouth I scream at him, "*C'mon, Will! We need help, not more trouble!*" His next lunge hits the door, several voices inside shouting wordless strings of curses. Belting alarm swarms inside me.

The main voice yells over other muttering voices, "Get the hell away from here! Last chance! I said we got guns, and we ain't afraid to use 'em!"

"Will! Come on! Come on! You're gonna get us all killed!" I fling myself at his back and feel something break through his dumb concentration as futility marshmallows through his limbs. I shove in desperate effort against his slackening weight.

The fury gathering behind that door, suddenly he feels it, too.

I drag him by one arm, and we both turn to run. "Asshole! Assholes!" he shouts back at the blank wall, but I'm pulling him past the pumps toward deeper darkness and the desert beyond. He grunts out profanity, but at last we're both running flat out.

I careen against him. "Shut up, Will," I hiss, giving him one last shove. "Just shut up and keep moving!" and then I break free of whatever he's going to do and stretch out in full stride as the station door scrapes open behind us, sheering across distance and time.

I leap to desert. Voices cry out, there's a blur of furious volleys. Two shots cut the air close around us, a third whizzes past at ear level. Bullets slice darkness into new pockets of terror, and I run without thought, body sole owner of my flight. Will slams along to my left, and suddenly we're pushing through curtains of sleet that descend without warning. A veil, ice bullets that dance and sing on the ground at our feet, it's our last vestige of hope. It plays out in the thousand pelting missiles, visibility snuffed, our final protection.

Somewhere in the not so far away a door slams. My legs go to rubber, melt to a wobbling stagger.

Where is Cora? Where's Cora?

Despair twists, and I stumble ahead. A fetal-shaped mass takes form on the ground, next to Cora's discarded pack. I drop to my knees without fully stopping. Sobbing wrenches rise from the muffle that's Cora. I reach out to sweep her long, heavy hair from the sodden muddy ground and cradle her head in my lap. I look around for Will. He stands sullen a few feet away. Throbbing malice emanates all around him.

A sharp rage rampages through me, threatening to explode as I look at him. But I turn away and bend low to Cora, who's beginning to sob out of control. "Sh. Shshshshhhh. Cora, Cora, help me, we've got to get you warm," I say. I look up into the freezing sleet that shafts down now in earnest. The thick mud will freeze, soon if the temperature keeps dropping. I bend low to her ear. "Sh. Sh. It's gonna be alright." I look up at Will, who's moved closer, glowering like a sulking child. Cora is shaking so hard I feel her lifeline spinning out of grasp. I bend lower to cover her body with my torso, turning my head up to Will.

"Will," I call sharp, then sharper. "Will!" He raises his head and looks at me, blank and savage. "Will! Look! It's wet and getting wetter. It's freezing." He sweeps his gaze up to the sky and back. "She's hysterical, going into shock. We've got to get her covered, warm."

"Yeah," he says flatly. "We're not gonna last out in this anyway," and continues to stand and scowl.

"Look, Will. Start with something. Now! I need help!" The fury I feel toward him stabs through my voice. He flinches. "C'mon!" He steps to Cora's pack, yanks it upright and starts to undo the straps. Cora's shaking so hard it scares me past the shock that's already ferreted deep in us all. "Sh. Sh. We're gonna get you warm, Cora. Dry. C'mon. I need your help now. C'mon. Sh. Sh. It's okay, it'll be okay." I pull her upright, and she leans into me, dead weight.

Will bends down to pull her sleeping bag free and unfurls it in my direction. I grab a corner and drag it around Cora as I look up again into the sleet. Stinging, stabbing it melts rivulets in a race down my face. A hard shudder quakes through Cora that matches a shudder rattling through me. I shift my own pack off my back to rip at the straps and free my bag. As I pull the bulk around my shoulders, half-tenting Cora beneath it, sleet hits the surface, and crystals turn into water seeping and massing in the canvas pores. I gag on the burgeoning scent of army surplus.

I look up at Will. "She's going into shock, Will! We've gotta do something to get her warm!"

He towers over us, his own bag lying limp now across his shoulders. Shaking his head he looks around. "We can't stay here," he ruminates. I nod, encouraging him. "We've gotta get outta this weather. We won't make it to morning if we don't … there's no light at all on the horizon … she'll only get worse not better." I nod again. He's got it, then. Hypothermia. It's not far away. Not for any of us. And Cora for sure won't tolerate much more. I drop back to soothe her. Will kicks at sage and looks around. Sleet thins, and he suddenly points back to the underpass. "We'll have to climb up under there. There's nothin' else, it's the only place outta this weather."

Relief floods, and I lean into Cora. "We've got a place out of the wet, Cora, you've gotta help us, you've gotta get up and help us get there, we're all cold, we have to move." Her sobs drop a decibel. I look up at Will. He grabs her arm and pulls her upright.

"Let's go," he says. Will swings his pack over one shoulder and reaches for Cora's hand. I stand and take Cora's arm. Sobbing whimpers break and die, break and die as she leans into me. I struggle to keep the muddy bags around us. Exhaustion buckles through my body. Waiting a moment, the heavy weight of making the distance looms against muscles gone crazy. I watch Will gather and juggle all three packs. When he starts out I manage one step then another, straggling behind to guide Cora across muddy ground. I almost cry seeing her bent like an old, old woman.

I'm suddenly so tired that I'm willing to let our sleeping bags fall and lie where they may. But then we're at the underpass, and the foot of a steep incline leads to cover below the interstate. The climb is incomprehensible to me. Cora and I weave together precariously. My legs feel like lead. Will slides down to pull Cora up to a barren camp he's laid out. I nearly drop to all fours to follow them, clenching at what it will mean to crouch for hours on this cold, cold ground, every one of us already chilled to the bone. We all must be near some state of shock. I watch my arms quiver and verge on useless. At the top I stuff Cora's sleeping bag into a pad beneath her as Will lowers her down. Then I try to do the same for myself, hunkering into sickening weariness on the slope below them.

Will sinks down next to Cora and spreads his bag to cloak them both. His body heat will pull her through. I feel grateful for that and sit staring into what's left of the night. But there's no light at all seeping on the horizon. I know in a sudden flash that night will last forever. Hours don't exist at all, only the dark and the cold. Clouds open up, and freezing rain pelts the desert floor in earnest, hail pellets bouncing white on road and mud and sage. Only vapor winds and whispers around us. The gas station hulks beyond. We don't speak. There's nothing to say in this drenched, frozen fracture of eternity.

I stare, willing something decent into form. Horror at what daylight will bring drags. In the shiver of cold, misery thickens. Shame festers and skirts endless outer limits. Cold, cold, cold goes on forever. I sit listless before the shattering facts, so cold I hurt. I can't imagine facing anyone for any reason. Hauntings set loose in the sleet and pain slice. Night streams on and on and on, nightmares bunch around me. The horror of what my sister and mother might have had to endure, the horror of what has happened, the horror of where we are and what lies ahead are banshees of fear and disgust and dismay. They gather around us, pressing, pressing.

The ancient sea in the sand of this unknown place shifts and stirs. Forever dwindles unnoticed into the soft, diffuse light of a breaking day, sneaks past my tortured reverie. Vague shapes take hold in the shifting haze. Frozen to where we sit by things more heathen and rank than awful cold, coming light begs for action. There seems nowhere to go, nothing to do in the prescient ooze. I shrug it all off to hunker deep into dark and impossible thoughts; circumstance lies bleeding and broken in every direction. There is *nothing* but this misery. Why chase more?

When Will's voice finally clamps on a word, it's not quite clear to me. Another croak and the word splays out, hollow like a dead or dying thing: "Help," he says.

No kidding. I'm astonished and annoyed by his intrusion. Hasn't that word — that effort — proved nearly fatal? There's no meaning to it.

As though out of nothing but ethers and breath, at a second stop sign just across from the gas station, a school bus sits idling on a road that winds into the roots of high desert mountains. In the hazy, slight dawn its yellow bulk is dazzling. I stare, blank to its meaning or charm.

Will stirs again, mumbling, "Bus ... help ... " I ignore him, refuse to comprehend the significance of what this means. A pause and then he coughs, "One of us should go, ask for help."

Help. There it is again, that meaningless word. I turn it over, feel its burn as it hovers then boomerangs through my body. I'm revolted by it. I wait for one of them to rise, walk down the incline and make the approach. I wait for Will to claim his own idea. In the waiting and watching a pickup truck pulls up behind the bus and idle vapor meanders a rise, wends to curlicues that float and kiss the back of the bus. I contemplate the vapor and its path. No one moves.

I feel angry with Will and Cora. Humiliation takes root in my bones, clashing against Will's imperative. It's his. Let him act on it. I'd rather die than stand and walk to that bus. Will croaks again, "We need help." Resentment bridles, I wait again for him to get up and go for it. Cora stirs, whispering. The world turns. I sit waiting them out.

Then I get it. Neither of them will take this on. Their resistance meets my own. I look to the yellow bus, the line forming behind it. I reel with the thought of the strangers sitting out there. Mud plasters our clothes and gear. I turn away to imagine other options. Nothing comes. What can I possibly say? The appalling night clings to us, siphoning off my will. Someone has to move.

Real dawn stacks the cards against me. Light is growing. Restless, edgy tension shimmies down my back. We're nowhere, nothing. How much more nothing can there be? This vies with a dim but razor-sharp awareness that cuts at the edges of thought. We won't be allowed to stay here forever. *She could get worse, will get worse, we'll all get worse, worse than what?* The chill, the dread, the agony strains on my mind and snaps the wait.

I stand, muddied sleeping bag sliding to the ground, and teeter forward in stiff descent. Alarm pulls in my gut when I reach the bottom. I keep moving, knowing a pause spells trouble, disaster of one kind or another. The only thing I can trust now is motion, so I trust it with the full weight of walking the road toward the yellow bus with my hands deep in my pockets, drooped head lifting to assess the woman who sits in the driver's seat. Sentences string together in my mind, fall apart, string together, fall apart until they dissolve out of reach or comprehension. Another car, a truck, a car pull up, one by one a line lengthens behind the bus. I steel away from panic, have trouble breathing, give up knowing what to say. If there's a point to this it will come.

The driver of the bus stares straight ahead from her seat over my head. Given the path of her gaze you would never guess that someone was walking the road toward her. At the front of the bus I veer left toward the accordion door where passengers normally board. It is closed. Tight. No one is inside but the driver. No one approaches from the waiting cars. I stand looking in at her. Nothing. So I knock once on the glass. The driver doesn't move.

Knocking again, I pause then call out, just loud enough to penetrate the door, "We need help. Please." Nothing. "We've been out here all night in the cold. There's another woman back there who's hurt." Nothing. The driver sits staring straight ahead as if I were a ghost in another universe she can't see. I look in, for a moment bemused. "Please," I try again, "We need help." She never once looks my way.

Her small meanness penetrates into awful grief gnawing on me. Anger spikes ever so slightly, pushes me around to her side of the bus. She sits just above my head looking into a distance so vast it clearly does not include me. Her indifference twists in my gut, her face an insult. I reach as high as I can and rap on the glass by her ear. She doesn't move. Sorrow so deep I had no idea it existed anywhere in the world wells from a stark place inside me. I study her through my pain.

"I'm, we're not asking to get on your bus. Please, just, where is a phone?" I call out. "Or, or someone who could help us? There must be something, a phone, someone, somewhere near here." I stare at her. She stares off into morning forever.

I turn on my heel and walk back to the truck idling behind the bus. Shame looms from the gooey, rutted freeze of the road. In the pickup another woman sits in the driver's seat, her hair curling a frizzed bob, glasses in cat-eye glare, a child of 10 or so in the passenger seat across from her. They look to the bus ahead as though it were the Holy Grail shimmering in morning haze and I the one to steal it. She and the child are born of granite. I rap once light on her window.

"Please, I, we, my friends, we just want to get home, that's all, find a phone," I say. "We've been hurt, we need help." Her glass-eyed indifference mimics so exactly the driver in the bus ahead it would seem ESP is absolute etiquette, messy strangers the worst of affronts. This coldness seems to fly vehicle to vehicle, like precise instruction, an ironclad rule of the clan.

Anger flattens to gritty will. My mind grows sharp. I turn and press toward one more attempt at mercy. I walk to a low, white sedan, next link in this vilifying chain. Stark masks of one adult and three children face me facing them. They are stones. I stand taller and stare in at them. Sorrow for these children flashes, an extraordinary lesson on inhumanity. My heart swells. Alongside stubborn fascination reels my only answer to their silent ridicule: This is a bypass for fear, for pain. Theirs. Mine.

Straddling their ignorance I step past the sedan toward a next truck. Clarity lights in a flash half-way to it. Hands drop to my sides, not futility but resolve. I'm done. There's nothing here that remotely resembles help. Quick and clean I turn on my heel. Walking past car, truck, bus and empty promise, past empty eyes that stare and stare and stare, I feel a humming buzz like beehive transmission. I shift it off my back. I turn to look at all of them as I clear the front of the bus, freed of need or hope or return. Dread and all its clamorings melt away. At the bottom of the overpass I stride straight up the incline, pull my sleeping bag off the damp ground and set my pack upright, swinging it to my shoulders.

I look at Will and Cora huddled in the cold. "Get your packs, your bags," I say. "It's time to leave. There's no help here. Let's go. We gotta get up on the freeway and catch a ride."

I sling my sleeping bag over one shoulder, reach down one hand to take Cora's and help her to her feet. As she stands we look at each other a moment. She's present and clear in her eyes. As she grabs her pack I turn and slog down the steep incline in helpless relief. Will and Cora scramble their gear together and descend. I look up the muddy slope to the freeway, take a breath and stretch forward to climb to the shoulder above.

"We probably can't get a ride either, not like this. Look at us!" Will says, planting himself at the bottom of the slope.

Trying to climb in the slippery, viscous mud I turn to look at him. I look back for a moment at the bus and its lineup. No one moves. I look long and hard into Cora's eyes, she looks straight back into mine. I look at Will. "You wanna go back and talk with those people, Will, go right ahead," I say flatly. "Be my guest. But I'm gettin' outta here. Now. While we still can."

And then we're all slipping and sliding as we climb the muddy slope, grabbing at sage and shrub to pull ourselves up onto the edge of the freeway. I feel acutely aware of the way we're precisely silhouetted on this high point above all the idling vehicles. I see scatterings of buildings and sporadic houses strung out across the huge landscape behind them from this vantage point. Exposure feels less a threat and more revelation in the dim morning light. I know it's all just illusion. Things can turn on a dime. We're as obvious to them standing here as we'll ever be. In this moment, I feel neither baffled nor concerned. I feel outlined, certain, present, in place. A car whizzes past us, spray shoots out from speeding rubber like sparklers off a passing jet stream. One thumb goes out and up but too late, an unlikely chance anyway. We're a sight, a mess in sorry disarray struggling with the problem of three sodden sleeping bags. But we're alive. In the bewilderment of unstrung bags and equipment, disheveled beyond recognition, we stand in the mist and the muck waiting for the impossible: a ride. For the first time in hours, maybe days, I feel utterly perfectly clear. This is where we belong. This is what we have to do.

After lashing our packs as securely as we can, another car passes. Stuffing the ungainly sleeping bags into our packs seems beyond our capacity. Will looks at me with *I-told-you-so* disgust. I look back at him, spare smile and turn away to stick out my thumb. And a VW Bug appears in the near distance, shooting from mist, as unlikely as any ride we might have imagined. It slows. All of us have thumbs out now. The Bug pulls over on the shoulder, idling. The driver reaches across the front passenger seat past a large German shepherd calmly watching us and rolls down the window.

"Mornin'. Where ya' goin'?"

"Uh, trying to get back to Utah," Will says, as he leans down near the window, a pace away from the dog.

The driver looks unconvinced, but he kills the engine, hesitates a moment looking at the road ahead. "Well," he says, swinging his gaze back and bending down so he can lock eyes a moment with each of us, "Your best shot would be to just get outta here. Looks like you've had a kinda rough night. Hard place to catch a ride." He pushes the driver door open and swings out while we stare at the tiny car with greater doubt than his. He looks us over. The German shepherd grins through the passenger window.

He walks around the back of the car. "You're a mess. But I think I can probably get all of you in. Or maybe two of you and the other can wait for a second ride." We must all flinch, because he hesitates, stands quiet a moment. "Here's the thing: I can only take you as far as this side of Winnemucca, about 30 miles. I'd have to drop you on this side of town. Gotta be somewhere north of there really soon, it's all I can do. So if you're gonna ride with me you gotta promise now not to hassle me to take you any further, you gotta get out when we get there, when I say so. If you can accept that then we can go," he says, glancing down the slope to the raft of vehicles below with a strange look in his eye. "I'd take it if I were you. And I'm in a hurry."

"Sure, yeah," I sigh with relief. "Appreciate it. But can you get us all in there, with your dog, our stuff?"

"Yeah, yeah, think so, it'll be tight, what about the two of you?" he turns to Cora and Will.

"Yeah, sure … yeah, of course, appreciate it, thanks, thanks," they stammer in unison.

"Ok then," the man reaches down, grabs a pack, walks to the front of the Bug, pops open the hood and slings the pack inside. With skilled precision, reassuring even as it's unnerving, he starts slinging gear fast. He motions against handing him my pack and bag. My heart sinks as I imagine hitching alone, left behind. But he turns to Will, "That'll probably have to squeeze in front of you on the floor, or with the girls in back. C'mon. I gotta go, probably shouldn't have stopped. Climb in."

He opens the passenger door, leans in, "Rocket, back!" and the shepherd hops to the backseat, "No, back, keep going, all the way." Rocket whines once and hops over into the narrow space behind the back seat.

"Ladies," he turns and bows slightly, sweeping his arm as he pulls the seat forward. We climb in back, dragging my filthy bag and orange backpack in behind us. Self-conscious about the mud and his seats I try to cram everything to the floor, but our clothes are nearly as bad. "Yeah, drag," he takes a breath. "Don't worry, no weddings today."

He leaves Will to work himself into the tight front seat and hurries to the driver's side, swinging in to start the car. He glances once at the smear of buildings below the highway. "Not the best place to catch a ride," he says again looking into the rearview mirror at Cora and me, wrinkling his brow. "Kinda dangerous place to hitchhike."

And he's pulling out onto the highway, the weight of the full car lugging as it works up to speed. Skinny guy, long hair pulled back in a ponytail that flips around as he gets his bearings. When we're at a decent clip he studies our faces in quick glances in the rear-view mirror. Everything about him is kind of agitated now, in a rush.

"Not that far to Winnemucca, you'll do better from there, maybe," his eyes flick away to concentrate on the road. I feel relief to have his focus elsewhere. But I feel grateful, so grateful and sag in the seat, hyper to every nuance of man, dog, car and road, relaxing a little in the cramped warmth. The miles begin to roll away beneath us. Rocket whines behind my head. I startle but feel strange comfort in the dog's proximity. Cora is half-turned toward her window and slouched low, face pressed to the glass.

The man's eyes flick to both of us. I fidget in the seat and ask, "You live around here? Where are you going?"

"Yeah, kinda, I live kinda between a couple of places. Gotta be north of Winnemucca in less than an hour." A no-bullshit certainty in everything he says. His eyes flick back to the road again, he fiddles with the radio dial. The windows are starting to steam. Static strains a melody behind a scratchy guitar.

"Hey," Will speaks up suddenly, "You know we need to get a long way today. You could take us as far as Elko, that'd be great, past this stretch."

Utter disbelief shoots through me. "Will, no," I clap him lightly on the shoulder.

The man whips his head around to look at Will. "Whoa, man, did you not listen? I cannot take you to Elko. *I cannot take you past the west side of Winnemucca! Were you not listening?* So let me make it clear. I told you when I offered this ride I can only do this little bit, get you to town. That's it. That's how it is. No more."

Will counters, "Yeah, but we really need to get farther, can't be that much of a big deal." His voice is louder, belligerent and as the tone takes hold I shudder. I push against the back of his seat but he presses on. "We need a longer ride."

I flare out, try to hold calm in my voice against growing panic. "Will! Cut it out!" I shove against his seat, harder this time. "Stop it. You agreed. We all agreed. He's doing what he can. We're lucky. Give it up, it's enough!"

"No, it isn't!" Will's voice vaults to near-threat. "It isn't." He turns toward the man, massive in the cramped seat of the tiny car. "We just need to get farther along. You could take us!"

I reach over his seat, put my hands on his shoulders and press down. "Will! Knock it off! We promised, he told us what he'd do! He's going out of his way for us." The fury I felt toward him at the gas station in the night buckles in my chest now, a scouring burn.

The man's jaw is clenched. He scans the side of the highway racing past. The car slows. Will continues, bludgeoning over our promise as though it were nothing, nothing at all.

"Yes, he could, you could, wouldn't be such a big deal!" The speed drops further and I gasp. I reach up and pull on Will's arms. The man's eyes flick to the mirror, lock on mine for a second. A twisting knot in my stomach double-clenches. Will's bullying tone rises higher. He leers at the driver and opens his mouth, but the driver swerves the car hard to the left, hard again to the right and back across double lanes, throwing us all off-keel. Rocket scrambles behind me, claws scrabbling and a low yelp to a growl.

"Yes!" the driver bites, collected and steady. The last good-natured calm slides off his face, "It is a big deal. A very big deal!" Veering back across into the left lane his eyes check the rearview mirror. "Look man!" he snaps, cranking a hard right again, and we scramble. "You listen up! I got my dog crammed in the back of this thing, and you've got his seat. That, just that is outta my way!" and he rocks the car a couple more times, rough and fast. "I told you before you got in my car what I could do for you. Now you can take it or leave it. I can stop right here, and you can get out now and wait for another ride! Or you can shut up and go as far as I take you." He swerves once more. The car settles in the right lane.

Thick silence muffles us all for a moment. Rocket whines. I put my hand over my shoulder, and he licks it a couple of times. The driver clips in, "I can tell something's happened to you guys, it's obvious. I can see it … it's why I stopped, but it is not my problem. I'm taking you as far as I can go, and I'm not taking you any further! So, you wanna get out now — or you wanna go on to the edge of Winnemucca where I turn north alone? I can always find some help to get you outta my car, or I can drop you off at the cops if you want it. But there isn't any other choice!"

Will stares straight ahead, icy silence.

"Look," I almost whisper, "I'm sorry. We need this ride, please. We appreciate what you're doing. I'm sorry, I'm so sorry."

The man nods once, face stern and unflinching. His eyes flick again to the rearview mirror, and he nods at me. "You ok, Rocket?" Rocket whines once, wags his tail. The man puts his foot on the gas and his focus on the road ahead.

Cora cries into the sleeve of her jacket, face pressed hard to the window. I'm just trying to breathe. There is this promise we've made to get this ride. There was a promise made in the night. A promise. How will we carry this with us into the company of strangers, this way that we've come to be alive? I feel as alone as I've ever felt in my life.

The sediments of the old seabed are shifting, algae blooming red tide. Keeping my head above the toxic soup seems an endless journey and we each sink or swim as best we can.

17

El Camino

"Couldn't you just take us to the other end of town?" Will growls as we pull into the lot of a gas station on the western edge of Winnemucca.

"Afraid not — told you, I've got a schedule to keep," the driver barks back. "That's my route back there, road we just passed heading outta here going north. This is it! Everybody out!"

As the VW lurches to a stop both doors fly open, and we tumble out. I stand up trying to still the flailing sense that everything is scattering further out of control. In throbbing confusion I step away from the car and glance around covert then turn back to pull soiled, tangled gear out onto the pavement.

Our driver is civil, even kind in a tightly held sort of way. But he's all high-gear motion, hurrying to extricate us from this point in his life. His smile is taut and brief as he pulls our gear out of the trunk. Whatever lies ahead of him beyond this point owns him entirely now, our concerns of little note. He hustles around, invites Rocket back into the front passenger seat.

"You can ask for help or not, cops or anything else aren't far if you want them," he says. His thumb jerks over his shoulder across the lot.

Several men stand in a cluster near the swinging glass door to the station and watch us fixedly. Our standout arrival feels like a beacon. I've got no attitude to throw their way. Withering under their watch mortified, anger and shame torque deep inside me. Whatever plan might be spinning out of their conversation I want to avoid it at all costs. The VW man is about to disappear, gypped of any gratitude as place and circumstance pull and eat into my skin.

I ransack my mind for something to say, swivel as he crosses to the driver's side. "Hey, uh, thanks," I stutter, "uh, I, we, uh, thanks."

He flips a lean smile across the arc of the VW roof and says, "Yeah, see ya. Take care. Travel safe." The words sail over his shoulder as his door opens, and he ducks into his seat. The Bug chugs to life. Rocket pants and grins at us for the last time. The man's hand extends out the window as he swings into a sharp U, fires out onto the street and drives off heading back the way we came, brief wave flicked once then gone.

I feel paralyzed.

Shudders surge and rattle my joints. Morbid uncertainty shatters all confidence into a steaming puddle at our feet. Shifting, swaying we're finally able to look directly into each other's eyes. Will raises his eyebrows and nails us in a blue-iris spiral. The stampede inside me circles back, and I stare back at him, lost seeking direction from the lost.

"Ok," he hesitates, looking us over. "Shall we, uh, shall we find the, uh, uh, the cop shop?"

"What?" I'm suddenly riveted.

"Should we ask these guys how to find the police?" Will shifts around, slanting his head toward the group near the station door.

I look over my shoulder at the men looking us over. My blood curdles. Certainty catapults over misery. "No!" I retort. "We shouldn't!" I glance around and back, look at Cora. "You wanna talk to those guys?" Her eyes slam up to mine as I continue, "I don't. I wanna get outta here. I'm not going to talk to these guys, not to any cops!" the last words sheer out of my mouth like a whirring blade.

Cora looks from Will to me. Will opens his mouth, closes it, opens it again. "But you guys need help," he says.

I glance at the men again. My eyes ricochet back to Will. "You really think these guys are the help we need — really?" I pause. All my focus bores into Will as I watch his face for a cue, a clue, for some solid answer to counter the certainty that's set in my gut. He looks from me to Cora and drops his eyes. Nothing rises out of him to counter my conviction. Who do we trust? What?

I stand in our mire of pain and watch the two of them, ferreting around for an answer that rings true inside me. Will's idea clamors an absolute no. So what do we do? Panic is near, so near.

Suddenly my brain snaps clear. "I don't think so. In fact, I'm absolutely sure. I think we should just get out of here, find a ride and get home." My eyes drop, I glance left to right then flash back to Will. "I'm not talking to anyone here!" I pick up my pack to turn away. "I'm going to the bathroom to change clothes," I say with a low mutter.

Will flicks his head toward the men and sneers, "Don't think these guys will be too happy about that!"

A helix of anger wraps around rising panic and the broken everywhere feeling. I stand for a minute and try to breathe. Slightest hint of lingering in this place for even one extra moment cuts against that precarious hold. And the feeling of filth that coats and strangles every inch of me feels just a hair worse.

"I don't give a rat's ass what they think," I fling back and start toward the bathroom door at the side of the building. After two steps I stop and look back. I gesture toward Cora, "C'mon, let's get cleaned up and get outta here," I pause, "unless you really wanna talk to these guys."

She grabs her pack, and we head for the chipped bathroom door.

The room is close, other women come and go from stalls, and we're right in the middle of what little space there is. When I've changed my clothes I step to the sink with a bandana and wipe myself down with the shock of cold water, murmuring to Cora, "You ok?"

She moves to the sink and looks into my mirror face with the slightest nod. I flinch at the lost look in her eyes, watch how it echoes in my own. I try to smile. In the focused effort of hurry and pain, it isn't possible. The best I can do is nod back at her. Hurting everywhere makes it hard to keep moving, harder and more dangerous to stop.

We finish up, grab our packs and push out of the dark room into the grayed light of the station lot, vision scattering in pinwheels. The cold that slaps against us is bitter but barely distracts from the basic good feeling of clean, dry clothes. But it registers sharp on the damp skin of my face. Cold day, and it will be another cold night.

One man approaches out of the swing of the station door, looking all lecture and insult. Will exits the other bathroom. We swing our packs on our backs and cross to the other side of the street. I half expect a shout or some challenge, but there's only silence full of sharp eyes. We move along the narrow street toward the eastern edge of town.

Will's voice hacks out into the chill, "He said it's not far."

"Yeah," I rasp back.

Cora murmurs, "Yeah, sure, not far," and catches stride, almost smiling.

I'm glad we have us but can't think as far as the end of another town. We're about as obvious as we can be. This makes a ride once we get where we're going seem impossible. But the town's end is there before we expect it, the abrupt finish to a forlorn place. We stand on the shoulder of the empty road, like kites waffling in need of wind or string. Winnemucca stretches behind us, long ribbon narrowing to a nothing point. I ponder the disappearing act of the road and wonder if this is a town at all. Was it there? Was anything really there at all? I scan the immense horizon ahead of us.

And move closer to Will and Cora.

An El Camino erupts out of nowhere, pulls over next to us, solid apparition. I look back to the town, turn to look over the black half-car and its truck bed. Where'd it come from? A huge man, with apple-happy cheeks, smiles from the driver's seat. A Doberman sits next to him, panting.

"Where you going?" he gives the dog a friendly shove as it turns to lick him across the face, then he grunts and wipes his face with his sleeve. All three of us look over the car-truck, man and dog, uncomprehending.

His second question sails out the window, "Where you trying to get to?" The apple cheeks swell upward another notch.

"Uh," Will licks his lips, "Salt Lake City. We need to get to Salt Lake City. Utah."

"Well, good! That's good! You're in luck! That's the way I'm goin'," and the driver heaves up and out of his door, engine still running. Like prey shying into cover, I step back, swallow and shiver.

Will, his arm slung over Cora's shoulders, looks hard at the large, friendly man. "Uhhh, you sure you got enough room, there's all of us three and packs and all?" he asks. Desperate as we are for it, the ride feels like the buckling of a mad dream.

The man leans forward, hands planted on the hood of the car. The black El Camino sinks a notch as he studies us. "I think it's doable. Packs in the back. Name's Dan."

Dan looks around and up at the sky. He's a very big man. "Let's see," he straightens and bends low to the door, studies the interior, "Dobie can get behind the seat. He's my buddy and I hate to have him cramped up like that. But we've done it before," he says, standing up again he looks at us quizzically. "Might be able to get us all in. Maybe not," he adds, looking back down the road into town, "but I'm not sure you're going to have a lot of other options." He swings his big head back and looks us over again. "You're kind of big, so am I, but the girls aren't much. Let's give it a go."

Will swings his pack over the side and into the bed of the El Camino. Cora stands watching, slow to move and I'm slower still. I don't want to let go of my pack, but Will takes it out of my hands, tosses it over the side and Cora's follows mine.

"Ok," Dan smiles. Will is taller but Dan's girth is notable, solid. A kind of exuberant, happy vibe rolls in his wake. There's a slight unwind in my stomach, but I shiver and can't stop. Wanting the ride not wanting the ride wanting the ride wanting out of here, I shuffle my feet.

Dan directs us into the car, me first to sit next to him, then Cora then Will on the passenger side. "If it doesn't work, you'll have to take your chances," he says, scanning the town. "Not an easy place, best of days." He sighs and makes his way back around to his door.

As he leans in from the driver's side to help his narrow dog into the tight, narrow compartment behind the seat soothing and encouraging, my heart is in my throat. I wait until he's eased himself into the driver's seat, the car leaning hard in his direction before I duck under Will's arm to slide across and sit next to Dan. Dan raises his right arm and lays it across the back of the seat as Cora slides in next to me. Trembling, I hold myself stiff.

"You're gonna have to move in closer than that," Dan smiles easy-going, jovial, "or we'll never all fit. I don't bite."

I nod and scoot over, struggling between rolling shock and the ease that exudes from him as a manifest force. Will crowds in. Now that we're in, the idea of another wait is unbearable. The doors close on communal inhale.

"Can you drive like this?" I croak.

Dan's eyes smile. "Sure. Yeah. At least I can try." He pulls his arm from the back of the seat, reaches below the steering wheel, turns the ignition over and puts the car in gear. Squashed now, I really can't breathe. "Got a long way to go. Good to have the company, it eats up the miles. If it get's too uncomfortable you'll at least get a little way down the `pike." His arm swings back to the seat behind us, and I inhale in quaking relief.

"Where you coming from?" Dan asks.

"Um, California," I answer. "We've been out to California. But we're from Wyoming."

"What about you?" Will asks fast.

"Montana. I trade horses and sell stuff. Get to Wyoming every little while, but not a lot, not enough. I like the Big Horns. Wish I could get there more often. But it's a long enough ol' drive without adding on any extra. So why California?"

"Friends," Cora coughs, vigilance moving like a dragnet between us. My heart rate spikes, Will twitches but Cora continues, "Got friends there. Went to see them. Been awhile."

"Long way to go for a visit. Was it good times?"

"Uh, yeah." Cora shudders but manages a small smile. "Yeah. Good times."

Will and Dan go off on a tangent about Will's job, electrical parts and mechanical piece-work, and Dan banters back and forth with him on the merits of this and that as my mind goes groggy. The warmth of Dan and the rolling car pull me into a muffled torpor that makes it hard to hold up my head. As their voices weave it falls sideways, bumps against Dan's shoulder and I startle.

"Hey," Dan interrupts Will, looking at me. "It's ok. Don't worry about it. If you're tired, just let it go. Sleep." I look up at him and half-nod. His smile, sincere enough, doesn't stop a tremor that runs through me.

They pick it up again, and I try to connect to Will's voice and concentrate. Their conversation rolls on. I can't keep the words from muddying together, disinterest nipping my attention into marshy ground. Exhaustion, comfort, warmth make my head grow wobbly again, falling against Dan's shoulder. He shifts slightly. Popping up again, I drop almost immediately into molasses ooze too thick to fight. In a fitful doze, never quite coming up for light but neither sinking into real sleep, miles and voices tumble and toss.

Cora's voice joins the chorus, syncopates, goes quiet, and they banter back and forth along strings of some complicated story Dan tells that I can't quite follow in the woozy neverland where I'm lost and gone. The miles spin away spin away spin away, tires a whoosh and whine along blacktop. I reach to pull myself to the vague familiar cascade of voices rising falling rising falling and locate Will's again and again. The dip and dive of the El Camino race forward like a soothing river, Dan's bulk like a dam against armies of faceless fiends that gallop the road behind.

Droning heaviness pulls me deeper, Will's voice melting away in a soundwave washing through the rolling car, as the big man beside me captains his low-slung ship.

The El Camino sways to the right and slows. I want to turn over and sink my head deeper in the pillow beside me, but a strange languor holds my limbs in a straightjacket. My eyes blink open as Dan's voice slips through the haze.

"Whoa …," he breathes. The El Camino cruises to a slow halt along the shoulder of the highway. With a banshee shriek I rip into instant flight, smashing against Cora who shoves against Will who slams and claws against the far door, terror wrenching.

In a dizzying exit we launch from the car in a knot racing before our feet hit the ground. Ten paces out tangling into desolation that extends in every direction we stumble as Dan's voice penetrates our rioting seizure. His voice barks again. We whip around almost as a single unit and still backing and half-running away we face him. He stands very still beside the El Camino, eyes locked on our frenzied flight.

"Whoa! Whooaa!! Whooooaaa, heeyyyy," his voice drones as we skitter further from the car. "Whoa. Come on back. Come on back. C'mon now. Settle down. Whoa. Whooa. Stop runnin', c'mon stop, c'mon, stop right there, whoa, whoa, where ya goin," the drone lifts to a croon to near sing-song pacing us. "Nowhere out there, nowhere to get to, nowhere to go, whoa you guys, c'mon, settle down. Come on back. Hey. C'mon back. You're o-o-o-o-okay, o-o-o-okay."

Gripped for another burst of speed, Will and Cora panting at my side my heart races too fast to comprehend the face of the moment. The big man stands on the far side of the car and watches us, chants out incantation, calm litany plucking our panic apart.

His voice falls silent. The car sits, hot engine click-clicking on the shoulder of the road. We no longer run but still back away, poised for instant flight. Dan stands rock-still. We study one another. I flinch as he raises his arms slow and steady, hands spread, massive palms open, facing outward. We look him over, glance at one another speechless.

Dan's voice cruises to us, "Hey," and he turns slightly toward the back of the El Camino. "Nothing to be afraid of. Nothing. Just gotta change the gas tanks. C'mon back. I'll show you." He drops his arms and turns to run one hand along the hood up the windshield across the roof and down to rest on the side of the truck bed. He stops and looks at us.

Face flaming I untangle my legs from their will to run, forever flight into wild wide space. My hands jam in the back pockets of my jeans. Forcing one step in Dan's direction, I pause. Cora and Will struggle next to me fighting for a semblance of calm. Dan motions with his head. We watch him close as we wind slow-motion, an indirect meander back to the front of the El Camino.

Bending low beside the truck bed Dan straightens and looks directly at each of us, a commanding light in his eyes. "Don't be scared," he says. "Come on back. C'mover here so you can see what I'm doin'. I drive long distances, see, like I told you before. I like to drive as far as I can between gas stops. So here, see here," he bends low again and I flinch slightly, "I got two tanks on this thing." He waves us around to his side. We slide over keeping distance but in range to see. "Gotta switch the tanks over. Rigged 'em myself, works like a charm," he says as he fiddles a minute. He looks at me and flicks a switch.

The flight in my blood flicks like lightning cut loose. But the urge to run drops to bewilderment, and I stand embarrassed, uncertain. He stands upright, his hands out again, open. I lean slightly toward him, watch as he bends and flips the tanks over once more. "Like that," he says as he looks up at me. "It's done. Simple. I can get down the road miles and miles and miles before I gotta stop. We were just runnin' outta gas in one tank. That's all." Standing straight he looks me over then Will, then Cora and nods.

"Ok now," he walks to the driver's door, and his voice takes on a bit of an edge. "I gotta let my dog stretch his legs, pee and stuff before we drive again. Having all of you in there is hard on him. So it'll be a minute more," and he pulls the seat forward enough to ease Dobie out of the car. "It's ok. Just be a minute or two. Then we'll go."

He and Dobie start to wander ahead along the shoulder of the road, but Dan stops and looks back at us. "Look. I can see something's happened to you," he says. "If you want to talk, great, if you need help say somethin'. If not, fine. But I'm not gonna hurt you. I'm just giving you a ride." He starts to follow behind Dobie, who prowls the ground eagerly but turns back once more. My hand fidgets with my pack in the back of the El Camino, uncertain. The three of us don't look at each other. "I pick up people all the time," he says, "every trip I can because it helps me stay awake, pass the hours. Talk and stuff. That's it, that's all. I can leave you here to catch another ride with someone else." He turns to his dog and looks back over his shoulder, "but I think you better let me get you as far as I can. Might wanna relieve yourselves if you need to. I'll be walkin' the other way."

My hand falls from my pack, and I look at the ground in shame and confusion. I look at Cora. We turn from the car and walk off the other direction.

In a short time Dan whistles Dobie back, gets him watered and stowed again behind the seats. He directs Cora to slide in next to him then Will in next to her so Cora half-sits on Will's lap, then it's me by the window. There's a semblance of slightly more room.

Without the comfort of Dan's big self so near I feel a vacancy. A kind of throbbing misery sets in that has burst through the roadside debacle. I want to help Dan with the drive, talk us through the miles, but if I open my mouth I know words won't come. I'll begin to weep and never ever stop.

Miles pound away. A numbing daze sets in that slides along the edge of indifference but sharper, meaner with a permeable fog of dread fast at its heels. No words exist to counter the deluge beginning to rain down. The only beacon in me says "home", wherever that is. Vacant prayer is misery and hope scrambled together. Talk is spare. Dan drives as fast as before, 100 mph or more, but there's no lightness, no escape in the speed. Swept along grateful in his able wake we are without compass to pilot his trip or our own. Daylight dims, fades away and on we rocket through gathering dusk into the belly of another vast night.

––––––––––

Where would we have been without Dan, without that man in the VW? The Nevadans who shot at us, the bus driver and people in the cars and trucks, why didn't they help us? It would take a very long time for me to face all these questions. The fear and ignorance we encountered that night would remain a deep haunting for years to come.

But in time I would come to some understanding. Ugly things happened along the highways of Nevada in the `60s. In the year of our journey in 1971 Charles Manson was heavy on most people's minds. People living simple lives in small rural places were afraid. Minds and hearts can be small or large in any time, and any place, but there are reasons that simmer beneath the surface of things, and sometimes they reach beyond narrow thinking.

Group mind, crowd mind and no breaking the code, that's another thing entirely — and it harmed us that night. Hidden in my cells I carry the memory of lives ended at the hands of crowds. Lives stack on lives. Some rest in the old soils of Nevada. I came to this life to put large swathes of history to rest. Each of my friends carried their history too. Stories link. More stories than ours played out on the desert that night, every player a continuum of their own.

We are strong. We are weak. We are light. We are dark. We are journeys. We are stories. We are notes of a song. The barrier of time is permeable. Each moment curls along what will be and what has been. Kindness and courage, generosity and cowardice, overwhelm and violence and despair, it is not always easy to tell which is when.

Is this story the means of a shattered soul trying to comfort itself? No.

As Dan carried my friends and me out of Nevada into Utah, my journey was not just a journey to reach home or to find home. It was a journey that tied strings of a massive tapestry into a finished form — a story that could wake up from the dream. I was a soul seeking resolution through great sweeps of time and history. That is what I came for. This is what I chose to do.

———

A tapestry is fraying, re-weaving a story that winds on the bobbin of time. Threads to these patterns wash out of my family. Some threads are filaments all my own. I've come to this life to make peace. Yet there is more, much more beyond the surface of things. In this strange, lost place where we find ourselves, the new story is not just up to me.

18

Keys

Moving toward a destination we long for past reason, we're dropped off in Salt Lake City along an eerie stretch of deserted night interstate. The parting with Dan is painful, impatience knifing through his exhaustion, the ineptitude of our confusion. We spend the night again with Cora's cousins. The next day Will has to hot-wire his car because he's lost the keys. This bummer fades into unspeakable freedom as we drive across southern Wyoming reeling with joy. Skywalking jokes mamba out the car windows. We whoop at slightest provocation. Simplest things feel like miracles. We laugh and laugh.

Inside the crazy zoom of our travel a single new leaf unfurls inside me. It turns on the powerful desire to call my mother. My thoughts braid to the moment I'll dial her number, hear her voice and tell her what every turn of every mile beats out now. *I'm ok, Mom. I'm ok. I'm fine. We're fine. Everything is going to be fine.* The refrain hums like invocation inside the rhythm of spinning tires.

Will pulls up hours later across from Cora's house. For a moment it's as though none of us have any idea how we got there. Will looks wrung out. We stare at the very normal house familiar yet vague. A boy and a girl play on a slab of driveway, front door yawns open, autumn sunlight fades as trees drop last leaves onto the fenced expanse of a brown-tinged back lawn. We can't imagine ourselves into any of it but sit watching in the stillness of the street until the facts imprint through our hungry, needy pores. The two children skip, turn and recognize Cora. A high-pitched squeal and she spills out of the car, quizzical joy bursting past autopilot stupor to hug her little brother and sister. Will steps out stiffly to open the trunk and pull out our gear. Cora's mom appears from somewhere, a materializing genie of concern. I tumble to the sidewalk unsure of purpose or direction but grateful for the bustle and the change.

Evading questions, the crush of hugs and laughter, I hang back aching to reach the telephone inside. The girl and boy toss Cora's name into the sky over and over. In the sparkling mercurial light of late day it's like walking on water, this heaving picture of the world. Cora, pressed into her mother's greeting, nods at me then at the door of the house. I push past them into the cool, dark interior, my eager pulse matching the light beams outside. In a stride I'm at the phone. I lift the receiver, and new life seems to percolate at the turn of the dial. I quaver on the final spiral as a ring begins to beat out in a house halfway across town. One ring. Two. Three. They saw against hope.

The music of my mother's voice clips in, voice thrilling, how it almost sings. "Hello!"

The corners of my mouth twitch up. "Hi! Hi, mom! It's me!" Silence. "It's Cat! I'm back! We're back!" Silence. Full-steam exuberance skips ahead, "You know ... back from San Francisco, back from the trip with Cora and Will. Remember?" Smiling, wishing I was sitting close enough to take her hand I see her in my mind's eye and remind her, "This was it, you know, the weekend we were going."

A beat and the always music of her voice drops to flat dull lethargy. "Oh. Yeah. You're back." Sandpaper scrapes along the skin of the world.

Unfazed I go on, "Yeah. Yeah. We just got back. We're at Cora's house, uh, dropping her off before I call someone to pick me up, to take me home." Celebrating my return runs a delirious joy through my veins.

"Oh, well. That's good. Glad to hear it. Sure." Her indifference blooms to a waft of antagonism that flirts across space and time.

I stagger. "I, well, I just wanted to call you, let you, uh, know. We, well, we just got back." Silence. "We're alright. We're home, and I'm alright, mom. I wanted to tell you first. I'm alright!"

"Oh, well. That's good."

I gulp, "How are you? H-how was your ... week?"

"Oh," mom's voice barely rises past vague hostility. "Well. Fine. Ok. It was fine." Her last words land with indifference so stark they erase even the enmity. Tumbling boulders cripple the fragile narrow bridge spanning between us.

I cringe as I hear myself continue, "Uh, well, I thought I'd come by to, to see you. But I'll, I'm just going to, well, I'll just have Will take me." Silence. Only silence. On a deep inhale that I can't quite orient to my lungs I let the boulders finish their work. "Ok then, just, I wanted to let you know we're here, I'm back and ... ok."

"Well that's good. Call me sometime," she says as her voice drops to complete vacancy.

"Yeah. B'ye. See you then, I guess."

"Yep. Bye."

The clatter of the phone receiver settling into its cradle rattles in a house I can picture, but have no idea how to reach, try as I may, in this life or the next or the next.

19

The Party

My friends and I do not go to the police. My reasons are complicated. There's our promise. There's the influence of someone who's told me that rape in Nevada risks capital punishment. I don't believe in capital punishment. There's denial. There's shame and humiliation, the depravity of what we've been through, the fear of exposure, the harsh layers of the years leading up to this experience, bound so taut inside me. We do, though, with assistance from friends of Will and Cora seek medical aid through Public Health. In so many ways, the aid feels almost as bad as what we've already been through.

At the meeting with Public Health the three of us are separated out from each other. I don't tell the whole story of our ordeal to the officials who question me. None of us do. I can't hold the reality of our experience in their presence. Their hearts are not in the room. I don't expose myself beyond most basic detail. We're all too young, too fragmented to remain anything but half-hidden under the glare of their harsh lens.

There is also this: Beneath all the damage I believe the man who harmed us was changed by what happened between us. I believe he will not repeat what he did again. I rarely speak of this foolish or wise perspective, few would understand. It's a hard thing to hold. Where does truth lie at the heart of travail? What are our struggles and violations spun through the harshest views, an eye for an eye? I know well enough how harsh life can be. I don't believe struggle and violation are only that harshness. I believe they are more. They are vines that might bear something worthwhile over time.

One night not long after our return, Will and Cora throw a party. I arrive and wander through a small crowd gathered just inside the front door, jump to the early pulse. It's hopping. I like the feel of the groove, but there's no music. Where are the tunes? Some people are familiar as I wend my way toward the kitchen looking for Cora. I want to catch up with her before things get crowded, and she'll be too busy for real talk. I want to see how she's doing. It feels good to be in the mood of the crowd, lighthearted. The past couple of weeks have been harrowing. Maybe tonight I can make it all slide away.

The meeting set up by Will and Cora's friends with the head of Public Health slugs through my thoughts. I push past a group jiving in the middle of the living room, and for a minute I catch their beat. But in my mind the head guy at Public Health haunts me, I see him as he leans back in the chair behind his desk in his button-popping, grease-spotted yellow shirt. He was a pig to us. His strange sense of power, he treated us so badly. I try to shake off the residue that still clings from the meeting with him. It disgusts me every time it jolts or wavers into my thoughts, which is thankfully not often given the landslide of everything else.

I shrug, throw it off, move through the rooms, laugh and smile at strangers laughing and smiling at me.

I get it that the medical checkups and penicillin were necessary. But I sneer at the memory of the hard, nasty swipes that came with those inoculations, like it's a justifiable price, to have despicable attitudes doled out with treatment. It seems to go with the territory and that rankles and festers. I ponder what I've experienced over the past two weeks. It feels like a common distemper that eats away any humanity in the guise of help and assistance. It makes me feel empty and sad.

I want to shake off the gross intrusions of it all. I'm still furious at the way the supposed authorities divided us into solo interviews, then brought us back together to rake us over the coals, saying our stories didn't match up in perfect detail and therefore must be a lie. Why would we lie about this? Hell, my sister, brothers and I never get the same thing out of the same hour in same room on the same day in the same way. What does that mean? Do I care what those jerks think? Not a whit. The frustrated, poker-faced abusing bores can eat it, for all I care.

Jamie waves from across the room. Good. I smile at him, raise my hand to indicate a later catch-up and note he's still wearing his lab coat from his med tech job. That reminds me of the doctor I saw last week, and I cringe. His starched knowledge and vague diagnosis confuse me the most. He seems caught in a magnitude of crass misunderstanding. But he also holds a key to the only claim I've got for figuring out how much my health was affected or not — and starting over with a different doctor makes me want to cry — or go to sleep for a long, long time. It all frays in my mind, so many deceits and prevailing conceits. I look around for Cora in one room then another. The laying on of ignorant values about what the hell all of these people have decided that we are makes me tired, so tired. The rage barely muffled all week in the morass of confused dramascapes feels sharp. I move around the happy chatting clutches of people and try again to let it all go.

My tension finally dissipates into the early party hubbub. I smile again pushing, pushing it all away. There's still the big, the truly BIG thing, this enormity of being alive. It cuts away the petty crap daily. Stuff that used to cut and pull at me all the time spins powerless now, a kind of massive perspective. I see other kids around from high school, the dumb, mean things that go for social jockeying, how small it all was, still is, how small when we could be so large. I feel grateful for this at least. Who do we think we are haunting one another with despicable judgments, false claims — ego agendas blind to truth outside the small and the narrow and selfish? I feel sorry for us all. And grateful, so grateful, for this other thing, it's so big, so good and so free. I want it to last.

Will suddenly lands in front of me with a guy I barely notice at his elbow. They block my way forward. I'm glad to see Will. A smile breaks across my face, feels bright after the harassing ugliness of past weeks.

"Hey, Will," I say, grinning, as he stops me in my tracks. "How you doin'? Been a good week? Job ok?"

"Yeah." Will offers an actual smile, way more than he usually musters. "It's been ok. Pretty much ok. You need anything? Chips and drinks and stuff are over there on the counter," he says, sweeping his arm toward the opposite side of the room.

"Yeah, yeah, I saw, thanks. Just thought I'd find Cora before it gets too busy in here to pin her down." I swivel as our friend Susan comes in close then circles away, a slight pinch to my arm motioning toward said counter and all the food. I nod at her.

"Snag you at the chips in a minute," she says, winking.

I'm hungry and want to catch up with her, but I swivel back to Will. "Whatcha' been doin' this week? Hey, where's the music? Seems kinda quiet for a party."

"Uh, work and stuff all week, the usual. There is some really good music, gotta bunch of albums over there. Ray's stereo just got set up, he's loaning it to us for tonight, but we got sidetracked," Will says as he hooks his thumb over to the wall where albums stack next to a nice-looking set of speakers. Then he leans his head back to indicate the guy at his shoulder.

I nod, "Oh, gooood." My attention zings to the stacks of albums with longing. "I'll check it all out. Great!"

I give Will a pat on the shoulder and start to turn again to find Cora, catch Susan and Jamie, get some chips. I realize I'm really hungry now, and investigating the music for the night is another hot new attraction.

Will stops me with a quick tug at my arm. I turn back, distracted.

The guy standing behind him seems fairly jumping out of his skin as I throw them a quizzical look. "Yeah? What's up?" I ask.

Will seems at a loss for a minute then jump-starts his voice, "Uh, hey. Yeah, I just wanna introduce you to my buddy here, we work together. Ray, this is Cat. Cat, Ray."

Ray throws out his hand, a kind of flailing gesture that fails, big goofy grin as his eyes ferret into mine, wild behind thick glasses. "Oh, yeah, hi," I reply as I stand with my hands in my jean pockets and give him a partial smile, still half-distracted as I look around the room. "Sure, hi Ray. Good to meet you."

"Well, yeah, baby, me too!" Ray gawks across the space between us. "Really good to see you!" He looks at Will, flashes a gritty smile. I nod at him, uneasy. His next line skewers between us. "Hey, you're a sight for sore eyes, looka those legs hey, oh yeah!" He nudges Will in the ribs. Will grins, a kind of strange delirium crossing his face. I pull back a step. Ray gushes on, "No, hey, stick with me, baby, I'd love ta see ya naked, no clothes, hey, bet that's a sight ta behold!"

Will flicks right in, "Oh, yeah, man, I can tell you, that is a sight to behold!" Crackly grin beacons across his mouth and slaps me full in the face. Dumbstruck and staring at the two of them, their onrushing wreckage slams into me, singeing the air between us. Dismay strangles on loathing as meaning sinks home, a slow-motion spike from Ray to Will that arrives with complete knowledge in my reeling brain. Their ready, easy banter hangs putrid between us. My smile cripples away.

As happiness shreds I don't even look at Ray. I stare at Will, his mouth agape with an unbearable leer as he stares at me. Rising like a banshee between the two of us is the one and only time he could base such a claim on. As this curdled understanding slithers into the room I watch him go pale. We slide into a crushed and mutual recognition. One night on a Nevada desert. The room tips.

Agony flames through my mind, burns stark disbelief at the scope of Will's horrific betrayal. I can't fathom it, barely able to recognize the frantic gasp of colliding thoughts branding us both. Ray's disregard and stupid anticipation grin through the debacle, buddy-buddy arm jostling tilts forward, a wide-mouthed ghoul with lewd prankster hopes. The sick light of comprehension waxes in Will's eyes and turns my stomach. I turn away.

Blind and raw and without direction in the sordid intrigue of their torpedo blow, I walk away. Their ignorance savages its way to my heart and out the other side. Everything in front of me lists as the room turns to ash and drops away, twitching on remorse and pain.

I find myself at the stacks of albums beside an empty turntable. Sinking to my knees my hands reach listless to comb through blurs of albums. A kitten-like mew weeps up from somewhere I can't identify.

Then I know. It's coming from me. I rock back on my heels, stare at multitudes of silent, shiny-black discs and their bright cardboard sleeves, a wild kaleidoscope hanging in a field of nausea. It fades, returns and spins, my frozen mind lost and gone somewhere far from this place.

Pain wrings me back to the mirage of a party. The vast selection of music beckons inside the smothering room. Kneeling, staring at one black vinyl disc grasped in my hands, a splotch of wet shimmers along spiraling grooves, and my frantic blood flattens. I staunch the threat of tears, curl into a ball near the speakers shuffling through artists and heartbreak, setting the score for the night.

It will take years before I find enough grace to come close to understanding Will on this night, the choices he made throughout our hitchhiking journey. Eventually, though, I will come to it. When I can finally find my way back through the layered dregs of time I'll rediscover the pain and the rage I felt toward him. I'll walk through it to the other side and forgive him. When I do I'll release us both. My forgiveness condones neither his ignorance nor his actions, but it will be possible for me to see how they may have come into being: how as a male he could have floundered in the extremes of our ordeal; how the helplessness and impotencies of that night might have twisted in him. Unjustifiable as his leering betrayal was, I will be freed from its burden. Healing will come. And for Will, his journey to awareness or not was his to claim. By the time I searched for him many years later, he had died.

20

Aftermath

The world is in desperate need of a new story for our times that must arise out of new stories catalyzed from the core of our individual lives. To arrive at a new story, the past must be understood. It must be balanced and cleansed.

For many years ahead I will manage the big episodes of my life as a series of separate events, compartmentalized and held down.

My questions will spin on the edge of time. Justice, does it exist? Who in this world cares about truth? What is truth, what is true? (My parents seemed not to have a clue.) Where can I turn to discover anything solid in what seems endless abstraction? Is anything solid or true or dependable? Does anyone anywhere hold answers to these questions?

How do you pick up the pieces of a life after repeating loss ... betrayal ... tragedy ... violence — over and over again?

I stayed by Cora, though the years eventually pulled us apart. My growing chain of extreme events was taking its toll, each one, each its agony. A person can only hold so much.

It may be that what saved me, besides the love of my grandmother, besides the constancy of friends, my sister and brothers, besides the luck of relationships, whose power I often could not see or had no idea existed and did not always know how to trust, there was this: I did not experience myself as a victim.

I did not view myself as hapless. I did not feel my life as finite. I experienced my life as large, a journey, a pilgrimage — a string of events and circumstance, catalysts that could make or break me. Life was clay and within it I was the artist, the sleuth on a trail of great mystery. I was a player. I could shrink or expand. It was up to me.

Despite the crushing train wreck and near-death of early independence I did not feel I was living on borrowed time. I lived with a sense of purpose, though the damage was great, the living through it hell, and weighty costs built to a pitch inside me.

Somehow I knew in my core that there was more to life than the things that happened to me.

I sensed there was a pattern that could be decoded. You don't see your experiences clearly when you're within them. It is time and distance that bring us back to ourselves. Understanding the patterns of our lives can bring us home. Some part of me remained engaged, curious and so, I survived. Time passed its clues. I learned that there are times when distance or forgetting keep us sane and are what save us. And there are times when the only thing that can save us is the act of remembering, living intimately with our stories. I never forgot what happened to me. But there was so much that went underground. It would take the intimacy of memory to find the most important answers.

And so my path would be the path of recall, the demand of claiming my whole life in all its brutality and all of its elegance. I would decode the truth buried within the whole. Wherever and however I had become estranged from life — that would be my path through.

Yet there was more beyond this early understanding. There are threads of other lives strung out across the spectrum of time that also hold truth. In parallel cycles, within parallel lives lay other clues. And these clues tied to restless bloodlines of my past. There were cycles in the long ago that called for forgiveness, cycles that had yet to be redeemed. They echoed within me, inside current time yet beyond it. The layered history of my one life to the point of my 19th year held clues to not just this history but to other histories as well. Keys buried from childhood to young adulthood that could free me linked also to keys of cause and effect that trailed through other lives and other times. Spilling into the now, these keys fit the lock in the puzzle of time. They held my answers.

In 1971 I had a long way to go to take hold of this knowledge. I was not home yet. I was still in reaction.

The people who stand before you and suffer, the people around you who have been harmed, the people beside you in need, these are the people who are your way through. *They are not bad karma.* They come as offerings so we each might learn. They give themselves for understanding. They reach to extend their hands so that you may extend yours. We are all here on a journey. It is the journey of the heart. It is the only journey that can save us.

Part III

The years, of which I have spoken to you, when I pursued the inner images, were the most important time of my life. Everything else is to be derived from this. It began at that time, and the later details hardly matter anymore. My entire life consisted in elaborating what had burst forth from the unconscious and flooded me like an enigmatic stream and threatened to break me. That was the stuff and material for more than only one life. Everything later was merely the outer classification, the scientific elaboration, and the integration into life. But the numinous beginning, which contained everything, was then.

Carl Gustav Jung, 1957

21

A Life

In so many ways, I came to this life to make peace with death, to understand its dimensions. Not intellectually — I had that grasp early — but as pervasive spiritual veracity. There is only one path to integration like that. One must live fully.

So there was my journey from the beginning. At 19 years old could I survive, and not just survive but learn to live well? Within each cycle could I understand how and when to let go? Could I release my past? The ultimate surrender of death exists in subtle form within every nuance of our lives. We are born. We expand. We contract. When we die, we let go ... such is life's virtuosity.

These were partially realized concepts for me in my early years, but they were threads that carried with me from the beginning. In the midst of the violence, horror and cataclysmic events I survived, sometimes with decency, sometimes by desperation. And through each agony I reached for something more. I was a child, then a girl then a woman who struggled as all people struggle against great odds. Our wisdom may live within us from our beginnings but our paths are metamorphic journeys linked to its rediscovery.

What alchemy transforms diminishment into possibility? What force inherent to the nature of living alters limitation — limitation made manifest in words like won't, can't, don't and hate — into possibility? Could I meet fear, pain and betrayal straight on, convert them — and sustain the conversion? Through the years before my mother's worst betrayals I understood at some innate level that I had to push back against limitation, against litanies of criticism and condemnation that wove through my family, against entrenched negativity that seemed inherent to the fabric of our lives. By my late teens all my questions turned on one question: *How much farther can I stretch beyond limitation?*

That was before the worst of the violence. But after that terrible night in 1971 my questions were absorbed in a continuum that rooted inside me and moved beyond the heinous realities that seemed to grow out of nowhere.

On the Nevada desert I had tapped the only force that outreaches everything. Or had it tapped me?

Though a sense of expansion had carried with me out of the agonies of Nevada, it grew dulled and contracted over time with the ongoing effects of disturbances that continued in the years ahead — as though the weight of epochs bore me down. Through all the dark and the light, intense violations became encrusted into a kind of barrier or wall that divided the *before* of my life — all my childhood, the joys, betrayals and losses that led up to that night — from the *after* — everything in my life that followed beyond it. This division thickened to a formidable presence. Invisible to my day to day it determined every move I made. Fixed in my depths the trauma of the past paired to seizures of flight and fight trapped in my cells, adding to the density. In time the barrier would crumble, dust mixing to dust in the old ruins of time, but the effort to bring it down would be seismic.

In a most disturbing, despicable way I had become a woman the night I was raped. I knew this in a way that connected my spirit to the ages-old bitter history of women and long eras of violence. Was that part of what I had come to challenge, to change, to resolve?

That night on the desert I learned much about my humanity, my capacity for decency, my ability to endure, about courage. And much about qualities more challenging to define — attunement, presence, deep listening — the truth that runs through the channel of every moment.

I began to learn that what we fear rules us. All survivors are complex constellations; intersections between gift and challenge, expressions of weakness and strength.

Within the blazing horror of my past, a finer me dueled with nightmare and disassociation. And as time wore on my questions deepened. Blistered and singed, an instrument tempered through fire, how much more could I bend and return to identifiable form?

I am five or six. Our Nonnie has come to visit my family in Mexico. She is my daddy's mommy, my other grandma. I am sitting very close to her in wooden stands that ring around a circle of trampled earth. She calls it an arena. On the earth just below us men shove roosters together until they fight and tear each other apart. A packed crowd of strangers rage in a din around us. I can't get my breath. The claw and rip and cry and smell of the raging roosters mix with the smell and sounds of the men who grasp them and the crowd. Tears run down my cheeks. I cling to my

Nonnie. I feel sick. She holds me close, but she is also shaking. My father laughs somewhere nearby. In a reel the crowd shouts, "Matador de torero matador de torero!" Men in gold, glitter, in black and red enter the ring. One walks to center. The claw and blood of the roosters spin through my heart. There is a twirl, a flash of red cape. A bull races into the ring. Another man follows. Lances covered in flowers hurl into the bull. They stick and sway in its hump. Blood runs to dust. One lance gashes a horse. Matador approaches the bull. He twirls the red cape. The bull paws and runs. Matador dances. Cape spins. Again the bull runs. Again the cape spins. Again and again the dance until the bull drops to one knee. Sweaty, tongue hanging it faces the matador. A sword drives to its heart. The order of the world grinds to dust and blood. I might be screaming. Someone takes my Nonnie and me out of the stands. We move away from the ring on narrow dirt streets. Shouts erupt. People flee around us. We run to a small courtyard and crowd in. The street fills with bulls racing with a clot of boys and men. The running of the bulls, someone says. The river seems endless.

My family moves back to the States. My daddy buys our first TV. It is the only one in our neighborhood. White, black, gray shape into an ancient city and on the shiny screen a stone palace ghosts into form. A terrifying creature appears. It is a bull with a man's body. It speaks. Gruesome and suffering it rages in a cave or pen. In horror I watch as a woman runs into a dark maze. String winds through the maze. The woman follows the string. The bull with the man's body enters the maze at the other end. I cower, crushed with fear.

I am nine years old when I see this scene. At nine years old, I am the scene. Each generation plays out its horrors. Unresolved horrors wind in contortion. No shred of wisdom carried out of childhood with me from the Minotaur story. Only cruelty. And fear. Why don't we stop long enough to lay it all down? Why are these the stories we choose to live by?

A few months after I return from Nevada I turn 20. The things I don't know are legion. I don't know that I don't know. Life is unraveling threads out of my hands, into my hands. I let go, pick up new threads, half-interest, half-desperation.

I no longer live in the communal household. The artist boyfriend half of the couple has tried to seduce me. I've exposed his ruse. Living in my mother's empty house I have a short reprieve. She's left town with her brute of a husband. She's selling the house. I have four weeks. There's no furniture. I need to find work, a place to live. From here on out, even this tiny hint of home is gone. The house reeks of its history. I shiver in the night.

Brad comes to me a number of times. The trauma of the moment of his death stops slicing me wide open without moment's notice when I know for certain he isn't suffering anymore, when I know he's ok. The hole in my heart doesn't close. It goes underground, bleeding at a deep and cavernous level, buried beneath the weight of too much.

The crushed part of me is not taking hold. It has to take hold. I can't imagine. I must imagine. I have to move forward. What is forward? I don't know. Something's broken. I'm broken. *I can't say this. I cannot say this.* I feel like I'm drowning, unworthy. Unworthy of what? I don't know. All my relationships spin in a maelstrom. My mother, her husband, the communal couple, their kids, the Falls Creek crew are all half-detonating mine field and half-foundation. I can't tell what is real, what is possible, what is safe. Too much feels real. Nothing feels safe. I make a beginning and it ends, over and over and over. Old threads from gaping rents in the tapestry dangle and fray. Patterns lie hidden, hard to get at. By purpose or design? I can't tell. Where to now? I don't know. I don't know. It's hard to breathe. I'm drowning. There's no one. No one. I'm alone.

I read an old English novel. It seems never-ending. Right now that's good. But I know it will end, it will end soon. I make potpies because the scents that rise off the pages of the story make me hungry. Baking feels like someone's home. Home. But it's not me. I'm not home. I'm barely anywhere. A man my mother has hired to replace the kitchen floor crawls around ripping up linoleum, pounding nails and always half-drunk. I cook around him. He asks me if I'll bake some potpies for him, so he can freeze them. He likes the smell. They'll be good when he's alone and hungry. I think, why not? Why not? I make him three big potpies in foil pans he can put in his freezer. He pays me for them. It helps keep down the frantic deluge that's coming. It is coming. It's always about to hit. The waves will finally pull me under. And then for sure, I'll drown.

22

Dog Bite

My older brother, Tom, is back from Viet Nam, out in California. Here's what's happening to him, but I don't know it yet. I won't know it for another 39 years. Our paths are converging. They have always been converging. They're converging as I struggle alone to find a place, a way, a path out of menace and a maze that's closing in, and I can hardly breathe.

Tom is with his girlfriend. They're trying to get back to Wyoming. They're making their way across Nevada. She is desperately ill. They're hitchhiking. They're going to get married but they aren't married yet. She walked half-way across San Francisco to find Tom, to get to their apartment after being released from a hospital that did her more harm than good. But they can't pay the rent on the apartment she nearly killed herself to walk to. They have no home. Time to leave California. They don't know what's wrong with her. But something's wrong. Something is terribly wrong. They're broke. They're desperate. They just want to get back to Wyoming. Find help. They're laying down cairn after cairn that link between us but they're as ignorant of these salient markers as I am.

They don't know what they're doing except hitchhiking. Like me a few months before, hitchhiking. I thought I knew what I was doing. Hitchhiking home but landing in hell. A ride drops the two of them off on the east side of Lovelock. I wonder if the air sizzles the moment they step on that ground. It should. The weather is bad and getting worse, freezing. Sizzling and freezing, that air. Her health is going downhill fast. Tom is terrified that he's going to lose her, that she's not going to make it. He feels helpless. They're leaving dry, silent tears in a place where the sweat and blood of my terror and sorrow drench into sand not so far from the place where they stand.

At the edge of the small, forlorn town they wait on a freezing day at the end of one desperate ride, praying for another. They huddle in cold and agony. Life slips in precarious balance. Why do some make it, some not? In time, just in time a car crammed to overflowing stops for them. Stuffing into the packed car, her pain rockets to wretched at a whole new level. It's all she can do not to howl. She has no energy to howl. She hovers fatefully close to a brink. What saves her hurts her. Hurts her so much. They're lucky. Oh so lucky. Out of the wet and the freeze they're carried all the way back to Wyoming. She makes it back. Just in time. A tubal pregnancy is revealed. Just in time. All in the nick of time trails a harsh hair's breadth between life and death. But I don't know any of this yet, not for a long, long time. Close, so close we all dance to the edge.

In 1975 they will marry. They'll have a child, a son. He'll come in the early hours on Christmas morning, my first nephew. When my sister and I get the call we'll leap from our night beds without thinking, collide in the kitchen, grab for the phone and dance in wild abandon in the auspicious hours of predawn winter. The delirium of becoming aunties brings riotous happiness singing through our blood. Several months later I'll visit mother and babe, vibrant crawling boy on the fourth floor of a retrofitted mansion turned walk-up. I'll turn to the family dog, Suzie, an effort to bypass tensions that always crackle in the presence of my sister-in-law. I'll ignore my better instincts and lean down to nuzzle the dog. A show of some kind of truce, for what, I don't know, it's always this way. I make amends for the unease that runs hot currents through the rooms of my sister-in-law.

Her own pups hidden away in the bedroom closet and half-crazy besides, Suzie will land a ferocious bite that'll rip through my face halfway to China. The sound will be enough to stop a heart. Half a dozen deep and jagged lacerations will split and shred, shooting blood across floor and carpet. I will be a train wreck without sight.

My sister-in-law will shriek and scream. In a mad dash to the bathroom, feeling my way, I'll find the mirror somehow. Hands clenched over my eyes will lower to discover a miracle. I'll be able to see. I'll see that I can see. Through the gore and the pouring blood I can see. First thought, and it's all I want to know. Vanity sidelined, I'll stare one moment, two, and go quickly past caring what the rest of the awful damage might mean. My sister-in-law will be overtaken with blind hysteria that sirens through the house in full abandon. I'll look in the mirror above and below each brow to horrific rends that gape and snake to the edge of each eye where the long gashes stop. I'll admire the dog's handiwork. Through the scarlet blur two other long gashes gnash across the lower half of either side of my face. Something will drive through the flooding blood, speaking below thought as I enter a tricky zone.

My sister-in-law's howls will rise to a new pitch, reminding me that the baby's diapers need to be changed and that there's something probably more important even than that. I'll turn to leave the bathroom. Through the haze of blood I'll find, then coax my sister-in-law to gather the baby, gather the car keys, get down three flights of stairs, no, four, to the car, strap babe into car seat and drive fast to the hospital emergency room. For some moments I'll be unclear why exactly this is important, but I'll know with hazy conviction it is. My sister-in-law will scream every time she looks at me so she'll drive with her head out the window as a towel soaks blood in my lap. Even I will know the blood is a problem. When she can talk without howling my sister-in-law will mention that the gashes might be, too. I'll hardly care.

At the ER two nurses will take one look at me, and it will become clear what the rush is all about. Concerned about rampant infection, they'll also be horrified about the overall effects to my ravaged face. This will send them helter-skelter on a search through the halls of the hospital — but not before vehement coaching to fend off any treatment by the doctor on duty who they predict will enter the room I'm in at any moment. They hit me up with a massive shot of antibiotics then streak away. As fate will have it a plastic surgeon is somewhere in the nearby halls making his rounds. They mean to find him, before the doctor on ER duty can add to the debacle of my face. I think this is all kind of interesting. I start to feel really strange. I don't really want to sit up anymore. I want to lie down. But I've been told, bad idea. Shock — is that what it is, what they said — shock is locking in at a fast pace, obliterating what they've told me. It spreads uncommon stupidity across all my senses. I feel too much. I feel nothing. I feel relief that slushes into a blur.

The on duty ER doc walks into the room. He doesn't say so, but I know it's him. He's small, thin and old. He peers into my face, avoids my eyes, pats my knee. He seems friendly. I know I should have words for him, words that will affect his approach to me. I can't find them. I watch him move around. *Distract him*, the nurses said. *Distract him*. I'm not conversant. I stare, feeling mild interest then confusion then I feel peaceful. He shuffles silver things around on a metal tray. The fact that I can see him at all brings extraordinary joy. I smile. Smiling is a jagged sensation. He shoots me up with something. Then he begins to dab at a deep gash, and I feel conflicted about that.

The two nurses walk into the room. They're just ahead of the plastic surgeon. They look at me and relief pours over their faces with a double wince. They lure the old doctor away. The young plastic surgeon goes to work on my face. He cleans. He prods. He stitches. The stitches are very precise. He tells me over and over again as he works. *Be prepared. We'll probably have to rip all these stitches out later. The likelihood of infection is high. Very high, extreme to be exact.* Because of this the wounds may have to heal in their original ghastly state. I don't dare nod. I listen. I can see. My eyes can see. So I'm prepared. I can handle this. *You're too young for this*, he says. He keeps on saying it. *You're too young. You're too young. You're too young. If the stitches have to be ripped out, something will have to be done.* I nod without moving some more. Euphoric.

But his work is superb. The prep of the wounds, the stitches all done with concise precision, they will not be removed before healing is complete. Every rip, gash and tear heals clean. His work disguises and repairs the frightful detail of the dog's work. But I already know this will be so. I've known from the moment he took his first stitch.

Before the healing is complete I look like a monster for weeks. I see the plastic surgeon often. He's very kind. He knows I'm not much more than a kid on my own. He charges me little, so little for his miracle. *A young person should not have to live with this kind of damage,* he says. Because of him I don't. I'm lucky. I work at a bookstore. My boss keeps me on the front counter despite everything. He figures the customers can adapt because he knows I really need my job. He also likes to see them squirm in the face of grim reality. Our customers prefer not to look at me — or approach me at all if they can help it. But they can't help it because they like their books. I'm the main channel to their books. I get their special orders. I take their money. And I become very, very clear about what the surgeon meant as the weeks progress, as the looks on the customers' faces stymie and arrow in, sharp and not always kind.

I'm so awkward in myself that I don't know how to show my gratitude to my boss or the plastic surgeon. *Thank you,* I say. But it never feels like enough. I'm tough by this time. The surgeon cares for me through all the healing and aftermath. No small thing. In all the machismo I've accrued, just to walk down the street, just to look for a job, just to keep one, just to manage the kindness of strangers, I'm a serious and sometimes sullen young woman. In the face of the surgeon's thoughtful concern I become a little softer and a little tougher all at once. I don't know exactly what to make of it. I don't know what it might mean. I wonder when it might turn, that kindness. But it never does. Years later it will be impossible to tell the scope of the real and great damage that the small jaws of a half-mad border collie can do, on my face at least. You'd never know it happened. The surgeon tells me that as I age the scars will start to show. But they never do. Impossible kindness, two sides to every coin. For months, a year, I flinch hard whenever I'm close to the face of a dog. But in time that passes, too.

The wheel turns and makes what it will of the patterns of our lives. Years after the events of most of this story, and long after his parents have separated paths, my oldest nephew, who was a babe during all these events, will move with his mother and his half-sister to Lovelock, Nevada. In a strange repeat marker of history, they will settle in that place. Their mother will marry the sheriff of Pershing County. The past will be mostly quiet for them there. Their lives will be mostly good. They will have no idea that a potent segment of my life is buried in the soil of that place, so near to them. Brother and sister will grow to young adulthood. We'll be out of touch for much of that time. Ignorant of most of the details of one another's lives, only small bits of news will filter through the roots and vines of family and time.

––––––––

Scrambling to keep my own life in some semblance of order I will not look too closely at what I'm juggling. I'll keep juggling. I'll keep moving. I'll be running wherever I am and however long I stay. I'll be running even standing in place. But I won't know that, not for a good while, I won't know it really at all because it will feel normal. Lovelock will fade as a reference for me of any kind.

But later I'll learn that this same sheriff of Pershing County will break the lock on a gruesome chapter of Lovelock's history. Unrelated to me, or my family, yet skimming unnervingly close.

23

Ship in Full Sail

Between 1978 and 1980 a predator couple will stage ten known serial killings in an area east of Lovelock, Nevada. The victims will be mostly teenage girls from the Sacramento area. Abducted, brutally assaulted and murdered, they will be buried one by one in a valley a very few short miles from the near-death site of the ordeal of my friends and me nearly ten years before. A few short miles from the sand where we dug our own graves by hand on a bitter autumn night, spurred on by a different madman. My nephew's sheriff stepfather will break the cycle on that chain of horror and bring as much justice as can be found to the murderers of those ten girls. These girls have nothing to do with my friends and me. Yet I am linked to their lives as I am linked to the sands of that place, as each human being is linked to another. I am linked to them as I am linked to all women. The exception between them and me is that my friends and I lived, and they did not — and this other odd link through the interstices of time and family. Coincidence, it's said.

It will be thirty years and more after our time of torture before I'll come to know of this twist of chance. Even the whisper of the deathly ordeals of the girls will remain hidden to me. It will be more time yet before I'll understand the close skimming cross of our trails, such a narrow line. But their voices sing across space and time. They speak the world and need to be heard. When I stop running inside my own skin, I will be one that turns to listen. I'll find them in their stories. Painful as it is to hold them, excruciating as it is to imagine, when I've captured my demons and broken their spell I will turn and listen. Beyond scorching terror, it is not just horror I'll hear, a given by then that is useless as sterile soil. It will be something else that I'll receive.

On an upward draft of wind I'll catch the songs of small girls at play that will rise in a waft across time. They did play once, like me. They did know happiness. And it echoes. Dream running laugh singing girls in simple song. Young lives half-lived, both seen and heard. Guileless girls stretch to women, hungry ghosts. We all carry their tune. Each particle song is a history time holds. Through fire and time, voices speak and rise on the breeze. We can choose not to turn away. Each day holds impossible beauty. Hearts inside song at the center of the world allow them to be set free.

But it is still 1972. And I don't know any of this yet.

The land heaves and turns up its ghosts. My ghosts from this point are close, close and so very close. They are heel-biting ghosts. They are ghouls. That outpost limb of my brother's family is barely at the edge of my awareness. I'm still just surviving. They've had no trek yet across Nevada, not stopped in Lovelock on the side of the road, no marriage to sheriffs, not yet a nephew, none quite yet dreamed. There's been no biting dog. I'm alone. I have nothing. Time for solutions wears thin. I'm terrified and can't admit it. If I do the world will fall down forever. Hope and ideas pull paralysis, dead weight. The water grows deep then deeper. I'm forgetting that I know how to swim. I can't imagine myself out of the vacated house of my mother. I can't imagine a life with any wings. The last time I flew, near death and disaster.

I reach for a lifeboat. I call the only adult I can think of that I might have half a lifeline to. It's a lifeline mired in confusion, still smoldering on searing pain. It's the man who called me with his calloused news about Brad's death – pain so deep in the underworld I can't touch it. But I call the man. Appalled by my circumstances and not knowing even half of it, he thinks of his cousin in Colorado. She has an au pair coming from Europe. She might need some help in the meantime. She lives in Denver with her architect husband and three boys. *Do you think you could do this,* he wonders? I'm staggered. The lack of imagination stifles me, juxtaposed to my once-grand hopes. But I say yes, *I could do this.* Unexpected. Unimagined. Tame. Dreams spin away into ethers. Jake checks with his cousin then calls back to say that she wants me. At the end of three months there will be a second family I can work for. I think I can be good at this. I was good with the kids in the communal house. I can be good at this. I move to Colorado.

Old, nightmarish feelings rise about living in a city. For no reason I can name they link to New York. Since they make no sense I decide that they are like all the fear I carry around, something it's best to push down.

I adapt to the family, enjoy the boys, take on the city without loving it and ride my bike everywhere. Within three months I move to the second family. They are also wonderful with a girl and three boys. I find things to like about Denver. From the beginning I spend my free days exploring the new art museum. I search out bookstores, fabric shops and interesting nooks, cannot explain odd, shifting feelings of unease that seem part of the cityscape for me. I begin to view the city as its own kind of wilderness. The central avenues of tall buildings are like canyons out of time. I learn the ins and outs of getting around in them. As months pass I worry about my father, lonely in California, my younger brother living with him now, and I worry about their loneliness together. I cry for them sometimes. I realize peripherally that I am also crying for myself. Yet life is knit together again into some kind of a whole. It will be years before the full grace of the time in Denver comes clear in my awareness, family extended where I had none, surrounded by love and care, plenty and purpose where the world seemed only frightful and vacant.

On my first visit to the art museum I come upon a large painting of a ship in full sail, sitting in a bay. The painting arrests me so forcefully it is hard to move past it. I revisit the painting again and again, whenever I'm at the museum. The effect is always the same. No matter how often I feel its power, my logical mind is taken by surprise. I experience first a sense of arrest, then of being claimed by something potent and meaningful. I become lost in deep reverie before that painting for easily an hour at a time. I feel no active curiosity about the painting per se, I don't even question my experience - there is just the uncanny arrest and intense engagement with the scene portrayed in the painting – and then I pass on. I revel in the museum as a whole, but there is nothing else quite like this.

When I stand before the painting I feel as though I'm on board a ship with sails full and masts piercing sky. A city skyline shimmers across a bay. I feel myself tumbling into deep water, a penetrating sadness, desperate, unable to affect my fate that waits in the water below. I'll drown. I know I will drown. There is no stopping it. Again and again the scene plays out like living history I'm watching, within a living experience I am having. My mind eventually picks up with a story to account for the sensations. *Oh*, I think, *like a sailor, lost at sea.* But there are always unsettled questions just below my awareness. How can the sailor be lost at sea in a harbor? Close, so close to the city? Near, so near to the ship? The falling figure does not feel like a sailor. In fact, I have a strong aversion to any allusion to sailor or a sailor's life at all. My mind barely picks up this thread.

Finally on one visit I shake off the effects of my reverie enough to step forward and read the painting caption. The hair stands up on my arms.

"Ship at Anchor, New York Harbor."

I back away, mind reeling. Some larger part of me knows. The story that my mind has conjured is not the story in the painting at all. The real story is much more chilling. A story I can't hold in my consciousness. Not yet.

Ever since childhood a profound unease that bordered on terror in regard to cities in general and New York City in particular has plagued me. As a child I had no context for this, no way or reason to vocalize these feelings. They just were. There was no real locus for New York in my life, at least none that I was aware of. Yet in odd moments the old fear would arise, stark and uneasy.

Near the end of the year with the second family, when I'm home alone with the family's toddler for two weeks, an attempted break-in occurs. Wild terror leaps out of the night. I hurdle past fear to race for the baby, pull him from his bed, chase through the house turning on every light as I go and call the police. Policemen arrive with flashlights, check around the grounds and tell me there's nothing to be afraid of. *Sure,* I think, *sure.* I shiver in the night air holding the little boy close. I thank them, turn away and lock the door tight. I sit up all night in the middle of the main floor in the middle of light blare and hold the dark-haired toddler who sleeps deep in my arms.

The electricity does not leave my system. When the family returns, it's over. I leave the city soon after. I run for Wyoming. Another family wants me, and I go to them. I go toward two boys, two girls and a set of parents full of innovative ideas. Smart and riveting, unusual interests that match my own, they intrigue me. I reconnect with a man who is my brother's friend. Sparks fly, and I have a boyfriend. He and my brother are both musicians. We all have a really good year. Lost, but for the moment I'm found. There is laughter and play. Life moves on. On one startling night, though, a woman who once dated my boyfriend calls to taunt me while I'm alone with the children. Overwhelmed in the face of her mocking threats, the children in bed, I hang up the phone and cower on the stairway between basement and main floor with a table knife gripped in my hands. I talk myself out of my overreaction. I go to bed. Dread that smokes just below the surface of life cripples through the rest of the night. By morning the old terrors are pushed down, muted into the muffle of daily things.

Tougher still by this time, each family keeps something inside me soft and knit together. Connections breathe where I had none. Another year, another cycle, another partial whole.

As a prized asset in each family, I let life fold in around me. The harsh disconnected parts of me drop their wariness, subsumed then submerged. Life feels like enough. And then, suddenly, it isn't. A pressing need for change overrides every satisfaction. As with the family in Denver, I'm offered a dozen different treasures to stay on.

This time it's 40 acres of land. The terms are just one more year. *Please*, they say, *one more year*. I think, *ok, this will be easy*. But it isn't. My spirit won't settle. I can't stay. For more than two years I've been living the lives of other people. I have to claim my own life now. My story is calling. It's time.

———

Ah, my story. We all have one. To this point, few know the full story, the real story of my life. I barely know it myself. You have to stop and look back to know your story. I'm trying to stay alive, stay ahead of mine. Some few know my story in fragments and disparate chapters. My sister and a small handful of friends know more, but they know it as one knows the surface of a river. Points stand out along curving banks. Hints. Fascinations. Dangerous snags. They have rivers of their own they're navigating. In mine hot springs hiss and blister, pressures spew from far below surface. Inner channels carve to cauldron center, places too hot to venture, impossible to touch or tell. I cannot linger in these places. Crushed in a vise of kept fury and pain, roiling coils of contained forces writhe and simper. Within them resides a Pandora's box with a trillion drawers. I don't open any of them. I throw away the key. I know no one with a story like mine. I move on to the next rung of the ladder up and out of this place, treading ever so lightly.

24

Abyss

Beneath the magma-hot history that strings out behind me, other deeper elements are converging. These are lives for which I have no reference, stories for which I have no name. But they spill, overflowing into my one small life. Lifelines thread parallel paths, making way toward resolution. Deep time expands toward the now.

There are tributaries that cut wide swathes through what is now known as the Great Basin, that long-dried bed of what was once a great inland sea. Long ago, other lifetimes ago, these were nomadic pathways, dear and familiar to me. Lives stack on lives stack on eras, and sometimes, the stories spill out.

I lived a life in that long-ago time that links to my mother and her second husband, a cycle centuries old. In another era we were a family triad. I know this not by the ways that I know them in this life now but by the sense and the sound and the feel of what we left unresolved.

In that earlier time, Carl was a man who was a leader among a nomadic people. My mother was my mother then, as she is my mother now. I was their natural daughter. Of all my mother's work in this life, and I do not begin to speak for what is only hers to know, an unresolved thread ties to me and ties back to this nomadic life. Stories repeat. The past returns until it completes.

Within our life as a threesome my mother did not stand up to her husband, who was then my natural father. Though similar to our lives now — when she married him in this life as her second husband — the circumstances then were different. She made a vow that she did not keep and she did not protect me. Because she was female and he was male in a patrilineal culture? Because there was some aberrant trait in him that in time separated us from our people? Did we walk alone, a tiny unit? I remember us this way but these aspects are unimportant now. I was a child. Our work in this life, my mother's and mine, was to complete that old cycle and to resolve her vow. From that old, triangular enchantment, there were unfinished threads to weave.

That life in the Great Basin held much joy for me, apart from the tensions within our tiny family. I was connected to soil, rock and sky, water, plant and insect, bird, animal and their seasons as I was connected in my own skin. The twisted authority and aberrant power that were rife in our movable dwelling were qualities that swelled out of my father. But in deep, timeless memory they linger only as a strangeness that jars against the rhythm of the wild world, a world I felt so complete within. So I ducked beneath the aberrant strangeness in every way possible in order to relish what I loved. I can still taste the helplessness within the abuse within the deviance that laced our triad together, traveling the old seabed and wild, wide space, wandering tributaries of what I now know as the Humboldt River.

My mother's husband, the man who was my father, murdered me. He left my bones to bake in the ancient sands. In time he murdered my mother as well. When my death came, it came quickly. I did not die within cloying terror. I died with surprise. I feel myself most clearly in those times when I feel the love that tangled up in all of it, the land and the sway and the sweep of that country. It never stopped singing in me. The joy of place, bright and alive, sings across time.

In this current era, in this current time with my mother, we both survived her second husband's brutality, though barely and by separate strategies. Time repeats but outcomes alter. Later in her life, in this life, this man would try to kill my mother again, but this time she would escape — and I, a long time before her.

Did my mother succeed in some way in this life to resolve her old role of motherhood, her old vow? It doesn't seem so. Is it possible that her act of throwing me from her life was the best she could do, saving me from much worse? Is that what she had not accomplished in our lives before? Or did she fail utterly? My mother carries her answers. Her path is hers to speak for. We each complete our stories as best we can. Did I complete my walk with my mother? Yes. By the end of her life, I was resolved with my mother. Was she resolved with me? I don't know. Through many years I did what I could to help my mother lay down the demons of her history. And what of the man, what of him? His demons for a time became our demons. Though at last, in 1971 I laid them down for myself on the same old, dry seabed under a cold October moon with another madman. Through the last decision of another tortured soul, that man who had abducted my friends and me, the past was released.

In some distant past I was violated. I violated. I led good lives. I redeemed lives, and I failed.

Repeating cycles of violence against women hinge alongside other cycles — themes of devastation tied to ages-old racial bigotry. We are weak. We are strong. We struggle for intelligence. We sleep. Themes merge in a life, born of long patterns. Like all patterns, they can be altered. Like all patterns, they can be released.

But I'm ahead of myself. This story and its patterns circle back to 1973, before I'm conscious of any of this.

I'm 21 and I've left my work with families and children and picked up a job at the Pahaska Lodge outside of Cody, Wyoming, near the east gate of Yellowstone. This opportunity comes through my mother's mother, who knows the owners of a tourist lodge where I can work for the summer. I sign on to start early and open the buildings for seasonal operation.

When I arrive the place seems deserted. I wander with shy uncertainty looking for someone to tell me where to go, what to do. There's a restaurant along the roadside and behind it a large log building that stands on a river-rock foundation among other nondescript buildings. A half-circle of A-frame tourist cabins, all painted the same medium-brown, hang in the background. I want to get unloaded from the ride here with my mom and her creep-out husband. I don't like the invasion of them anywhere in my life, the clinging rat-out fact of our shared history. But I still don't drive, and wonder of wonders, they've given me a ride here. Being around them sets off a jangle of intense feelings, an endless conflicted tailspin. I want them to drive away and be gone.

Where is everybody, anybody? Some of the old buildings don't have foundations at all. They meet the earth along undulating lines, buckling of soil and gravity. And I feel it. The gravity. I can't shake it. It pulls on my mind, a twist in my gut. I can't get back in that truck with my mom and her husband. I've gotta find somebody, anybody to tell me where to go, what to do. First wave of early season crew looks like a single, lone ripple. Me. There must be someone else here. I wander from one building to the next knocking on doors shy and awkward but determined, praying I haven't missed something in translation that came down through my grandmother. I don't want to fail my grandma. I don't want to fail period. It's just a seasonal job. That's all, a start.

New beginnings line up behind me like bated breath. Maybe this one will catch and hold, a path that moves forward.

Across the way an old, log lodge looms. Two stories high, pitched roof and a wide wrap of covered porch. Though it sits right in the middle of the rest of the buildings in the midst of all this wild country, it's secluded and oddly apart. Windows wink within its covey of ponderosa pine. The lodge and ponderosa catch hold in me. Logs slump and sigh, lost in time like a figment, a dream. Still and hushed among tall, swaying long-needled evergreen gods, it seems both there and not there at all. Fragrant pine wafts on the breeze, soothes. I step forward, pulled like a magnet but stop and stare, uncertain.

The lodge seems entirely deserted. Air streams through boughs, a sound like high water. Sunshine holds crisp and cool along grass and gravel. I tip into the mirage of someone, anyone who can help me, tell me where I belong. In my first stride forward a whisper like a sigh runs through my body and it turns away of its own accord. I'm surprised to be moving in the opposite direction, abandoning the lodge in its ponderosa embrace. I walk to a small cabin on a grassy knoll behind the restaurant building, climb the steps and stand bemused before the cabin's door. I raise my fist to the door frame. Shy, now doubly shy in the catch between buildings and something unnamable, I pause bewildered. There's a shift, fleeting but sure. I shake my head, push past dismay.

What am I doing here?

About to give up but uncertain what giving up will mean, I study the screen door in front of me. Poised for the echo that will follow my knock and thinking to just walk away, the inside door flies inward before I can raise my hand. The stern gaze of a fierce gray-haired woman grabs hold of me. Our eyes lock through screen mesh. She pushes the flimsy screen door outward, and I step back to the edge of the steps.

"Irish eyes," the woman states flatly. Her eyes flare, aloof irritation to hot interest.

"Wha -at?" I stammer.

"Irish eyes. You have them." Her gaze doesn't flinch.

"Oh," I shuffle and look around behind me, turn back with a fast glance into the dark room behind her. I return her gaze with a wince. "Uh, my sister might look more Irish than I do, her name is ... I dunno. I'm supposed to be here now. To work, for the early crew."

"Right," she says, intent on my face. Odd kindness brightens her eyes as though she knows me, really knows me. Certain she's got a direct line to the center of my brain it's not worth the effort to cloak swirling thoughts. Something clips together in her mind. She nods sudden and curt at a long, low building across from the cabin. I turn to look.

"There," she says. "That's it, the bunkhouse for first-timers. That would be you. I haven't seen you here before. Must be your first year. My husband's the cook. Go ahead. Move in. Come find me when you've unpacked your things." She gestures at the main building that houses kitchen, restaurant, gift shop and bar behind her cabin.

I back away, nod and half-stumble down the steps. The obscure
kindness in the middle of the woman's bite unnerves me. Her eyes
plaster to my back as I turn to leave, a feeling that will grow over
coming weeks. When I look back, she's gone.

I walk around to gather my gear off the side of the road where it
was dumped half an hour before. I thank my mother, refuse their help
and say good-bye. As they drive away I haul everything in a couple of
trips back to the bunkhouse. Which turns out to be a cheerless, dark
room with concrete floor, cheap paneling and six metal-framed beds
hardly bigger than cots that mirror to either side. A little natural light
spills in from narrow windows high along the upper, west wall. I take
the cot on the far end below the windows, sling my stuff to the floor
and quickly make up the bed with worn linens stacked at its foot. I feel
both lonely and thrilled. Anticipation runs a fast current, one notch
above vague, weighty sorrow. I take hold of the thrill and make my way
back outside to my workaday world. Promise rifles out toward the rest
of the summer.

Four, maybe five months here stretch ahead. There's something that
buzzes in the sunlight, hovers in the shadows. I move toward it, a sense
of mystery. Work is the way, but it's not the why of being here. It's the
place, this feeling, the reason I've come — not the tourist crust and
crow of it all that will build as the season builds — but something
tumbling together beneath. I can't explain it and I don't try to. My job
starts the moment I walk through an open door that turns out to be the
kitchen. A couple of introductions put me on my way to bailing out A-
frame, winter-closed cabins. I go at it full on, glad to catch the wave
and ride. The smitten something just below the everyday world flares
and calls, a persistence that has no form.

Happy. Belonging. Somewhere. The air the trees the quiet sing
through my skin, percolate, penetrate, float through my blood. Every
breath hints a decoding to which I feel bidden. Attending I work.
Working I linger. Lingering I listen. I think it's the ripe enchantment
that swells each time I remember how close this place is to the Sunlight
Basin — I feel as though I could touch into it with slightest reach, and
I want to. I don't know why. It's something deep. So near so far it
ripples, a longing, a pull like a song lost or song not yet written. My free
time is spent outside wandering. Then I think it's the sheer wildness of
place flowing out of forest, off ridgelines and over boundaries of kept
space on indecipherable currents. Then I think it's the solitude. I'm
sure it's the freedom. In the midst of the call to work, schedule and
demand, freedom croons. It's none of these things. It's all of these
things. Nameless. Formless. Sure.

I roam where I can when I'm not at work, which is seldom and not
very far. Work is the constant. In all the exposure and newness I'm

ignorant of most local history. I just took a job that seemed possible. For the world past the workplace, longing whets appetite at subterranean levels. I want to wear what I feel like a skin.

Leaves sparkle morning and evening light dapple, court sunrise, flirt afternoon. Waters gurgle in miniature cascade, a melody transparent from gravelly depths of the river. Clouds shape, unshape and reform. The recent past stirs old chronic unease, rustling within the ply of this place. Everything layers. Worlds beneath the surface wax mesmeric. This edge of unknowns is a soft collision. Make new the world, all seems to whisper.

The pace picks up, and though I miss the solitude of the first weeks, I love making new friends, the laundry cart that I have a blast driving around and running with the cabin crew. The summer swells. My boyfriend drives up from Casper for a couple of visits. We explore the woods in the evenings. I get lost in cacophony of forest, carried by the dream of earth and shadow. Dazed and illumined by the power of merged natural forces we expand beyond self into place as connected as roots rising and diving through humus and soil, funneling trees that soar to heavens. The unceasing call to the wild courts, sirens and woos through these nights and into the day-to-day.

It turns out that Bill, one of the crew members, is the key-holding caretaker for the old, retired hunting lodge of Buffalo Bill Cody that sits at the center of the bustle and noise. Two-stories, the lodge, long closed down, hovers in its separate reality among ponderosa at the heart of the other buildings. Built in 1904 it predates our time by 70 years. I don't know it yet, but this lodge is the spiritual ancestor to another place that links through family and time and a great-uncle of mine in Canada.

One morning, up early and wandering through willows along the river on the opposite side of the main road that leads into Yellowstone, something stirs along the outer edges of my cells. Comes a shuffling up my spine. I turn to gaze in the direction of the Sunlight Basin, imagine a time when I might explore there. Lingering along the water's edge, I long for baptism in that distant basin sanctum. But here, now, river flows through willow. Lilt of morning light weaves space into changing patterns. There's a waft of movement. I turn again. Mother moose with babe lingered here yesterday but not now, not now nothing here but willow, water and grass waving on banks in morning lowlight, beneath the sweep of towering ponderosa.

Movement like a breath, like a spiral as though flame to be fed shimmers on light air turning. Currents drift through shadow. Some counterweight topples to a second pitch and I startle, listening into the keel of change. Limen of opposing forces, time parts and bends quicksilver among swaying willows — out of sight, out of rhythm, portents hang on still air. In a quivering back turn I face the old hunting lodge across the road.

Bill and his friend Joe move from bunkhouse across grass to the covered porch of the aged building. Boards squeal as they take to the steps. No one else in sight, I step out fast and cross the road to join them. Kim, another friend, appears out of nowhere. Hushed we hold our breath as Bill works the key into the lock. When the door swings open musty scent puffs out on stale air. We step inside. The door swings closed. White sheets cloak furniture that stagger in clustered humps across a large room that vaults to a high ceiling, stone fireplace at the far end. A staircase climbs to the left. Steps seem to crumble on the casual force of our glance. We scatter. I cross to a blind corner behind the fireplace. Peering around, wondering what I will find, I hear Joe yelp. I whirl to see him climbing the decrepit stairs, wood tinder falling to the main floor beneath.

Kim, Bill and I gather on the floor below. Joe cautions us back, continuing up. Bill fidgets, unnerved and speechless. Boards threaten and squeal beneath Joe. Deft he's halfway to the top when Kim steps with care onto the second step and begins to climb. Joe pauses midway, stares to the floor below that gapes through a shattered hole in the step above him. He takes the step above, another and another then leaps to the upper landing. Tiny fragments of flooring spin and splinter through the dusty air. I'm halfway up before I realize what I'm doing, astonished to find myself making the climb. Kim takes her last step to join Joe. Heights and precarious perches unnerve me, yet I climb with unaccountable focus. Bill, frantic below, squawks in warning as though he can stop us. The sound is ludicrous in the dense silence that claims the old lodge.

Like Joe and Kim before me I step around the yawning fracture in the step halfway up, move fast and light to the top. Bill's misery is silenced to a curse, as last and largest of us all, he begins to climb. He lands beside Joe, sweating and very unhappy.

The floorboards on the second floor are far worse than the floors below. They sag across the landing, a large fracture gaping in the center. The boards cry out beneath our weight. We move closer to the walls. There is a row of closed doors and Joe, Kim and I make our way toward them. Bill stands at the top of the landing in a tight fury. I want to open every door we come to but Joe's first and I'm last. He turns each knob, holds us back as we strain to see over his shoulder. Sheets cover furniture, dust whispers. He closes each door, and we move on. I barely see even the plain furnishings, but we move as though we are glued together. Joe continues room to room, as though they are trophies he wants to capture. But there's something here. I feel it. We round the end of the hallway and begin the sweep along the other side.

I want Joe to slow down, stop, linger. But the place itself holds us silent. Bill, at the top of the stairs, hangs on the instant we will leave.

The last door and a single-faceted knob glimmers against old, blank wood. Joe reaches out, and the door swings slowly open. Snags of memory bottomless and insufferable slouch through swirling dust as we step to the threshold and the door cries into a room. The room is filled wall to wall with enameled chamber pots. Pitchers and basins crowd and stack on bed, bureau and floor. Joe turns away disgusted, crowding us out as he has at each room. But I resist. As he pushes past us out onto the mezzanine I take a step forward. The floor whines. I stay where I am. There's something about this room that's different, beyond the old chamber pots. I lean forward, holding onto the doorjamb to hang deeper into the room. Kim stares and Bill jeers from across the landing. I scan the floor of the room for an open passage between all the speckled pots and basins. Boards sag, crying beneath our feet. The air is thick. Recollection stirs electric wizards up my spine. I have no names for the old familiarity. My heart skips a beat. Something echoes.

I lean in further. The echo wavers, faint but full-throated call. Speckled pots seem to speak in tongues, a whispered incantation that is not from the pots, not exactly. Crowded and close they sit, mediums for something … something … dry, abandoned whine keels just past hearing, old cadence building. I want to move toward it, not away. Floor is crowded, too crowded. Strange treasure, chamber pots, they waver. Will the boards hold? I place one foot forward. Bill mumbles frantic mumbo jumbo from his perch at the top of the stairs. A ripple among the pots, decoys for a faint beckoning that tips and shudders. Room wobbles and rights itself. A glisten. A glare. Revulsion at the unpleasant utility of these vessels has dropped away. The old floors moan. I stand inside the doorway unmoving. Kim steps out. I look past her over my shoulder. Across the landing the floor sags at the middle with a cry; sallow warning.

That slumped floor is a conundrum I want to cross. Why? Bill's panic is building. I turn back to the room and stare into melting recesses past the present moment. An exhale, then intake of breath laments. Faint, shifting reek suffers from walls and furnishings. Not scent, not even imagined, yet what exactly? It's as though unseen worlds meet clashing. A puff, like a memory, something on the verge of showing itself that sparks and dissipates. I step back, close the door and step away.

The longing of morning willows sings, murmuring along hallway borders. I see and feel the cadence from the river flow through the air. Bill pants, nearly choking. My hand falls from the door, facets of the knob imprinted on skin, on memory that shivers and swells. Cold and heat flow together. Then I see it — the last door across the landing, not far from Bill, a room unto itself. I want to go to it. Next clue, next treasure, next threshold. Bill sees my face. He turns red and gasps. I take a step. The sagging floor screams. I step back. Bill strangles on words.

"Down!" he croaks. "Now." He shudders. "We have to get out of here. We shouldn't be up here at all, shouldn't even be inside."

I look at the last door, so near so far. The three of us skirt back along the hallway the way we've come until we're standing next to Bill. Walls murmur secrets around us. I look down the stairway. Regret drags at my back. That final room hunts my name. I turn.

Something here knows me. I want to know what it is. I lean toward it. Bill grabs my arm. I turn to watch Joe then Kim make their rickety descent. I want to be alone for the final moments up here. The room pulls and whispers. Bill makes me promise I'll stay where I am and follow him down. I nod.

Down is the gamest risk of all. Each faltering step lowers weight to fraying wood and feels like the last. It's not the same balance as climbing up. Keeping real distance between each of us looms a little nightmare, urgent and sharp. An entire descent before the next person starts. The staircase sways rotting. A board that cracked beneath Joe threatens, and he's the lightest of us all. In a graceful leap he lands flat-footed on the floor below. Kim takes the final steps on her butt, lying back. Bill follows in mimic.

For a moment I feel stranded. Wishing I were anywhere but making this descent, the near-tragedy of every step taunts. My mind, more dangerous than the stairway, finally settles. The three call from below soft then softer. For a breath fear is gone. I take one wide, downward stride to cut over two steps, staying light, descending on air past two more. Somehow I miss the breakaway hole. Elation bears me down the final cascade. The lower room seems to respire.

Jumpy we fling across the room as Bill walks unheeded to the door. At the back near the fireplace I make for the blind corner, step around into gloom, a smattering of light dances beyond. *A kitchen?* Bill's hand lands on my shoulder. He grabs for Joe nearby and herds us to the door, Kim at our heels. I look back as the shrouds gust and settle. Bill pushes us over the threshold. The door swings closed, his hands trembling as the key turns in the lock. He turns and waves us off the porch.

Duties and morning light swell like a claiming, counterweight quarter note done. We scatter.

By evening distraction claims me. Unable to focus, I go to bed early. The next morning brings a day off for all four of us. Kim is driving home to see her family. I'm going with her. Bill and Joe will catch a ride as far as town. I can barely track our plan. Everything feels convoluted, ungainly. When we gather at Kim's car Bill is thrilled to nab the front seat when I get in the back. Pressed to my window I feel like I'm losing control in a way I can't name. I say little, my friends a burble, talking so fast my head spins. Our first day off in three weeks and we're outta this place. When the tires spin the road I jump as though glib with relief. It's a sham. Sharp pains stab through my abdomen. Clutching the door handle, I will the pain to pass. The guys start to tease when they notice how quiet I am. I can't even rise to the bait. I can barely keep my body together in one place. The three carry off in a garble of plans. I catch Kim watching me in the rearview mirror. I finally admit I feel lousy. I'm sure it will pass. *Sure it will. Sure. It will.*

We drop the guys off in front of the Irma Hotel. I climb to the front seat, and we drive on. For the first few miles I feel lighter, waves of laughter pass between us about mix-ups at work. We look forward to the night to relax. But I slide back into pain, lousy company. At her house I meet Kim's mom, little brother, we go to her room to hang out. I lie down on the bed. It takes everything I have to stifle a moan on waves of spiking pain. Kim's mom thinks we should head back to Pahaska and stop at the hospital on the way.

As we start to drive thoughts of contagion from the old chamber pots rifle through my thoughts with a ravaging twist. And then I don't think anymore.

Kim drives to the hospital ER against my wishes. I resist getting out of the car. She insists. The ER doc is young, dismissive but mostly makes no sense to me. He writes out a prescription to fill before we leave town. When we arrive back at my bunkhouse I have a bag of medication in my hand. Whirling concerns spin about work and not wanting to let my grandma down, and they fall with me into bed.

The night is bad. In the morning I imagine making my way into work clothes for the day. Misery holds me flat. Then Kim's at my side telling me to lay low: she's let the crew bosses know I'm sick. Everyone else has left the bunkhouse. When she's gone I rock against blinding pain that telescopes limb to limb, every joint locked into bands of tension. They bind at my head and feet. I doze. I wake on the upswing of muscle-strangling cramps. They lessen. I doze. I wake in a vise of pain and spin away into semi-consciousness. When I wake again the world feels dulled with weight and throbbing agony. I lie on the bed gripped by a pulsing agony.

I begin to come completely undone. My eyes roll back in my head. Panicked, I struggle to bring them forward. I fix a stare on the fake wood grain of the cheap wall paneling. I lose control of them. They roll back as though pulled on bands of steel. Horror bridles against an inexorable tension. It's as though ropes run taut between my head and feet. My head arches with the backward roll of my eyes, back and back and back as my spine, hips and legs bend in a backward bow. Eyes lock into darkness at the farthest reaches of my skull. In the torture of no control, panic builds. I struggle against the bending contortion. And bend further back, into a rigid bow. Muscle, sinew and cells clamp along sirens of pain. I can't stop it. The squeal of old history whines. My toes touch the back of my head, and I'm locked in an impossible backbend, completely out of control.

Panicked thoughts overtake everything. *If someone comes in and finds me this way, they'll think I've gone crazy.* I fight to gain control of my eyes. *If I'm found like this I'll be hauled away to an asylum.* The backbend deepens. Pain saws inside and out.

In silence, my body an instrument too tightly strung, the room slips away into thick darkness.

Tumult gyrates and slides on the hum of a massive hush. Plunging to nothing, faint hiss rises from beneath me. There is movement.

I see figures on the move below.

They race across barren, undulating landscape. Ahead is a woman. Some distance behind race three cloaked forms, amorphous, dark within dark. The woman flees over seam and fold. She runs up a rise. Her pursuers crowd from the distance, relentless. She pushes to a copse of close-growing evergreen trees and presses within them. The trees crowd around her, snagging. She pushes through and out the other side. She arrives at a knife's-edge precipice along a massive abyss. Open space plunges past sight, out of mind. Speeding, the dark triad waits behind her, waiting they come, approaching they drive the woman. She does not feel fear. She feels pressure, the pressure of their approach.

She steps onto razor-thin rock that stretches across the gaping abyss. She is me and all is darkness ahead and behind.

The way forward narrows; I drop to my hands and knees to crawl. Too precarious, I drop to my belly. I drag across luminous, sharp rock. Void space hangs in stark plummet, infinitude to either side. The dark three press through the copse of pine behind. I drag along the hairline edge of the endless. The triad reaches the precipice. Uneven balance, I hover, I cannot go further. Figures faint and ephemeral float in great darkness below me. The abyss drops in unending space. I grasp the cold rock, scrabbling. Small stones skitter into free fall. To my left the bottomless siren plunge lures into ricochet nothing. I inch my gaze to the right. Seductions of eternal whirling pulse within suffuse light. Mists pull and ferret. Forever rises, dives and separates.

I cannot go forward. There is no going back. Plummet is blank infinitude.

Suddenly, I understand. I have a choice. I can fall to the left. Forever. Or I can fall to the right. Eternal. Right. Left. Dark. Light. I must choose.

A chant to the left, faint echo, a speck in vastness, everything and nothing beckon. A pull toward perpetual, ceaseless gone. I sway. Forms appear and die by the millions. My body weights left. Biting rock burns. Lick and creep of limitless promise, limitless plunge. Scant hold slackens. Hands loosen, releasing their burden. I tip toward the nothing.

And a burst of awareness pops wide. A third choice explodes into clarity. It has a voice.

"Stop thinking. Stop thinking self. Stop thinking pain. Stop thinking."

Blinking infinity darkens. Spark in my core. Pain flickers diamonds. Stone cuts, bites into bone and skin. Magnetic beckon recedes. I tip slow-motion back to center on the sharp lip of eternity, hover on the knife of the ridgeline. Dragging backward from stark plummet, halfway from the center of nowhere I watch stones skitter and drop out of sight. The triad recedes, undulating toward silence and gloom. I pull myself back to the edge of the precipice. Beyond sight, out of mind the three tremor into the copse of pine and darkness. I stand upright on solid ground. Darkness hisses to nothing.

Plain room settles around me. Six narrow beds line on one side. Six line the other. I lie in one, locked backward in dreadful grace. My body begins to unbind. Vertebrae by vertebrae, stabbing liberation slows time. Nerves flex, scream, release and unlock. I tremble to a semblance of order, lie breathless full-length on the narrow mattress, at last no longer bound. Drone of the wire bed frame winnows along musty air.

Footsteps grind on the gravel outside the bunkhouse, cut approach to the door and cross over to enter the room. They make their way to the side of my bed. Relief floods through me, my body fully extended, though shivering in a bit of sunlight raining down from the narrow windows above. I shrink without moving, feel gratitude for this appearance of normalcy.

Blonde Susan hovers beside me, bunkmate from the next bed over. "Pretty bad, huh?" she says as her light touch pats along one leg. I nod.

She sinks to her bed and pulls a guitar case from beneath. Rattle of latch, scrape of strings, a claim and a pluck and the pluck becomes tune. Angel voice climbs into song.

> Babies' boats, a silver moon, sailing through the sky
> Sailing through a sea of sleep as the clouds pass by,
> Sail baby sail out across the sea,
> Only don't forget to sail back again to me.

Baby's fishing for a dream, fishing near and far.
Her line a silver moonbeam is, her bait a silver star
Sail baby sail out across the sea,
Only don't forget to sail back again to me.

Lullaby streams notes that capture the room, soaking through my pores. Pain goes on hold. Beauty and wonder settle like balm. On a final phrase, Susan rises. She stows her guitar away wordless, pats my leg, smoothes my hair and leaves the room. Last locks of tension release down my spine. Exhaustion cleanses joint and tissue. An enormous sense of return from across great distance takes hold. My mind abandons its bite and ache. I sleep.

The world outside the room presses. I wake to an awareness of work crews bustling about in early summer evening down by the lodge. Someone walks the gravel, calls out greeting. Friends and strangers inhabit the world beyond these walls and beyond this place. Tucked away in many different places people I love are caught up in the motion of daily life. There is laughter. I feel the world turn a notch. And turn one notch more.

I rise from the squeaking crease of the bed, shaky and weak. I make my way slowly to the outside door. At the threshold uncertainty wavers and holds me. Shell-shocked, without resource I wobble. I feel into what is outside beyond the door. Shy tenderness picks up my heart. I push out into evening air and look from left to right. Insects buzz, lazy in late-day warmth. Voices frolic and waft in the distance. Day's work done, evening chores are coming on. Gratitude lifts inside me on the evening cadence. I know this rhythm. In the late light and ring of wandering voices, the forest presses in from all directions. Each in their place, still points in time. It is too soon to move into this beating heart of the world. But I touch it. I hold it and feel how it's there for me. Time will bring me back into the fold of belonging, and I will choose it. Frail and sore I breathe once, twice and turn back to the spare healing silence of the room.

25

Riding Stable

And so I begin to return to myself. Memory plies forward like a new awakening. What was lost to me in the years of greatest violation and confusion? What is still to be found? Time wrinkles, time stretches, and old remembrances unfold.

When I was a girl I rented horses at a stable to ride with my friends on the prairie at the foot of the mountain outside our town. We would ride off on mild adventures in a cluster of chatter and dream through sage and open vistas. The horses were docile, dulled by time and changing riders, but I chose the most spirited among them, each of us vying for our favorites. One summer day after I turned 13, we returned to the stable from riding and found the owner waiting. He wanted us to know that one of the mares was near to foaling. He asked if I wanted to watch the birth the next weekend. If I came very early in the morning and the timing was right, I could see it happen.

I was horse-crazy. I returned to the stable the next Saturday at 6 a.m. to find he had our horses saddled. I was confused. I thought the mare would foal in the barn. He said we'd have to ride out to find her on the prairie. I swallowed surprise. We rode off on the search. Normally reticent, the man chatted with great animation about the mare, our timing, our luck and the early hour, how we might just come up on her giving birth. Or maybe find her already with foal in the lee of a hill.

Like a needle in a haystack, he said, *to find her.*

We rode out of sight from road and buildings. The beauty of the morning and chance, the wonder of birth and the lure in his voice gathered to a gesture as he waved out in front of us. There was a swell, then a hill beyond.

Just beyond that, he said.

With those words I knew at once that I did not want to ride with him to that swell, never beyond it. I did not care to see the mare. I had to get back to the barn, in sight of the road and the house. I hung back.

Oh, no, he said, *just a little further. It's just up ahead. You'll be sorry you missed it.*

I knew that I wouldn't. I shook my head. Surly, cheated, his voice went hard and he turned in his saddle, pointing again toward the hill. When he looked back I was already turning my horse, riding away. I knew that the mare was not where we were going.

I rode back to the road, back to the barn, back to the house and stable. I dismounted, tied my horse and left for home. I never went back to the stable again. For years after, I shuddered anytime we passed the place on our drives to the mountain. My mother asked why I never wanted to ride there anymore. Each time my answer was vague and oblique, outside the realm of clear understanding. I felt ashamed about my last experience at the stable. I didn't know why. But I never doubted my decision to turn from the chance to see the mare and her foal.

What happened to the intuitive guidance and core knowing I trusted as a girl that day on the prairie?

Four years after that day, my mother married Carl and betrayed my younger brother and me to her new husband. Parent-to-child trust was impossibly broken. There is nothing more vulnerable than the trust of a child to her parent. Betrayal like that distorts native senses. Betrayal like that wrenches native talents apart.

Like a needle in a haystack, finding a way through the collision of past and present.

26

Fey

Instinct and intuition, set at odds within twists of reality and betrayal, were part of what I had to set right. Critical senses had slipped from my grasp, turned inside out by confusion and circumstance, blighted and torn by ongoing overload — the very senses I needed to trust, above all.

For the span of many years I tried to bar the door, keep the floor from falling out from under me, stop the slide down into a dark undertow, save boys I would meet in a children's home, or anyone else I could. And I tried to reclaim my natural talents and skills.

After my experience at Pahaska, I was left to wonder, what had happened to me there? Had I experienced a nervous breakdown? A psychotic split? Was it spontaneous kundalini? Or was a shamanic vision carrying me along a pathway of healing? I was aware of no such interpretations at the time and none then were useful to me.

What I did understand was that the wisdom I carried within me was trying to break through into conscious awareness, a force that informed and pulled toward wholeness. This felt impossible to explain to most people I knew at the time and I seldom tried. The weight of the past, the underworld of my experience drew me toward resolution — connections that were making way on the outbreath of time. As they filtered and shocked into waking awareness I could hold them at best, though not yet articulate them for what they were. In Wyoming in 1973 there was little within the culture of my world that supported the wisdom I held. Though I sensed truth and power within me I was on my own to understand what it was, and I knew it. Revelations laid down new challenges and life carried me on.

What did it mean, truth and power composed within deep disruption? How did one find the way to the center of that? New questions layered onto old questions. So many threads tied in a complex tangle. Yet the Ariadne's thread within me wound steady out of the bestial lair of my experience, if I could follow it. I would discover much in the years after my time in the old hunting lodge that lived on my inward plane as guidance. And I would also discover a spiritual lineage that linked to the old lodge itself. But I knew none of this then. Each layer, each its time.

My body bent backward on distortions of my past, my progress forward trapped by fears held in my mind that distorted my present — I was an instrument too tightly strung. Yet the awful contortions gave me one key. How can the mind be stopped from its overwhelm, its fearsome gyrations? A mind like mine, fertile, creative and full of terror, rooted in lived experience? Could I use this new key, and learn to control my mind? The tuning fork so alive in my childhood was an exacting vibration that bent me backward toward clarified form … hinting at the need to look back.

But in 1973, I'm caught in that torque of severity. I feel ill or fey half the time. I can't do my job. I can barely function. Abdominal pains return and redouble anytime I take up my work with the cabin crew. The cook's wife keeps me on dishwashing duty in the restaurant kitchen — a kindness but also a demotion. I hang low before the stainless steel sink, dreading the next step that's cued inside of me. It's time to give notice — leave my job, leave my friends. Strains of guilt and heavy regret hang on this decision. I had committed to stay the full season, early on, late off, close the place down. But today I'll let my boss know I can't keep my end of the bargain. I feel pathetic.

I'm barely able to look him in the eye at the awful meeting. But afterward the dragging heaviness relents. I feel a little lighter. Small bursts of fuzzy anticipation for the change rise up like little fireworks that make me feel hopeful. On my last day as I sit in a meeting on the grassy knoll outside her cabin, the fierce gray-haired woman watches me closely. The cabin crew is gathered around her in a bubbling cluster, yet her sharp gaze still seeks me out.

I feel unmasked from things I don't even know I'm holding. Her look is full of something more than ripe concern. I flinch away and lean in all at once, wanting to cry or run. The dreadful past that lies hidden inside me curls deeper. Tensions left from my experience of the abyss hint around my eyes, insinuate through my cells. I'm fragile. I don't like it. My gray-haired guardian maneuvers along the grass until she's next to me. And when everyone else is distracted, she asks for a promise: *Will I please keep in touch, no matter what?* No matter what, and she presses a small paper into my hand. No matter what, and her eyes fall to the paper. A list of addresses and phone numbers fill the little page. She talks on about how she and her husband travel and where she'll be when. I look up and nod into her mother-hawk gaze. I feel willing, grateful. But a hole opens up that plummets into the underground of our exchange.

As I look away, sorrow blooms deep inside me. I know I will never see this woman again. And then it's the next morning, and my brother Tom arrives to pack me up, and we drive away.

We wind and float our way down the long canyon away from the lodge. I can barely focus through my fog of malaise and uncertainty. But it feels good to sit across from my brother. I call out landmarks here and there in the growing sunshine. He asks if I want to stop for coffee and breakfast. Just like that. It feels like unmitigated freedom, and I smile for the first time in days. We pull up to a log building that sits in a cluster of tiny, log guest cabins, just where the canyon expands into the laughter of wide-open space. Swinging from the car on a light note I feel a quiet sense of adventure. I've never stopped here before. I've never had the confidence to do it, though I've admired it in passing.

As we climb the steps the tight canyon hunkers at our backs like the open exit of a birth canal. The glib proprietor is welcoming, offers seats, pours coffee and leaves for the kitchen to prepare our meal. He's owner, host, crew and cook this morning and happy to see us. No one else here; we're glad for the privacy.

My brother watches me over the rim of his coffee cup. His own half shattered gaze, still fractured from time in Viet Nam, takes in the splintering way I hang back, let him order and direct our meal to this point. "Bad, huh?" he winces through spirals of steam.

I try to find words for my state of mind. There are none. I look down into my own cup. Caffeine and cream swirl, probably not a good idea, given the way I feel. I think maybe I'll change to decaf, black, as my cup rattles back to its saucer. I mention this, which gives him an idea of how unstable I feel. I search for words again, but I know it's ok. The ease I feel with my brother unwinds the tight place inside me. I relax into my chair with the closest thing to peace I've felt in two weeks. I still can't entirely control my eyes, and they drift left, right or backward all of their own accord in random moments for no particular reason I can fathom. It's like shame but not shame. I can't define it. They make it hard to look directly at people. I've learned to work this in the company of strangers by dropping my eyes, turning my head or letting my hair fall forward, whatever it takes to avoid a direct gaze until my eyes right themselves. But here, now, today, they behave as eyes should behave, and I look at my brother with a half-smile. Our food arrives, and we begin to eat. The rightness feeling settles deeper. About halfway through the meal I'm able to tell him some of what the past weeks have held. He listens and nods, making a comment or two.

"There are spiritual aspects to these things, you know," he says.

"I know," I say. "I'm workin' it." It's enough right now just feeling that someone understands even a little.

We leave the cozy cabin and drive through the valley then on through the many miles to the place he shares with his girlfriend outside Powell. They've set up camp in a blasted-out migrant worker's house on a farm in the outskirts. Somehow they've befriended the farmer and his wife and enjoy free rent for an occasional chore, though little seems expected of them. But then the house is hardly a house at all. The place is an overgrown, downtrodden, bare-earthed blight. With no actual doors on any of the three entryways, the house is scoured with hard use and the grit of blown-in sand and dust. There is no stove, no refrigerator in the kitchen. They cook in an electric frying pan. Plumbing is mostly worthless. The bathtub doesn't drain but water hauled to it makes it a kind of cistern, and the toilet can be flushed with buckets of water scooped from the tub.

Tom's girlfriend has added still more sand to drifts that blow in with the wind to create a rock garden of skulls, assorted bones and cactus on the enclosed front porch. This makes the constant need for sweeping the rest of the house in maddening regularity an easier chore: just add sweepings to the inside garden dune. The place, though, is no kind of a midden. Beyond blown dust it's neat, clean, earthen and spare. Quilts stack on quilts on the double bed in the single, small bedroom. An ancient chenille couch looks shabby elegant in the worn surround where it hunkers against a living room wall on clawed feet. Bed and couch are the only furniture except a chipped, yellow Formica table and four matching chairs in the kitchen. This surreal household makes strange sense to my own inner landscape and, in truth, can't hold a candle to it. The severity of the place absorbs with ease into my fragile, humming equilibrium.

My brother's girlfriend, though, is another story. I'm glad when we decide to go to a drive-in movie on the first night, to shift her intensity off me and onto the screen. When Tom realizes what movie she's picked, he shoots a frozen look at me and falters. He's grown up with the results of my nightmares. He's aware of what I'm juggling now. But I tell him it's ok, and we watch *Soylent Green,* a movie that would normally chill me to the bone. The story revolves around a society that holds dark secrets about climate change and the terrible source of its food. The movie hardly fazes me. Like the house, it's nothing alongside the reality I'm carrying. The capacity to affect the movie's effect on me is a new curiosity. How can I hold it? How can I broker each experience into a whole, if fractured containment inside of me? It's a mystery. Observer and witness, sacred and profane, I'm casualty and vanquisher all in one. We laugh a lot that night. We shiver and gasp.

The next day when my brother and I meander along sidewalks of the nondescript town, I pull out my cool, hip-chick veneer and wear it with extra vigor and style. I have to. We stand out big-time in this provincial little place. My eyes are still unpredictable and a problem, especially in public. But I manage a mask on a mask, keenly aware of all the masks that smile, frown, blink and nod on the other faces we pass as we wander by, cruising our route. I'm glad to be in this place with my brother, however insular or vague or strange. It changes everything.

That night, a little bomb drops. It's time for them to make a run to another town for supplies, a regular part of their routine. It's especially convenient because now I can stay and take care of the kittens they've been trying to keep from a tomcat that prowls the grounds each night, the mother killed fighting for them. I'm to put the kittens inside a large metal milk can every night before dusk, secure the cover but leave it loose for air and release them to roam each morning. This sole responsibility settles into the fact that I have nowhere to go, to be and nothing to do. They'll be away for a few days, give or take — probably give, knowing them.

The bizarre and extremely exposed fact of the house and the edge upon which it sits, between the moderate prosperity of the farm and the conditions of poverty to which their workers must submit, funnels into the extremities my mind must hold. I can't close or lock any entrance, not windows, no doors. I can't secure anything. I can only be. I'm not actually waiting. Except for them to get back. I haven't any idea what's next. I just am. I find that what's threatening here is no worse and no better than anyplace else. It all lives inside me. So I accept what is. Doors that can't be closed can't be locked. Windows ditto. This adds fear to fear in the night. But fear's in the night anyway and I sleep. It's been this way since I was a child.

The place and its scoured purposelessness take on a meeting of psyches. When my brother is gone and true isolation sets in, I settle in to a desert of the soul. I find I'm home. The hallowed and blasphemous walk beside me. I can hold both places. Many places. Here I hold the extremes. In this place they're just more apparent. I look at the stark, varied nature of life and don't flinch. This in itself becomes healing unguent on wounds laid out inside of me. Alone isn't lonely, it's alone. This is the one thing I know, I have always known. I can let aloneness be whatever I want it to be. Now I want it for its simplicity. So I set tasks for myself. I ride my bike into town for groceries. I buy an ice cream cone just for lightness, play. I chat with people in businesses or on the street who stop me with question or concern. If I don't feel like it, I don't, I keep to myself. I master the art of the electric frying pan. When panic rises, I walk. I read — though never for long. Concentration is nefarious and unaccountable. I fit the extremes of the thing called loneliness when it hints or caws or claws, to an aloneness that's as natural as the sand that blows and drifts into the house on hot, dry summer winds.

At night I place the kittens in the milk can. Each morning I rise grateful for early light as it hints beneath heavy quilt layers. I step into the cool bite of morning. And each day I find a single kitten lying lifeless on the pounded brittle earth. There have been no sounds in the night. There are no tokens of battle. There is just the simple still form, stretched or hunched on bare earth at the break of dawn. The tomcat manages his work. The first morning my heart flips and I grieve. I make ritual of humble burial. I study the security of the milk can lid, find it faultless. I release the other kittens to roam. I take up another day.

Four days, four nights, four kittens and then there are none.

Still no signs come of my brother. Not a word. On the fifth morning a message arrives from the main house, impossible to see from within the cloister of Russian olive surrounding the disintegrating migrant shell. My boyfriend is on his way, driving up from Casper. My pulse quickens at the unexpected news. The endless days are now finite. By evening, he'll arrive. And he does, outraged that my brother has left me alone in this miserable place.

I can't explain how fine I am. I can't speak to the tragedy of the kittens nor of the tenderness of life, but he sees them breathe in me. I can't name how, somehow, the margins of this place have helped knit my own back together. How it is that life always turns on a molten precipice. How nothing is for sure. But I can say how glad I am to see him. And how much gladder I am still to leave with him — and go home. I can't imagine the idea, home, but it rolls over the lip of my mind, oiled and bright and breathing. One night, no kittens, no death, not here in this place at least, and we're gone with the first light of morning. It's just a walking away from the blasted-out shell of the house toward the creamy glint of a Plymouth sedan waiting just past the yard. My boyfriend slides into the driver's seat. I curl up on the passenger side, lay my head in his lap, feeling both lost and found. He turns the ignition. The car sputters to life. He murmurs, stroking my hair. And this is the way of the rest of our long drive day. We tell each other secrets and listen. But words are few and matter little.

And so it is. We return and set up a narrow apartment together that he finds on a blighted street that appalls me. But I've made a choice to be in my heart, and this is the essence of what the abyss is teaching me.

I go to work at the state children's home as a housemother in charge of preadolescent boys. Most of the boys trust me right from the start, the rest follow in quick succession. I'm good at this. These are boys who have no home and little hope of one. And unless they're released to return to their original family, so they'll remain. Because the slippery slope of state law makes this so, only one of the boys is up for adoption. His particular medley of quirks and debilities keeps his appeal to adoptive parents minimal. Fond of them all with their hair-brained energy and eccentric ways, the work is exhausting and hard. I come to love these boys in the complicated way of caregivers whose job is a job. It's not easy. Their suffering eddies constant storm.

The terms upon which the orphanage (whoops, we're not supposed to call it that, it isn't after all really an orphanage anymore) — the terms upon which the home rotates are a gross improvement over past incarnations, yet they're dreadful all the same. Lines of abuse are crossed regularly by some staff, couched in treatments like knuckle therapy from the headmaster, lockup that too often pushes to extremes to deal with discipline problems and other disturbing, disgusting methods. There are some really good people that work in this place. And there are some really bad, most of the latter from the past order when conditions were truly monstrous. This group likes to reminisce about the old days as though something to yearn for. It's chilling. I never know what I'll find when I return for my next shift.

On my watch I can keep the boys from most if not all the worst of it, build bridges between them, with them, tell stories, share chores and make them laugh to draw them from their solo shells of disaster. But I can't save them. One boy, Tom, is an Indian kid from a reservation or broken family somewhere. It will be years before I realize how much he looks like Brad, how Brad must have looked like Tom as a boy. All Tom wants is to go home. He trusts me, but it's hard for him, harder than most. The trust he gives to me, that they all give to me, comes from the innocence of boys who still have a kernel of dream left in them. Tom's is hairline thin. The system and their realities are like a massive beast that hovers tooth and claw over us all.

My reality, resonant to the boys' hopelessness and hidden violence, finally reaches a breaking point.

By the end of a year I know several things. Rage is building inside me. It's a rage of hopelessness that I can't yet fully define. Efforts to bring change at work mostly fail. It's no different at home. My boyfriend is an alcoholic. There are probably drugs besides. Well-meaning, in love but with no common ground, shared vision, dream, interest or intent between us, we could not be more opposite. He's kind. He loves me. He also likes the bars. I can't stand them. He goes out to drink one night and, fed up, I find him at the bar owned by the man that my mother had an affair with when I was in high school, the still-married father of a past classmate. This wrenches my heart in a frozen horror. A day or so later I come home with groceries to find the

antiquated refrigerator again melting water from the tiny freezer
compartment all across the kitchen floor of our sad, little apartment. I
barely manage to save myself from a hard fall as I slip in the mess, then
hurl a full bag of groceries against the wall in a blind fury.

Decay is unfolding all around me.

At work I start to take my shift breaks on one or another of several
mostly deserted stairwells between ward floors. I sit and play dirge-like
laments on a wooden soprano recorder, until one day, on a pure, high
note that dies into silence, I recognize that I have to leave. I can't do
this anymore, not any of it.

The resonance of the music has found its way to the truth inside
me. The burden of my own hidden history is too much, juxtaposed to
these boys, to the unhappiness in my life with my boyfriend.

On the day I tell the boys that I'm leaving I scramble across the
floor on my knees, pulling them out from under one bed after another
where they've scattered; to reassure them of my love; to remind them
of their gifts; to tell them I'm not leaving because of them; to say that
I'm sorry. *I am so sorry.* It's Tom who is the most undone and most
undoes my heart. It takes forever to get him out from under his bed,
longer still to get him to speak. He lets me know what a traitor I am.
Hearts break by a fracturing dozen.

It's the spring of 1975 and my sister invites me to join her and her
husband. They intend to leave college to travel with a loosely formed
commune of other students who plan to head north from Laramie into
Montana and then west in search of the 40 acres of their dreams, a
back-to-the-land lifestyle. I split with my boyfriend, move out of the
apartment and say good-bye. I arrive in Laramie to join the communal
group, enthusiastic and on fire with the thrill of entry into a long-held
dream, one that I can actually belong to. I'm quickly slapped silly for
the temerity of thinking I can enter this tight circle as an equal. They
have a pecking order. I'm at the bottom. They agree I can go with
them, but I'm not allowed to assume or have a vote on anything up to
and including any place they get serious about. The crush of this works
as it's intended to do. I'm taken down not one notch but 20.

We travel for two months, backpacking in Wyoming and Montana,
working farms for cash with migrant workers in Washington and
Oregon, and in time, my sister and I break from the group to travel
south through Oregon and on into California along Route 1. We return
to Wyoming in early fall. I move through a series of jobs and at last go
to work at a bookshop where I'll manage the next two years of dog bite
and pulling life from old ashes. And here there is respite as I let the
revelations and extremes of my past fall into background and from
there, a deep dive into underground.

Late in 1976 I make a plan with a friend to hike the Pacific Crest Trail, a 2,700-mile trek from border to border, Mexico to Canada. Once again Canada is a beacon on my radar with Mexico a subtext frequency. But we decide for logistical reasons not to start at the Mexican border after all and instead begin a bit further north in the Mojave, knowing early that we want to experience the country we're passing through and not just grind out trail in a counting coup of notched-up miles. And with this as our philosophy, we also don't make it to Canada. We come off three months and 800 miles of the Pacific Crest Trail and, I become involved with a musician. Our paths wind in and out of each other's lives for months.

In 1977 I move to Arizona, where I live on a ranch turned back to native grassland and in 1978 to Boulder, Colorado. From there I buy a restaurant in Pinedale, Wyoming with a friend and move back to my home state of Wyoming. From Wyoming to Arizona to Colorado and back to Wyoming I live out a seven-year cycle of love and heartbreak with my musician boyfriend. I can't see that I'm patching together a way to keep my past in check, to stay ahead of it and bar the door. I'm just embracing life as best I can. But just as it was in the migrant shell where I stayed briefly with my brother and his girlfriend, my life is now like an open house with no safe barrier or boundary, unknown forces lurking just beyond the threshold. And because I have a business partner, work at our small restaurant allows certain freedoms. I can travel to see my boyfriend.

On the face of things, I'm doing well. I put my heart in my work and do well by all my commitments. Still, the wandering life of musicians and life on the road is an unstable way to belong. It carries me between the restaurant and many trips to be with my boyfriend. One of these leads to a small, western mountain town where the band has booked a weekend job. All through the night before I leave to meet up with them and the next daylong drive to our rendezvous point, a tempest of wild energy shifts inside me, jumping between agitation and leaden weight. Each time I imagine what the time ahead will be like, a harsh, sharp edge of something unnamable winnows through my cells. By the time I reach our meeting point, joyous to see all of them and longing for time with my boyfriend, I'm fraught with impossible tension. The next morning we drive north in a little convoy toward the town and the bar where they'll play. As we wind toward our destination along old, narrow roads I feel intense and clammy dislike of the place. Dog-hair pine crowds scruffy and thin, and a sense of bleak hostility seems woven to the place. It reverberates through gray weather. Yet by the time we find the town and our lodgings, a truce has settled in me.

This is just another dingy small town, another bar clientele, a short weekend gig, and we'll be out of here. I let go of tension as we make our way to the bar. Muffled by too much history, glad to be with my boyfriend, I don't read the signs and walk straight into someone else's nightmare.

27

Mountain Town Madness

We start out our lives in all innocence. Like me, like my mother and father before me, like all children. And in time, life breaks us, dismays us. No matter the age when the breaking comes, it's the buried places, the broken and dismayed that hold our gold, trapped and crushed within sediments and seams; layered geologies of old circumstance.

I contemplate forgiveness. How fierce it is. How far it lies from pastoral concepts. Forgiveness, neither fuzzy nor champagne-bubble light, does take us home to expansion that is inexplicable and far-reaching — and sometimes when we land, it's soft. But the journey to forgiveness is sharp, filled with quagmires and landmines. And though forgiveness does redeem, it neither condones nor allows further trespass. To truly forgive, one must first forgive oneself — and that's the mightiest task of all.

In my late 20s the simple longing to be with the man I loved blinded me. I could not see that a need to forgive myself would be part of the long road ahead. A road not soft but jagged and sharp. After one chance moment in an obscure western town I would have to attain forgiveness for something I had no power to control, that did not originate with me nor spring from actions played out by my hand. On this irregular night in a window of time that seemed all too regular, my heart would be crushed, my spirit shredded and parts of me scattered to the winds. Though the worst that happened that night did not happen to me, it wedded to chaos already alive within me — and to a night that would haunt across time.

In the fall of 1978 my friends and I make our way along the dirt streets of a town tucked into high-altitude pine, to set up for the night's music. The place looks a mimic to an old Western movie. We find the saloon, unload equipment and the guys go to work in an alcove off the main bar where music is staged. The lead singer's girlfriend and I set up to shoot pool on tables in the main room. The bar itself runs the full length of the main room along one side, opposite the pool tables and an open aisle running between.

Three people sit on barstools at the far end of the bar. They huddle close over drinks, one woman between two men, and their backs to us. Not far from where they sit I rack pool balls and take in the scene. The voices of the trio rise in sudden whoops of laughter then drop low into a hunched knot of private humor and talk. The bartender moves between them, getting his bar set up for the night, laughing into the animated conversation. The woman's long dark hair flows heavy over shoulders and down her back, rippling in low light.

I grab a pool cue, and we concentrate on our game, settling in. Half-bored with the all-too-familiar scene, I think about whether to stay and listen when the band starts playing, or go back to our room. It's hard to say what the crowd will be like. Billiard balls click and glide, echo into net pockets. *It's cool*, I think, *I'll figure it out, play it by ear.* The band mutters in the alcove behind us, dragging the speakers, wiring the sound. I shift the cue from one hand to the other as the 8 ball flurries across green felt. Daylight pales another notch, beyond smutty windows. One brilliant ray of light shafts through a cloud, beams through dirty glass panes and gleams in quick luster on the flat shine of the bar next to the three drinking together. Transient brilliance fades as late afternoon sheds to evening.

Banging caseloads of this or that under the bartender's watchful eye, a handful of patrons and bar crew wander through the far end of the room. The bartender polishes glasses from the rack above his head, winking patterns of light that fracture along bar top and out into the larger room. Two guys step to the table next to us and take up pool cues. I hear a couple of new voices pick up with the band in the alcove behind. Our guys shoot back friendly but edgy replies to questions they've answered hundreds of times. They are pressed to be ready to play on time. I glance up. The minute hand on the clock over the bar jumps ahead. The front door swings open.

A slight, tense man steps into the room. Brown hair is choppy in the low light as he glances around the room. His eyes burn. Chiseled features focus on the three hunched figures at the far end of the bar. Laughter burbles and yowls aloud from them, dropping back into private conversation. The slim man at the door moves fast, head up eyes fixed as he strides the length of the bar. A guffaw shoots out from the tight-knit threesome, oblivious of everyone beyond themselves. In a last stride the man stops behind the woman. His hand shoots out. She sees his reflection in the mirror at the moment he grabs her dark, thick hair in a tight wrap around one hand. Her hands fly backward, her face a grimace as the two men beside her fall off their barstools to either side.

With a yank the man pivots the woman like a doll to face him. I shove the bandleader's girlfriend into the alcove behind us, hissing for her to stay out of sight. My eyes are locked on the couple as I step to the end of the pool table. A gun flies out of the man's pocket to within an inch of the woman's face. I freeze where I stand.

As her mouth opens in surprise, eyes popped wide, a macabre slow-motion dance unwinds. She wrenches left, right, the man follows her every move, his hold in her hair keeping exact beat to his hand holding the gun. Bending to her bend, swaying with her sway, they move as one.

"No! No! You wouldn't!" her voice cries edgy but sure. "You can't! You won't! Put it down!"

His voice bites, "I told you. No more. No more. But you're here and now so am I." His hand in the tight shock of her hair yanks hard, back and up, her head pulled to impossible contortion.

Pleading now, "No, no, please — don't — you wouldn't   you couldn't — you can't," jerking hard right, harder left to escape the aim of his gun, her disbelief shrinks to desperation, "No, don't, don't, pleeeaasse ... "

The man sneers, marks time, and the barrel of the gun flares. Between echo and strike his grip on her hair holds her upright. She twists and the gun follows precise. He's crooning, "I told you, I told you ... "

"Please," she flails, "No, please, please ... let me go ... "

With a hiss and a curse the second shot rips from the gun. The woman cannot fall, he doesn't abandon her, and they bend in a low, dipping dive. Shattering through the room, disbelief wakes us all to confusion as he twirls on the crack of a third shot. Hand jerking free he tosses the woman to the floor. Head high he steps back and turns to stride the long aisle for the door.

I step forward to block his passage. He raises the gun to my face with a laugh. "Wanna try? Go ahead. I don't mind two," he says as the gun stabs in my chest. I step back.

Keeping a bead on my face he walks backward. When he reaches the door he pans the gun across the rest of the room. "Anybody, everybody, wanna try? No? Then just sit tight. No one moves. No one goes anywhere. No phone, no nothin', just sit." Both hands on the gun, he looks the room over.

In a blink he's gone into the night.

I race for the woman. She lies 10 feet from the bar where she fell. I race back to the bar for clean rags and yell at the bartender, "Call 911!

Somebody, you! Pick up the phone!" I yell as he stares frozen. "Where are the clean rags? *Dial! 911 dammit!*" But his hands hang limp at his sides. I grab a wet rag off the bar and run back to the woman.

I kneel down at her side. One of the men who sat on the barstool next to her drops to his knees on the other side. She moans, eyes blinking. A black doctor bag pops open under his hand. I offer him the rag. "I hope it's clean," I say, relieved by his presence.

He rocks back on his heels and snaps the bag shut, surging to his feet so fast my head spins. "There's nothing I can do," he says and walks away. Staccato heels break the silence as he walks the length of the bar. Without looking back he disappears through the front door.

I shake my head, stunned as I press the rag to the woman's neck. It's not enough. I run back to the bar for more rags, yelling at the bartender to call for help. He picks up the phone, slumps against the counter and crumples. I grab rags from behind the bar and turn back to the woman. She's dragged herself another 10 feet across the floor. People are gathering around her, a circle that closes as I approach. *Where have all of these people come from?* I wonder but again feel relief. They'll know how to help her.

I hear her struggling for breath. I can't get past the back of the circle. The group has closed tight. I hold out a rag to someone in front, feeling a small spark of hope. *This is her community. They'll know what to do.*

But no one takes the rag from my hand. I feel like I'm pushing through quicksand, dense and impossible. In the compressed space of split minutes a molasses-like energy freezes all movement and time. Why isn't anyone helping her? I try to push forward with the rag. I extend it again in my hand. Life seems to suck from the heart of the room itself. Frenetic, I turn to look for my boyfriend. He stands at the edge of the alcove, clustered with the rest of the band. I run to them and grab his arm to pull him back with me.

As we move away the band members hiss, "What're you doing?" They look at me askance, shaking their heads.

"A woman's been shot," I say.

"Stay out of it," they glare. "It's none of your business."

I pull on my boyfriend's arm. He moves back to the circle with me. No one at all is by the injured woman's side. *Why aren't they helping her?* It feels like a barricade, these people around her.

Frantic in still point, she cries out, *"Help me ... Help mee ...,"* her voice a distancing wail. *"Please somebody help mee,"* and nobody moves.

I lean forward, drop to my knees, and from the back of the crowd I look into her eyes. As they start to spiral, I can't get any closer.

"... Helpp mee please heellp me, somebody please heellpp," the group draws tighter around her. *"Pleeaasse heellp meee some bodee ...,"* weaker her voice siphons. My eyes lock to hers, *"Please, pleaeassse somebooddy heelp meeee,"*

and her voice trails down a spiraling tunnel, pleas moving now on a soundless thread. A vortex spins in her eyes. Suddenly their light goes out.

Bewilderment crashes through my chest. No! The finality knifes into disbelief. I search in her face for a sign. People don't die like this — awake, aware, present.

But there is nothing, nothing I can do. She is gone. The cold room lies colder across her as life evaporates into death. Her empty, blank stare sears the room.

An outcry erupts from the front door of the bar. A storm of cops breaks through the room on a wave of high-pitched motion. My boyfriend grabs my arm and pulls me back to the alcove. People surge left and right.

Dazed and shell-shocked I wander deeper into the alcove, adrenaline streaming. I can't get my bearings. Heartsick and stunned I stagger from one group of people to another. Rattled chatter bursts all around me. Rumor and intrigue run high. Everyone seems to know something. Pandemonium flies through the outer room. I move through milling strangers. In the outer bar cops bar the door, breaking people apart. A sickening miasma of thrill pours around me, an orgy of news and opinion. As this trips into overdrive I raise my hands to my ears then cover my face and crouch to the floor. There is nowhere to go.

A heavily armed cop steps to the edge of alcove. I look up at his silhouette against the backdrop of glaring light as he spits orders, "No one leaves. No one moves from this room. No one exits the building. Got it? Stay put!"

A sensation splits at my crown. The haunting weight that I've felt for the past 24 hours suddenly flares into consciousness. The weight that dogged my steps all the way to this town — like a weather vane it foretold what has happened here, and what is happening around me now. Stunned in the glare of this, a second awareness follows.

I shouldn't be here. I shouldn't have come. I don't belong to this place at all. I reel with the knowledge.

The big officer pushes back into the fray of the other room. I suddenly see what the cops are doing. They separate those that they know from those they do not. In the alcove, we're mostly those-they-do-not, but not all. Confined to our ugly billet of space in the half-light glow of the bar, a skinny greasy-haired man has a small crowd gathered around him. Totally ripped out of his mind he rants about the woman who just died and the man who shot her. He knows them. He's gleeful. He splays out their history, his conjecture, *her husband, their children, two little boys, new vows, second try, just last summer, they couldn't make it, couldn't make it, couldn't make it, couldn't, just wouldn't stay apart.* I crumple to my knees. He laughs, throwing back his head in a maniacal howl, gone on stoners of one kind or another. Glee and thrill mottle his skin.

He knew! I stand up and stumble away as he rips into a next stammering tirade. He knew!

His gone voice bounces off the circle of people around him and he rips on, "Floozy. Ha! Ha-ha! Ha-ha-ha! I never thought he'd do it. Ha-ha! But he did. He did! Yes, he did!" Words and laughter churn from his spittle-flecked lips. "Ha! Ha-ha! Ha-ha-ha! He said he would. And he did! Ha-ha! But I thought, I thought, he told me, he talked about it all the time. Ha! He said he would, said he would, but gawd I never thought I'd get to see the day. I knew he would. Ha! Ha-ha! Ha-ha-ha! I knew he'd do it. And he did it! He did it! He did!" his head throws back in a barking, gloating hilarity, regurgitation of the possessed.

I feel the room tip. He knew and did nothing to stop this! The band's soundman eggs the man on. I scramble to the edge of the alcove in search of a policeman. This man, he encouraged this mayhem all along.

At the edge of the alcove I flag one of the policeman. He ignores me. *There are children. Somewhere. Two boys. They're waiting somewhere for their parents. Waiting for parents who will never come.* Like machine-gun fire that doesn't stop, the warped detail chants through the alcove from the man behind me. Dry tears ice in my veins. I make my way toward another policeman, turn to point out the man in the alcove. He shakes his head. He turns away, waves me back.

I stumble backward into tables over tipping chairs. There is nowhere to go. I turn back to the cops and see that they listen to no one. Helpless against the mad prattle of this stoner man, I hunch in sharp solitude. The cops herd a cluster of people they know out into the dark that thickens the night to gloom.

There should be tears in this room, but there are none. Not a single tear stains this place.

In the hideous poem of death caught in the mantra of the living I die a thousand deaths as I turn toward the woman who lies alone just past the chaos. I'll die a few thousand more in the helpless hours that lie ahead. I can't see her, but I feel her in the middle of the madness. Alone as she's ever been, the pulsing heartbeat of the stampeding floor jumps beneath us. Police call sharp and biting. A whistle cuts the air. Everyone turns toward the front door. The stoner man slips out a back door behind us.

"You will all leave the room together and depart the building single file. You will walk straight across to the bar on the other side of the street. Everyone — *every one* — will enter that building. The door will be closed and locked. You will remain there for the rest of the night. Got it? You can't go back to any house. No houses. Did you lock your houses? A SWAT team is on the way."

We get in line, nodding as though we understand. But we don't. Not really. We plod across the night-gripped muddy street toward the foyer of the brightly lit building, shuffling like ankle-chained prisoners. Cold cracks through my senses as I slip down, down, down into the underbelly of a beast that prowls the town now at will. I glance back at the building behind us. A key clicks in the lock of the door after the last person steps out. But the woman is still in there, alone. I hear whispers rustling around me — there she'll remain until an EMT crew or someone arrives from out of town. I quiver and ask, "When?" But there seems to be no answer.

I shiver to no end as the lock of her eyes spiral into death before me, over and over again. *Someone should have been holding her someone should have taken her hand someone should have been at her side … Someone should have helped her.* Through confusion and pain I step through the door into the brightly lit building before me, lurch to a bench along one wall. Crushed with knowing that someone could have been me, my head drops in my hands.

Why couldn't I push through the cloying people around her? Why did those people do nothing but stare?

The foyer where I sit is muted in the glow of low amber lamps. The rest of the building blazes with light. Deafening noise from the bar beyond pounds. *A woman has just died. Why is this happening? Someone should be with her now.*

Red velvet-flocked wallpaper lines the foyer walls like the entrance to a brothel. Blaring music throbs behind a wall where voices whoop and scream. *Boogie-woogie.* The rough, high-pitched adrenaline pushes on a swell through the entryway and out into the night. As last people flow through the front door and past me, through a set of slatted white gates into the din beyond, frail amber light wavers on the velvet-flocked walls.

Alone on the bench I hear a key turn in the lock outside the door. Knuckles rap on the wood like a farewell riff. Heavy footsteps crunch away. The door is thin. These walls are thin. A man is out there with a gun. Two small boys are home alone. Their mother is dead. The father is on the run. I panic for the boys. *Did their neighbors get to them in time?* A SWAT team is on the way.

The thought of walking through the swinging white gates to the food and drink and gaiety of the crowd lacerates my heart. I drop my face in my hands again. My boyfriend walks back through the gates with a couple of band members.

"Come on," they say, smiling, "Come on. You can't do anything about it."

It's hard to talk. "No." I shake my head. "Please, just leave me alone."

"It's a party." They stare then stare harder. "Hey, it's a party!" And the party sprawls just past the gates and whips up a notch.

I see how it pulls at their backs. A long, high yodel splits the air, and their faces lift, sniffing the taste of the coming hours. My boyfriend grins as he turns toward the caterwaul, then turns back to me and presses, "Come on, come on." I get up and pace the small space. Dawn is a long way off.

"Look, I can't," I manage to speak. "Please just leave me alone." I stand away from them and choke out, "Please. I can't go in there."

The swinging gates sway on their hinges. My boyfriend grabs for my arm. I slip back down on the bench. "I can't," I say. "Go on. Go without me."

"What's with you? What's with you?" he cries. They all sniff and snort, ambling away toward the gates. "C'mon!"

"A woman died tonight," I say quietly. "In front of us. What's with you? She's lying alone across the street." I look at them straight. "I'm not going in there. Do what you want. I'm staying here."

Disgust crosses the distance between us. I turn my head to the window, and they're gone, gates swinging wild on the angry exit, one crippled now in the hinge.

———

I cannot see the way this night and this bar and the attitudes around me link to the party at Will's seven years prior, a similar pattern of violence carried out through acts of indifference. How it mimics the indifference of my mother. Will's party and the shuddering moment with his despicable friend, the legacy of experience with my mother — these memories are not lost but banked inside me beneath hideous pain. They are markers. On this night in this bar among my friends the violence of indifference plays out another hand.

Too broken with the death of the woman to see this repeating pattern — in the moment of the people gathered around the woman as she died doing nothing to help her; in the moment of my mother's horrible betrayal of my brother and me to her second husband; in my father hitting my mother while someone egged him on, no one stopping him, encouraged by indifference; in the men in the gas station in Nevada who wouldn't help us but shot at us; and in the people at the school bus with their children there is calloused indifference echoing too much too often through human lives, resonating through time.

Above the undertow of violence, do people survive on their indifference? Why?

A manhunt is about to begin here, now. The night rings with a high whine, menace and peril, life on its lowest rung. Low light glows through the faceted amber glass of the small, front-door window. It's hard to stand up, but I move to be in front of the window. I can make out the silhouette of building across the street. Darkness, no lights and the woman, they said they left her lying on the floor. Unmoved. Untouched. Forensics. Suddenly racing tires crush gravel on the road out there. They swerve to the side of the building. A split second later there's a second vehicle.

I shrink back into a corner away from the door, away from the window, away from the light, and stop breathing. These walls are thin. On the other side truck doors fly open. Feet hit the ground. Metal scrapes metal, magazines clip, and voices flurry just above hearing. I flinch as I feel the narrow division from deadly efficiency taking hold out there.

The intent of the SWAT team is palpable, gone fast into darkness. Silence settles, paces to the man with the gun in the forest on the run. These other men who race death against death outside these walls jar with the odd outpost revelry revving up in the room beyond, as though on cue. My senses track through the rimming forest, out into neighborhoods, hover over the scorched blight of this cinched-up town.

I rise from the corner and take up my post at the small window.

The pocked, wavy glass deforms the world outside. Warp against warp on the cold hunker of buildings beyond, my vision sifts in daguerreotype brown. Music blares up another decibel behind me, sacrilege curling across my skin. I shudder. Voices riot and launch to outer limits, a pulse like a crazed wedding rite. The wounded gates shimmy and swing.

Backlit at the window, vulnerable to whoever is out there, I keep vigil. The man could be anywhere, but he is surely running. Nerves on fire I listen, watch and wait. Someone has to stand for the woman who has died. Someone should be helping her to pass. I know this as sure as I know anything. An easy target in the window for a man with a gun on the last teetering brink of survival, I can't shake the conviction. *Someone should be with her, helping her to pass.* Of all the things that I don't know in the throws of the deteriorating night, this is the one thing I'm certain of. So I stand as close as I can get, falling apart and holding vigil from the amber glow of the velvet-flocked room. Though I don't pray this act is as much the same, it is in all ways the same, silence in a confused, tormented time. I imagine her boys in their crushed innocence; the twist of the woman's fate; her husband, hunter turned hunted; the scent and shadow of the woods beyond. One life tied to another tied to another tied to another. I hold these lives. There is nothing else I can do.

The minutes sag the hours drag, ache sets in that runs through my limbs until tension and pain wring like a rag. No undoing what's done, I tuck the pain and dismay and anger into a pyre that's building inside me. I watch the building. I bear witness. There are no stars; none shine, none glow.

The night turns. My body screams until standing at the window is beyond torment. The woman struggles more mightily than I. I feel further out into the night. A tight place in my heart holds two small boys whose lives have been stolen; the heart of a mother who cannot return; the insane choice of a father who may or may not recover his senses and if or when he does, it will be too late. I find a place where horror hints tender mercy, welling up from the panting mystery. Until all my focus is on the woman, alone, past death but not gone.

Pain spreads, my body wilts, the vise tightens. Outside there's a fading. The first fuzz of dawn hints. And then I hear them. The SWAT team rustles across brittle grass. Boots scrape from forest. Metal slaps, there is a low murmur off muted tongues. They have him. I know it. There have been no shots, no gunfire. The dampened pad of jackets push to doors, slide across seats, gear clatters onto floors and is hushed. One engine turns and catches. Then another. Lights flick to graying outline of trees across the street. A vehicle backs out, pulls onto the road and drives away on grinding gravel. The second follows. The bar crowd grown dull but far from silent shimmies in fatigued gaiety beyond the crooked gates. I drop to the bench.

Voices rise and fall outside the front door. A key chatters in the lock. No one enters. A gruff voice calls from the street like a bullhorn. I stand and look out, pale, the question in my eyes.

"Surrendered. Yeah, they got 'im."

I step back and slump down on the bench. The bullhorn voice blows, splitting into the room beyond. A pause in the revelers' yip and then people begin to flow out through the swinging gates like a dying river, cattle to feed. As the foyer empties I step in with the band and pass out onto the street. The big man at the door shakes his head at everyone.

"Go home," he says. "Just go home."

We stumble up the road to our ramshackle lodging. The padlock on the door is still there. Locked. But the hinged catch has been torn nearly free of the frame. So it's true. Gathered in safekeeping through the night, we missed a sure visitor, or he missed us. Everyone shudders. Maybe he started out here, looking for shelter. Maybe it was later.

Shuffling inside, gathering near the fireplace, plans start talking around. Time to tear down, pack up and pull out. There won't be music or anything else in that bar, not tonight, not anytime soon. Everyone scuffles their feet, surly and out of sorts. It's hard to speak and I don't try. As the group sorts out last chores, guessing about when we can pack up equipment I suddenly stand and walk to the door.

"I'll meet you back at the truck later," I say.

"Where you goin'?" They look at me like I've gone crazy.

"I'm going to the sheriff's office to report what I witnessed. It's the only thing I can do. I'll be at the truck before you leave."

A raft of voices heave across the room, "Are you nuts? What the hell good d'you think that'll do? Who the hell d'you think you are, anyway? Mary Poppins? Little Bo-Peep? Maybe you're Pollyanna," sneers bite at my back. "You think you're better than us? You're wasting your time."

I don't turn back. I don't say anything. I walk out the door and away to speak for the woman and her boys whether it makes any difference or not. I find the sheriff's office by instinct off the main road tucked in at the center of a stand of lodgepole pine. Dazed, dreading my purpose, pain past thinking, I walk into the building and push open the door to a large, bright office. The sharp glare of dozens of eyes turn, outrage spiking through every one of them.

I stand at the front of the first desk and state my business, stuttering over facts of the past night. The several women at their several desks turn away to their several tasks in a fury that swells with repugnance and a sound like hissing. This is their town. Inviolate. Violated. I must be guilty by the fact of being a stranger. Nothing could say this more plain. Clear that I deserve no welcome, no respect and no mercy on this morning that follows a murder, it has to be somebody's fault and it might as well be mine.

In the face of communal disdain, feeling tired beyond tired beyond tired I'm no less sure of my place. Murmurs run through the room like rabbits, *town up through the night, those damned bars, no-account drunks,* eyes cut and slash in a curse my way, over and over and over. Some few hover, curious and prying.

This hostile willingness to ignore the importance of someone's life — the life of the woman who has been murdered, my life as I stand waiting to do what I can rings through the hollow spaces of the room, the hollow judgments in the hollow hearts of the women gathered here.

I stand and sink into forever oblivion, strangely clear and collected. Ignored, I wait. Waiting, I stand. The minute hand ticks from the clock on the wall. And then one woman steps from a separate office, holding a clipboard. She nods at me with a soft look. I step forward. She waves me toward an office door and meets me halfway then falls in to walk by my side and steps with me over the threshold. I pass in at the nod of a well-groomed man in uniform sitting at the only desk in the room. The woman gives my arm a squeeze and pulls the door closed as she leaves.

The man nods to a chair at the front of his desk. Since this is all I can do I sit in the chair across from him trembling, colder than cold. I tell him why I've come. He asks a few questions and writes my contact information down in a notebook. He explains the process that lies ahead in the case. And speaks to the bottom line.

They don't need another witness. There are plenty that live in this town. The investigation and then trial will go on for months, the better part of a year, possibly more. It would pull me back from Wyoming again and again. There's no need for that disruption in my life, my testimony exists in the words of others.

I ask about the boys; he assures me they're cared for. I want to know what will become of the father. He can't say, but his outcome looks bleak. He asks if I would like a way to stay in touch and follow the case once I'm home. When I nod he hands me a business card with quiet respect. It's like a balm. I stand to shake hands. When I leave I have his card and what feels like rare kindness. I pass from his office and out of the building into a life that's waiting as surely as that mother lies elsewhere, dead and gone. But she's traveling with me. She will travel with me a long, long time. Hers is a life I will hold in my heart along with her boys, but she is also another weight that swings on a pendulum, a scale tipping low and out of sight. In time, she, too, goes underground.

———

It will take years for me to forgive myself. I will think endlessly of this woman's suffering and death. All that I have done right in my life slips far from my consciousness, next to what has happened. I can only see what I've done wrong in the face of this grueling reality. A long pattern of trying to protect others throughout my life — the band leader's girlfriend in the bar that night, my attempt to step in and stop the husband with the gun, my friend Cora the night we were raped, my friend in the bathroom attack in high school and a legion of others — they are lost in this spin of agony. All my efforts to be decent in the midst of indecency lie buried within terror and heartache.

I have a long way to go to discover forgiveness.

28

Third Presence

I go home and try to pick up the pieces of my life. My business partner and I decide to sell the restaurant. I don't know what I'll do, but I don't want to do this anymore. I'm starting to hurt all the time. My boyfriend wants us to commit to living together. When I consider his life, a life on the road with the band, I'm far less certain. I love him. But I'm lost, very lost. A kind of blurred panic spreads out before me — knowing one thing is over and needs to be by selling the restaurant, there is nothing else rising in its place.

And then a dream comes.

The dream repeats the experience of Brad's first visit to me after he died but with some variation. He's present again in physical form, clarified and vital. His eyes lock to mine across a room full of people. But in the room where the dream starts — a dream room I share with my boyfriend — a moldering skeleton lies beneath our bed ghastly and decomposing. The skeleton is the condensed agony of the many hauntings that repeated in endless litany after Brad died. They exude from the horrible fright: how I imagined Brad's last moments, the oncoming car and the impact, the destruction, the absolute loss. And there these horrors lie beneath the bed, a rotting grotesque.

I wake and understand exactly what the dream is telling me. The skeleton beneath the bed presents all the years of pain since losing Brad, pain that I have never truly put behind me. Crumbling beneath everything this old pain affects my relationships now, loss that holds me back from surrendering to love. I have to move on from this, move on in a way I haven't yet done. Be fully in life. Claim it. Claim love. It's past time. I commit to life with my boyfriend and agree to go on the road together. The dream repeats once more. This time the skeleton metamorphoses into light.

So we sell the restaurant. I go on the road and generally make good on shared lives. I've packed belongings away in storage and carved my life down to what I can carry in a single vehicle for inspiration, comfort and practicality. There are a couple of boxes of books, a sewing machine with assorted tools, fabrics, a bicycle, clothes, cross-country skis in season, sketchpads, journals, paints, the relics of dozens of interests and the black and tan quiver of my half-coonhound dog, Mariah. I've no romantic notions whatsoever about life on the road with a band. I've absolutely no illusions about the lifestyles of musicians. And I've no intention of spending my nights in bars with days half-slept away. I hurt too much to be wholly practical. Ache stacked on ache stacked on pain. I just want to be with my boyfriend and by this, still the terrible ache. The result is a knife's-edge balance. Moving toward love I stay ahead of the past and just keep moving. It's the right decision for the time and for a while it works out, allowing some part of me to heal.

For three years our lives are a driving flying constant motion. Roving between towns, recording studios, party gigs, fronting events and visiting friends and family during time off the road, time rolls by. Because I've no interest in bar life, don't like to drink and have no interest in drugs, I'm mostly outside the scene that holds the greatest presence in the band's life. Life on the road is what it is.

By the end of three years I can't stand the lifestyle and all the divided loyalties. My boyfriend is sliding into alcoholism. It's time for change, and this time my decision is clear: I move back to Jackson.

I eventually accept an opportunity as caretaker for a house on Teton Pass, the mountain pass west of town. It takes an agonizing year to fully break things off with my musician boyfriend. But I finally take my life back and move on. I begin to date another man, and we're together for nearly a year. But the past is bearing down.

I break off with him to fall instantly and headlong into another relationship. It begins in a conundrum of conflicted feelings when I go out dancing with friends one night and cross paths with a man who is far more edgy. His interest in me is like a lightning rod with almost searing heat. He isn't one of my dance partners. He works in the bar where the music is playing. I keep him at arm's length. I'm just there to dance, to get lost in the music. A day or so later we cross paths again. We talk. I feel a kindling on my side and the potency builds. Fire.

I fall into the third relationship and the heat of new romance full-bore. Soon after we become lovers he asks me to move in with him. I resist hardly at all. I move from my mountain pass home and into his cabin down in the valley. It doesn't take long to realize that the attraction is purely physical. I have almost nothing in common with this man. I'm stunted by my past, my legacy of betrayal and violence, but I'm awake to the world, intellectually engaged and curious. Our relationship distances me from the blossoming of old and new interests, chilling the new waters further. The longer the weeks play out, the more I find myself at crosshairs in something that has no bottom.

And then there is this. Almost from the moment he and I touch into serious involvement — I remember the moment exactly, I had invited him to dinner at my place on the mountain pass — there is something that seems to come out of nowhere. It's a dim, external third presence — I have no idea what else to call it. It emerges when he asks me to live with him. Like someone knocking on a door, pressing over my shoulder, whispering in my ear but so subtle as to go almost unnoticed. The incident is scant, like the buzz of a distant bee. When I agree to the move there is a faint, sharp outburst — and then the presence is gone. My mind dismisses it.

Once I move into my new love's cabin my dog goes crazy, cringing, tearing up doors to get out when she's in and in when she's out. So much so that after taking her from vet to vet for help and finally seeking to no avail another home for her or a ranch that will take her, she has to be put down. I can't bear to take her to the vet for this final blow. My boyfriend does it. I stuff my feelings of grief, confusion and guilt into the swelter of enormity that is my past, compressed and cordoned off behind me.

The feeling of the third presence returns in the weeks that follow and expands in a slow build. Though my mind can't acknowledge this as real, over time this presence becomes a constant whenever I'm at the cabin. The subtleties are hard to describe. There is a loving, caring yet grave quality that hovers around me in every room. I feel it most often when I'm undistracted, and so most commonly when I'm alone.

Parallel to these experiences, things are not going well with my boyfriend. He works in a bar. I hate bars. I despise the crazy life and duplicity they embrace, something I've learned all too well in the seven-year ache of my earlier relationship with the musician. Blinded by the heat of first attraction, blunted by my past I let myself slide past all of this. I'm starting to feel that I've made a terrible mistake. His projections are building, my blinders are coming off, but I'm confused. My direction is unclear. The perfect home I've left on the mountain pass is a thing of the past. I have a good job. But everything else is a spin of uncertainty. Like earlier years of my life, there is a growing muddle of bewilderment. There are so many dots I can't yet connect. What direction now?

The potency of the third presence grows. When I come into the cabin alone I experience something like a nudge that insinuates a push, a hand grasping my shoulder, a grip trying to propel me, something driving, always driving, silent but on the edge of a plea.

Soon it intensifies into pressure impossible to ignore. I have no idea what it is. I can't acknowledge that it's really there, something external. I understand my internal dilemma. It's not that. The pressure comes from *outside* me. Its disturbance begins to work like a premonition of something I'm missing yet have to see or find. But I'm blind. I can't understand it. I have no training for this kind of experience. I don't know how to sit down and listen, face it, draw out the clues. I don't know what it is. My mind tries to ignore it. Finally what I can only describe as an external strength of purpose — like someone else's will — is always pressing on me when I'm at the cabin, yet the purpose is veiled. I can resist it, try to avoid it but I cannot deny it. The presence builds to an almost frantic quality. One day I come home, and with no preconceived idea at all I move from room to room as though propelled, gathering up my boyfriend's guns and hiding them — a hunting rifle and knife, a handgun. I live in a hunting culture. Am I crazy? He has never been violent with me in any way. Yet there it is. I'm propelled to find his weapons and hide them. When they're hidden, the frenzy dies down. The presence seems to abate. I can relax.

I start to talk with my boyfriend about the doubts I have about us. He wants to work it out. I tell him I don't think so. I'm confused. I'm sorry. I feel unsure about where to move, I need time, I need to save more money. He says that there's plenty of time. We don't have to rush it. I take a breath and nod. There is time. I can work on a plan. I feel lighter.

And then the presence becomes a whirlwind of urgency. Being in the house is like being in a cyclone of furious efforts to urge, unseat, push. This time I get it. I talk to friends who manage monthly lodging on the north end of town. I start moving out of the house. My boyfriend asks me where his guns are. I tell him I've hidden them. He asks why and I shrug. I don't know. Quickly I'm packed and gone. We see each other a little after that — but soon I tell him no more. Within a month the people who own the house up on the mountain pass where I used to live as a caretaker track me down. They want me to return. I breathe a sigh of relief. Grateful and feeling like I've just missed a precipice, I move back in.

I move back wholly changed. I'm at last in a position to use the foundation beneath me now for the work I most need to do. I understand that the house and the time for reflection are a luxury. I don't waste them. I pick up my independent life again, continue with my job but step back from everything else. I guide my life by the sixth sense that has been with me since childhood. I settle into solitude and look for the markers that will help to guide me. I begin to see that there is a pattern to the past few years. Three men. Three endings. Two were abrupt. They link in some way. They feel like a long slide I don't want to know the end of. There is something else I can't name but have intuitive feelings about. It's hard to say what this is, but I want to make sense of it. I want to know what these patterns mean. I want to know the truth of my life, what has led to this point. I make a vow to myself: I won't date, won't get involved with another man until I understand what these patterns have to tell me — until I know where I stand in myself.

I have no idea that I'm opening up a Pandora's box I will not be able to close. I have no idea my questions and concerns will take me on a journey into places I've barricaded off, into the underworld of my history and down to the bedrock of my beginnings. I have no idea how close I will come to the brink of no return. I only know that something isn't right, and I want to right it.

I focus all my intentions. I do what I've done before when living in this house, but I take on more responsibility. And when the owner's dogs are failing and always in pain, the owners unable to face losing them, I pick up their burden, call the vet and twice ease a dog over the threshold into death, burying them as best I can in rocky, frozen ground. I accept this as a tithe for my own coonhound, feel the wheel of time shift, and I grieve for each of us. By all of this and more I balance the fierce focus of personal intent, spend time on the land in sync with the moon, sun and seasonal cycles and embark on the journey within, pushing off the shore into the wilderness of my innermost being. I dig into my past, ask tough questions and sit with myself. With these acts I begin the strangest, most demanding and extraordinary journey of my life.

———

Potent watersheds exist in the cycle of every life. I could not have said then what I know now. I seem born to touch the edge and return to tell.

In 1985 I do not understand how fractured I am. Yet the risks I'd taken or that had been forced on me in my youth are also my strength. In these focused years I seek internal clarity about the violence I've endured — what happened to me? Why? What can I do about it? I want to shift the irrevocable weight of the past into better channels of well-being. Once I'm guided by the directive of my innermost spirit, risk becomes my asset and critical companion. Facing and unraveling my history I rock my world, endure peril as great as anything by traveling the dark regions of the soul to pull myself from the fire and put it all back together again, mostly alone on a mountain pass, high above the great valley that is home. The arduous journey to the edge, the knowledge necessary to carry me through the fires of earlier times and back, are beyond my conscious scope. But they will return me whole to myself in ways I cannot imagine. They will shift my life from one of reaction to one of response. The oars of life's boat will return to me, pulled from the dark hand of the past.

There is an important footnote to the third relationship. An unexpected instance brings eerie confirmation to the path I've chosen. About two years after the relationship is over, a woman calls me. She introduces herself as the recent girlfriend of the third man and asks if we can talk. Though her call seems a bit mysterious, I agree and we meet for coffee. She wants to talk about their relationship. Her start with him was similar but even more radical than my own. She had come to the valley on vacation. Hers was a fast passion that leapt to a faster decision: She immediately moved from three states away to live with him. Our experiences separate there.

She goes on to describe periods of threats and abuse, when she or their neighbors have to call for police intervention. She wants to compare notes on all of this. I tell her I'm sorry for her pain. I haven't had that kind of experience with him. I don't know what to say. She insists that I must have insight into these aspects of their relationship. She says that he always talks about me. Maybe there's something I can tell her about how my effect on him has been so positive? I tell her I'm sorry for her confusion. I have no parallels to share. I don't know why he treated me differently. I feel bad for her and want to comfort her, give her words of wisdom, but I have none to match what she's experienced. As we part, I'm relieved but also puzzled. What can I offer her? What is the difference between her time with him and mine?

That answer will come much later. In a riveting moment I will suddenly recall the strange third presence, that unknown factor that drove me out of his house and away. It will take many years more before the pieces of this mystery will finally fall into place.

———

Other odd instances, outside reality as I know it, will arise in my life. My history is stacked with them. In the face of later occurrences I will find myself resistant to attach anything like paranormal experience, other lives or mystical phenomena to these patterns. It is one thing to imagine such possibility, as I had in my youth. It is entirely another to endure the unexpected shock of living experience.

Later the feeling that these peculiar events are real in some way throws my logical mind into turmoil and entrenched resistance. Yet the experiences in my boyfriend's cabin and those that came after are part of the fabric of my life. The more I battle against them the stronger they press against a door I try desperately to hold closed.

Digging into my past becomes full of riveting discovery. I learn to lean into my experiences, not away. Many recurring instances stagger throughout my life when time and space crumpled and opened. As though it has always been natural for me to be pulled from this world into others.

I'm 33 years old. The thirties are a natural cyclic time for a shift point, from living out the expectations of others — the conditionings of family, culture, whomever or whatever has determined our identity — to claiming personal autonomy; authenticity that aligns according to a deeper truth. Astrologers see the thirties as a time of adaption to the Saturn return that occurs at 28 years old. In this light the thirties are a time of challenge and integration, when changing dynamics push up from the fertile soil of internal life. At the time Christ died on the cross, he was 33 years old. Challenging the norms of time and culture, throwing the moneylenders out of the temple, speaking of a new expansive way of living — breaking down intolerance, orienting to love and forgiveness — Christ offers one archetype for the essence of the thirties. Life is full of watershed moments. This is my moment for reclamation. To break out of old patterns, I break into my inner life.

I take the risk to be myself, to reinvent myself, to challenge old history and take apart the old structures that bind me. I've no real idea what I'm biting off. There are so many doors to unlock behind me. The troubling pattern of the three relationships is the first catalyst to begin this leg of my journey, but there will be many more.

Why do some of us seem chosen or destined to walk difficult pathways? Are we here to learn something, work something out or serve in some way? Why do some of us feel the world so acutely? Is this a talent and skill, a gift that when developed has something to offer?

I settle deep into introspective life. I keep a personal journal, turning my thoughts and filling empty pages. I make deep inquiry into every facet of my life. I choose a life of investigation. The clear bell that rings through my history trails to this place of pause and chosen solitude. I begin to use deep listening to trust the wisdom inside me. It's a quieter life, but it's far from dull. As I immerse and take hold of it totally I discover a world more exciting and true than any I could have imagined. I spend time with friends and have many good relationships. I read, explore, discuss, and I think a great deal on my own. I remember my past with intentional focus. By the time I have coffee with the woman who calls about my ex-boyfriend I know I've claimed a life that's truly mine and I go deeper.

The house on the mountain pass is a sequestered area surrounded by wild country and few neighbors. Quietude, it has an edge all its own. I keep life basic, simple. My time turns into an archaeological dig of vast proportion. As I find my way I discover that I have a knack for this kind of investigation. I don't understand how dangerous the ground is that I'm traversing. Because my experience begins with rich and fertile returns, I don't realize that I'm just into the topsoil of my search for answers.

During this time a co-worker arrives at work one morning excited about a new play the local theater group is producing. It's called *Extremities*. The group is in search of women who are willing to talk with the acting crew about first-hand experiences with rape. She mentions calling the women's shelter or crisis hotline to ask for volunteers. I tell her I can help them.

"You don't need to bother," I offer, casual and confident. "I can talk to them. I know about rape." My out-loud confession reverberates through the bright light shining into our workspace from the full wall of windows. I hear the tone in my voice and recognize that pride swells in its cadence, I'm proud of something. I'm proud I've survived and more, that I'm thriving. I'm sure I know some things that will be of use to them. I offer to talk to the actors.

I think I know what I'm doing, that I've got a handle on it all now. But the personal work I'm immersed in, I've barely scratched the surface. The courage that has been my strength is now my weakness.

The enormous energy that is created internally by holding trauma, grief and terror at bay for so many years is a force of nature all its own. I don't grasp the implications or the illusions that are wrapped tight in my process. The actors take me on, and we set a date. Before the week is out I'm sitting on the floor of a close, stuffy room in the midst of the acting group. All eyes are pinned to me. Ravenous, these eyes of the actors — but I flinch only slightly.

The hunger to understand their subject moves quickly into hungry, sharp questions. Specific and immediate, they cut deep. On fire to capture the nature of the play and its characters, they leap query to query. I cannot keep pace. No chance for reflection. Before one answer can complete there is another and another. The questions topple over each other.

"How old were you when this happened ... who were you with, how many of you ... where were you ... why were you there ... why were you hitchhiking ... did you ever hitchhike again ... a man, you were with a man when it happened, how could that happen ... how did you get away ... who raped you ... what do you know about him ... what happened to him ... what happened that night after ... and after the ... after he ... "

The group cuts to dozens of moments I've never spoken aloud to anyone. Their questions pull against the myriad stories I've told myself and then strain past them. I have no capacity to answer any one question in full and then not at all. I cannot keep up. The kindness of the group, espoused at the beginning, is lost in a firestorm of curiosity. I begin to spin into panic. No one notices. Questions hurl fast then faster, my mind scrambling. The actors press close. One too many, a question hammers, and the response eludes me. The forever story that I have told myself and needed to believe is the not the real story of what happened to me, and this siphons into jilted riffs and mumbled stammers. I start to unravel. *No! It wasn't like that! Yes, it was! No! It wasn't. Yes. No.* I can't keep up and worse, I can't hold my story together. Confusion fogs into riptide. I'm drowning in lost memory.

The actors don't even notice. They hurl endless questions. Understanding has vanished in the rush and buzz. Stacked like sandbags against a massive flood my story splits open. And I'm out of the group in a flash, racing out the building and hurtling onto the street. Barely able to keep myself from spinning out of control, I'm desperate for one thing and one thing only: I want the answers to the questions I can't give. There's a small spiral-top notebook that has to be somewhere back at the house. I want it. It holds the only record I've ever made straight out of that night. I have to find it.

Staggering to my old, blue Saab I'm in the driver's seat with the engine roaring before I know where I am. Answers, real answers, simple answers to the questions that speed greased lightning now in my blood are in that tiny, spiral notebook. Dashing the miles out of town and across the valley I drive up the pass in a frenzy of links and connections that race through my fomenting mind. When I get to the house I tear through the front door to rip the seal off the wall into my storage bunker and scramble onto the gravel of the dank, close space.

I need the truth, what I knew at 19. The feelings that split and dive now are not that truth. I need the notebook that holds the certainty of how we made it, why we were there, how we survived. The flex and reel of life and death, banshees that choke free, are not those feelings. The tiny journal holds those feelings, holds exact words. They will say the feelings. They will name events. They will tell the story. They have the key to what was and was not.

I grab boxes, open one, then another, find nothing and push through to the back of the pile spilling onto the gravel floor.

Did you ever hitchhike again, the actors asked, after, you know? Fault lines swarm. Did I? Yes. Why?

With just this question my house of cards comes toppling, and it's still toppling as I claw through box after box after box after box.

I can't name the why of what we had and had not done, the exact why of any single choice I've ever made. Raw and ragged but on this one day a single small journal pulls like gravity, promises order, authority bound in spiral truth. Frantic I can't tell one thing from another. I make myself slow, breathe and look closely, go back through boxes I've passed through too fast. A large Ziploc bag emerges. Inside between letters and maps is a small, stained flip-top spiral. The bag quivers in my hands. Stepping back through the hole in the wall and down into the kitchen, I drop to the floor unsteady but with a turn toward calm. The little spiral tumbles out to splay open on the shiny surface of the table. Relief peeps through bedlam. I fold back the cover and search through dates and pages. I remember that old feverish desire to get down the sequence, make a record, to say what needed to be said. I remember feeling it would be important. And I remember how hard it was to try to find the words. Pages fan to September into October 1971. I bend to my long-ago efforts with a sense of gratitude.

And feel a jolt. This is gibberish, it's all gibberish! There's nothing on the first page or the next or the next that holds any answers at all. Self-conscious scribbling aches to be hip and cool. It strains past any meaning. Shame breaks inside me and cleaves to stark shock. I try again to grasp at stilted phrases that curl across every page. Conceits past meaning frame the words like a strangled cover-up. A thousand feelings burn. I remember this girl and her drivel, her self-conscious, endless prattle. I remember her desperate need. Take hold of life and be seen.

She withers naked in front of me on the lined, narrow page. In the face of frenetic, old anguish I stand up straight and begin to tremble all over again. Talons, so near to strike, descend on my mind.

Fast I slap the little notebook shut. Quick I hide the girl away. Back into Ziploc between maps and swirling images, back to the storage bunker, back to the bottom of a box. Scrabbling memorabilia on top, I bury her again in the past. I order and stack the boxes, slink back down into the kitchen; shove the panel back into the wall. More pain than I can fathom seethes and burns through my mind and body. Questions plunder answers. Events topple questions. My mind becomes paralyzed. Everything is thrust back into darkness out of sight.

Days pass. An extreme restlessness takes hold. A threshold has been crossed. Though I resist there's no fighting it. I can no longer use the old strategies to keep my history at bay. It's like a locking of vise grips down onto linked kegs of dynamite, fuse lit and already burning. The sense of impending devastation is wound tight against contradictory feelings. As though I'm standing at the edge of vast treasure I sense more than I see, and dread more than I can acknowledge. This conflict creates its own inferno. I'm dumb to the implications. I know only that I have to act. I don't know how or where I can find what I need. Help is not something I come to easily. Need is one thing, help is entirely another. But this time life pushes me past stark independence.

I know it's asking something else of me now.

29

Extremities

I've no confidence whatsoever in classic counseling. The public health scene is full of known hazards, a nightmare. I don't need more of that layered onto the mess I'm trying to pull apart. But I do know I need a key that is just out of my grasp. Experience tells me I already have it, masked and vulnerable to negligent approach. The answers lie somewhere inside me. I just need help to get past the opening. I can't name what this means. I'm finding my way in the dark.

I talk to my sister, who talks to a friend, Ann. When I call Ann to give a brief on my history she suggests that I keep a dream journal. She tells me she's not a counselor, but she'll work with me on a casual basis. She's about to travel, and we make a date to get together in two weeks. If I have anything by then we can meet to discuss it. Dismayed and ripe to begin I'm disappointed that I have to wait. She laughs as she fills in the date on her calendar. She suggests that I probably won't have anything by the time she returns anyway. It's not as easy as you think, she tells me. But the first morning I write my dreams from the prior night for an hour before work and have to skip my shower. I set my alarm to an earlier time for the next day. The second morning I write out dreams for two hours. On the weekend I wake earlier and I'm still writing at 11 a.m. I always have to stop before I have the full details of the night's dreams down in my journal. I learn to be selective, but I'm already aware that every aspect of any dream or dream series strings to new meaning and brings more meaning together. Inscrutable at times, the dreams always pop open in time to understanding and light. As conscious awareness builds in my dream life, spontaneous insights spring to clarity during waking hours. One dream will communicate through another. There is simplicity, and there is complexity, and they each have ways of communicating through image, color, feeling, humor, drama, story and time. It's thrilling.

A language new and all my own, it also feels ancient. My dreams are intense and sometimes playful. When I grasp this, it ties to ever more curious ways to understand what the dreams are saying. Each nuance feeds a river in me. By the designated date with Ann dozens of dreams fill pages in rich detail, all widely varied. Notations on the effects of the dreams and the added effects of my noticing them cram onto the margins of dream sequences and reams of random scrap paper. I'm gaining fluency and clarity, riveting and wild, though I don't know yet to fully trust it. I think Ann holds the key. She is taken aback by the many detailed dreams in my journal. I wait for her wisdom to flow.

"I see," she says, pursing her lips and looking at me over the rim of her wire-frame glasses. "You've done this before."

"Um, no, I haven't," I answer, confused. "Not in this life, anyway."

"Hmm," she mumbles and grumps, "hmm," and flips through the bulk of material with agitation. "I thought it'd be awhile before you'd actually get much of anything." And then it's a speechless moment as she sits back, watching me. I'm unnerved in the presence of this woman whose acerbic wit and tongue never seem to sleep. Eager, innocent I stare back.

"Ok," she says, "Let's see what we can make of this. Pick a dream or two and read them aloud." She flips on a cassette recorder. I feel flustered. Flush with success but not much perspective, I'm like a child anxious to show all her art. But I flip a page, choose a dream and just read. She suggests a book or two on symbols and archetypes. I take the recording home, and once a week after we meet I review the new recordings just as I review and evaluate my dreams. Within a few weeks, I'm on my own.

On the south wall of the main room of the office where I work there is a wall of windows. I have a dream about being in this room. When I look out the windows I see dinosaur bones stacked and tumbled in the alleyway parking. The image of these bones is powerful, evocative. When I wake the dinosaur bones press unrelenting in my thoughts. I puzzle and puzzle over them, can't understand what they mean. One day I suddenly realize that the dinosaur bones in my dream are not bones at all. They're old, rusted derrick parts. As I puzzle this out, associations begin to take hold. My father was an oilman, a land lease broker. My mother's second husband was a tool pusher on an oil rig, a derrick. Petroleum is a derivative of dinosaurs and ancient life that is transformed under great pressure. The use of petroleum is becoming an environmental disaster (as in the vehicles that park in the site of the dinosaur bone derrick parts in my dream, the parking lot where pick-ups and deliveries of all of our business shipping and supplies take place). The effects of my oilman father and my mother's second husband, an oilfield worker — human forces that were supposed to support my life with a strong foundation — are aspects of great pressure that crushed and transformed me, pressures that I'm now trying to transform out of the pressures of my past into new relationships with myself and other men. The dinosaur bone derrick parts also link to the main foundation of my time at Falls Creek where I met Brad — a place for social environmental awareness study — work that has deep relevance and meaning to me in my life. My subconscious through the dream is pushing the history of all these aspects of my past into conscious awareness. The elegance of the dream is stunning. Like the skeleton under the bed in an earlier dream, these bones are the essential nature of major aspects of my history.

And then a couple of months after my interview with the actors, the play *Extremities* is ready to stage.

It is scheduled for its first run at the Pink Garter Theatre. I note the date for opening night. Pleased with the earth I'm turning, the cues and clues arising from my dreams, vast jewels dredge out of the past to reveal patterns in the present. This play, I think, will give me new ground, but I also think it will already be ground that I've covered. I decide to go see it alone so I can savor the experience and whatever insights might come without distraction.

I drive to the theater intrigued. I keep to myself as I climb the stairs and choose a seat in a row at the back where no one else is sitting. The crowd packs together in the lower front section, theater less than half-filled. It's a bit like having a private box. I settle into the middle of a row.

The play unfolds sequence to sequence. A woman is kidnapped and brutalized but escapes. The authorities do little to protect her when she reports what has happened. She's lost her purse her wallet her ID her driver's license in the ordeal. Name. Address. Phone. They dismiss this as well. Her roommates are sympathetic but also don't get it. Though she's wary and careful the man finds her alone one day at home. He attacks her, but she turns the tables. She involves her roommates when they return to the house. As the characters unleash violation in eye-for-eye, tooth-for-tooth retaliation across the length and breadth of the stage, I come unraveled. From confident witness I become victim ensnared in rash terror. Hundreds of leagues deep inside of me a hot-magma bubble — pressurized and swollen with time — surges to the surface. Unhinged as the last act unfolds, a wild animal trapped in her seat, I cannot flee from the theater. My legs are rubber. I can't even stand. Mind shattered, emotions unlace to dread at every turn. As muscles wilt into floorboards beneath carpet beneath theater beneath my shattered mind, every cell goes into hyper-drive. I have to get out of this place. But just as it was in childhood in the movie theater in Mexico, only a thousand times worse, I cannot move.

Onstage, the drama wrenches on. Players leap and surge in the struggle. Applause breaks from the audience like shock waves — people I mostly know. And this awareness detonates into new horror that claws at my helplessness.

Yet something else — the threat of light about to burst through the theater — finally catapults me from my seat. I drag myself from chair to chair down the aisle, knees buckling; legs nearly useless. At the end of the row there is nothing to support me past the last seat. Open aisle yawns to the stairway. I have no control over my legs. Trembling, helpless I strain for control as the play reaches its stark finale. The crowd ignites to its feet. And I'm hurled across the open landing with the sense of impending exposure and throw myself down the steps. Only the banister saves me in the twisting slide to the bottom.

Foyer and open space are filled with glaring light. There is no support to cross it and no one there, this last part a relief beyond words. For a moment I feel a hint of composure, imagine I can walk across the room in all normalcy. When I hear an usher descending the stairs on the opposite side I'm wrenched to stagger in a burst through the outside doors and make it to the sharp pitch of stairs that drop to the street. As the audience fills the foyer at my back I cling to the banister in crazy descent, barely keeping on my feet.

At the curb and my car my hands shake so badly I can't get the key in the lock. Two couples descend the stairs. I grab my left hand with my right to force the key in the lock. Sobs take over as the door swings open, and I throw myself in the seat. I turn my face away from the questioning eyes of the two couples and struggle to start the engine. On a roar the engine comes to life. This is the last memory I have before I find myself pulling up the mountain road, panic alive in my blood and no memory of how I reached home.

I pour from the car to fight my way through keys and lock and front door with a host of demons flying down the mountain pass at my back, a volcanic horde of howling infamy. Locking the door I race through rooms, yank curtains, close blinds. But at the full-length windows of the sliding glass doors the venetian blinds, even closed, threaten with a thousand cracks. I race to the laundry room and grab sheets, race back to cover the blinds, haphazard and tenuous.

Horrible things gather outside these windows. Their numbers are growing. I back away from the windows as terror escalates.

The fear that fear attracts fear and what is fearsome explodes in my mind. Rigged sheets sway. Legions of ghouls mass. Mongrels shriek in the night. More will come. Their numbers are endless. The speed of the swarm gathers to a gale hammering on windows and walls. They'll never stop. I cower, exposed in the light. And race through rooms to douse all light. When darkness is smothering I race back to smash on each light.

At a sudden standstill, nothing I can do, the attack hurls in infinite number. Hostile eternity cramps through the doors and glass. The house heaves. And the gruesome assault intensifies. The glass won't hold. The walls won't hold. Nothing will hold. I can't stop the surging multitudes. Frantic electricity pumping through my body is reaching exhaustion. I turn like a top. At the back of the room where my bed rests there are blankets and a place to lie down. Too far too close too trapped. I back to my bed, grab for a blanket and drag it to the wicker rocker that sits before the sheet-clad windows. I sink to the cushioned seat. As wicker squeals my harrowed nerves into brighter misery I pull the blanket tight around me and try to sit very still.

The claiming throng will pull me asunder. I face the windows as the press outside builds and still they come. The sheets bulge into the room. There is nowhere to go. A moment of stillness, tense and silent, and the night outside goes silent. I dare to breathe. Banshees come screaming on wail and scratch and snarl. Breathless now, refusing them makes no difference. They come. And they come. And they come. The house withers and the stone beneath trembles asunder. I pull the chair away from the windows. Icy in the thick wool Hudson Bay blanket, a blanket from Canada that belonged to my father, I hunker deep in the whining chair.

For the first time since childhood, when I was caught in a haunt and had the courage to climb from night covers and flee to my mother's bed, but was turned away; for the second time ever in adult memory, it slowly dawns on me to ask for help. I have no idea where. I have no idea how. But I know that I have to find it. I can't imagine a form for that word, help. Alien, it echoes. The room settles slightly. Dread beats in all corners, throughout the house, and extends to the hellish pandemonium outside, expanding to the edges of all thought. But the word comes again. *Help*. I stare at the red writing table that sits in the opposite corner. A passive red hump looms on its flat red surface. It flickers, catches me eye. It's the telephone. *Who can I call?*

Slow thought curves around a blind bend. *I can call my sister.* I reel at the thought of standing up, of attracting the attention of the ghouls that smash along the windows. The lashing force is taking down the house. I stare at the phone. A phone somewhere outside this house is a phone that can ring. Someone can pick up a ringing phone and answer. The vision rears back. In near collapse I force my focus back to the phone. An answer wants words coming back. My teeth chatter. A clock past the phone ticks into view. It's late. It's so late. It's too late. I can't call anyone. A shriek carries off in the nightmare shredding the night into splinters, the press on the windows push hard.

I stand shaking and walk to the desk, pull the phone toward the chair. The cord doesn't reach. I set it with great care on the floor. Hordes slither, contort and screech. I shudder the blanket close then closer. I stare at the phone. Words start to form. The truth dawns hot in my mind. *If I don't ask for help, this night will go on forever.* I reach out to lift the receiver, turn the dial, lean over the phone, wait — and nearly drop the receiver as my mother's voice blooms in my mind, a cold answer, echo of a call I made so long ago.

A mumble like a miracle stumbles on the other end of the line, "Hello," I stop, stare, and the voice comes again as though through fog and mist, "Hello? Is somebody there?"

"Uhhh," my voice staggers. "I-it's me."

"Catie? Wha-what time is it? It's late, it's pretty late, where are you?"

"I, I'm h-home. I'm h-home a-at th-the h-house."

"What's up, why're you calling?"

"Uh, I, w-well," my voice quavers just above a whisper. "I w-went to the p-play tonight, the one I t-told you about."

"Oh. Well, what was it like?"

I can't keep my voice steady. I swallow but stumble ahead, "I, it was t-terrible. I can't stop, it's, I'm afraid, there are things, I'm scared ..."

"Scared? Why? You're at home?"

"Y-yes," I say, but it's like swallowing glass to keep talking. "I'm at home."

"It scared you. You want to come here?"

"N-no!" alarm shoots through my system at a higher pitch. "I c-can't come out there ... I don't think I can drive."

"How'd you get, never mind, what about Ann, have you talked to Ann?"

I shudder out a reply, "No, it's so late, she goes to bed early, do you think I should call her this late?" Thoughts settle and stop spinning so fast. Ann, who knew I might go to the play. Ann, who said she'd go with me. But it's late it's too late it's so late.

My sister's voice strikes in and I wince. "What's going on? Are you there? Are you ok?" I mumble, and she starts in again, "How bad is this? Can you wait until morning?"

Panic rips through my body. The night presses, yowling along the windows. "B-bad. No! Yes, it's p-pretty bad," I say as I glance around the room and shudder. "It's really b-bad."

"Are you safe there? Are you okay?"

I'm shaking so bad it's hard to hold onto the phone, "Uhhh ..., I, uh ...," I stammer as I begin to hang up the phone.

"Let me think," she says, her voice slowing my hand as it sinks toward the cradle. "You should talk to Ann. Just call her. Call her now. Before it gets any later. Try. Just try to call her. Then call me after you do."

"Uh, ok," I answer, feeling weak. "Ok. I w-will. Bye."

"Do it. And call me back. Call her. You'll call her right now, won't you?"

"Sure. Ok. B-bye."

"Call her. Just call her."

I drop the receiver in a clatter, stare at the pulsating phone. Tremors shake an unending clench. It's too late to call anyone else. The clock ticks. Fear shifts, changes form and swells. Sheets puff and wails rise in screams through eternity. I reach for the phone in dread. I dial but can think of nothing to say. One ring and a voice answers sharp on the line. "Hello!"

I squeeze my voice past dread, "S-sorry, Ann, sorry so s-sorry, it's so l-late," I glance at the clock.

Ann's voice breaks with its usual impatience. "Well. Yeah. It is late, really late for me. Why're you calling? Must be important."

"I'm, my s-sister thought I should c-call you," I say as I lose my breath and start again. "I went to the p-play tonight. I thought I was ready but I c-can't stop shaking and the windows, I'm afraid, I'm n-not sure what to do." The stammering takes all of my breath.

"Well. Oh. Oh! Well! Hmmph. You know I'm not a therapist. This is really not my ground. Hm. Have you — have you tried calling your sister? Oh, yeah. Never mind. Have you asked her to come up there to stay with you?"

"I, yes, no, she ..."

Ann nips in, "Well, why don't you just try getting into bed, see how that feels, are you in bed?"

"No! I can't, I can't do that ... there are ... uh ..."

"Hmmm, never mind, look here's an idea. Try this. Try calling Leo Sprinkle. He's the only one I can think of. You've met him, right? He might know, he's good at this kind of thing. Call him."

"I, it's pretty late d-don't you think? I don't know if he'd remember me."

"Yeah. No. Yeah. Doesn't matter. He'll remember you. If he doesn't don't worry. Just tell him what's happened, what you're feeling. I'll call him first then he'll be ready when you call. I'll call you back after I talk to him. Let me get his number."

"Well, uhhh ...," I say, shaking so bad I almost drop the phone. "Well I d-don't know," but Ann is reading a string of numbers out loud, asking if I got them down. I scramble to the desk for pen and paper. She repeats the numbers again.

"Ok. Ok then." Her voice barks relief. "You hang up now, and I'll call Leo. It'll be fast, and I'll call you back, probably five minutes or less."

"Ummm," quaking I try again, "Uhhh, what, what should I tell him? What if you don't reach him?"

"Tell him what you told me. I'll tell him enough of the rest. I'll call him. Then I'll call you back. Then you call him. Now hang up the phone before it gets any later."

"Uh, ok, bye."

"Bye."

I sag back in the squealing wicker, legs pulled to my chest. I grab the blanket, pull it around me and try to stop the tremors from wrenching my body apart. It's no use. I stare at the slightest gap between the hanging sheets as they list and sway. Chills run down my spine. I nearly tip in the chair. Jumping up I run to the laundry room to grab a clothespin, then back to clamp the gap in the sheets together. The fragile job threatens to cave. I back away. The sheets ripple but hold. The peephole is gone. I drop to the wicker and it squeals wild regret. My will shreds, and the phone rings.

I leap in a dizzy near-faint to answer, and Ann commands, "Ok. He's there. He's expecting you. Call him right now. You've got his number, right?"

"Y-yeah. Yeah, I've g-got it."

"Ok. So he's there. Call him. I'll call your sister."

"Ok."

"You are going to call him, aren't you?"

"Y-yes. Y-Yes. I'll c-call him."

"Ok. Do it. Call me tomorrow." A sharp click, and she's gone. I stare at the receiver, sit down, stand up, hang up and move the phone back to the desk. I rub my hands on my pants, through my hair and try to breathe. Ann's voice barks in my head. *Remember. You said you'd call. He's waiting.* The clock ticks. I jump. A wail outside builds to maniacal frenzy. Hell rustles hard along glass. I dial Leo's number. It's late, so late. I clench my jaw and hang on the edge for his voice, dreading that he'll answer, afraid he won't.

"Hello," a woman's voice chirrups. I stagger back. The voice perks a beat, "Are you calling for Mr. Sprinkle? He's expecting you."

"Y-Yes. Yes. I'm sorry, it's s-so late."

"Oh, that's alright, we're still up. Just a minute." Her voice calls out, a faraway whistle building steam, "Leo, Leo, Leo, Leo."

My hand descends microscopically toward the phone's cradle. A male voice answers, stern and hesitant, full of doubt, "Yes?"

"Uh. Y-Yes. H-hi, Mr. Sprinkle. This is, I m-mean, you w-won't remember me. Uh, I'm calling because Ann called you a few minutes ago ... I'm c-calling because ..."

His voice is calm as it breaks in gently, "Yes. Ann did call. You can call me Leo." Cautious he continues, "What is it? What is going on for you?"

"W-well, it's kinda late," I start but can't go on.

"No, don't worry, it's not too late," a little gruffness that softens. "You don't need to tell me everything. Just tell me a little, what you're feeling. Right now. What's happening there for you now?"

"Uh, well, I, uh, went to a p-play tonight. It, it was terrible, like s-something that happened to me a long time ago. I thought I was ready but, well, I kind of fell apart, not sure how I got home, and now I can't stop shaking. I'm afraid, really afraid. I've got sheets on my windows, things are out there, I can't seem to, can't seem to, Ann thought maybe you could help me. I'm sorry I've c-called you so late."

"Ok. Ok. It's ok. So how are you feeling right now, right this minute?"

"Scared. Really scared."

"Ok. So whatever happened to you, whatever it was that happened to you, that isn't you. Do you understand? That isn't you. You need to let it, for just one minute, you need to let it go. And the way you do that is, well, can you imagine surrounding yourself, right now, right this moment, can you imagine surrounding yourself with love? It's right there. It's always right there, with you. It's all you need. Just call in the love. Just call it in. Can you imagine climbing into your bed or a comfortable place and just calling in the love? So it will surround you the rest of the night?"

Through shock, terror and dismal agony his words cull through until there's nothing left in the room. It's quiet around me. The quaking slows. I breathe. My mind grows sharp.

He speaks again, "Are you there? Are you ok? It's love. It's love that you need. Call in the love."

And it's instantaneous. The sound of the word pops in my mind and expands. Fear disintegrates from my body, dread peels off my skin.

"Love," he says again softly.

Ghouls evaporate. The whole world grows silent and steadies. A tiny smile tips to wonder across my lips. I stand, listening to this man hundreds of miles away breathe softly into the phone. My body begins to relax.

"Are you there?" he asks. "Are you ok?" Doubt splays through his voice and hovers.

"Yes," I say. "Yes. I'm here. I-I can imagine it. I can feel it. The love." Impossible against the backdrop of the night the calm holds steady. My tiny smile vibrates. "I'm ... well ... I'm ... I think I'm ok."

Doubt edges again in his words, "Are you sure? Just keep calling in the love. Call it in any moment fear returns." There's no more quaking. My body holds still on the earth in the room in the dark in the night. It's quiet outside.

"Yes," I say, "Yes, I feel it. Everything's changed. That's it then, isn't it? Call in the love. Thank you." Crystalline joy sparkles and pings in my cells. Relief surges and knots unwind. It's almost ludicrous.

Unabashed surprise breaks through Leo's voice. "Uh, ok then. You're, you, you felt it then? You feel it now? You're, uh, ok?"

"Yes. Yes. I feel it. I am. I'm ok. Really. Thank you. Thank you so much."

Disbelief still laces his words, "Ok then. Call the love in all through the night. Just call it in to completely surround you."

"Ok. I will. That's it. Really. Thank you. I'm fine. I'll be fine. Really." Disbelief echoes through my voice, too, but it's a voice shining. My whole body is humming. Like a missing limb, fear is gone. "Thank you for taking my call so late, L-Leo. Thank you."

"Ok then," he stammers a little.

"Ok then. Goodbye, Leo, thank you!" I feel ridiculous and perfect. For a moment his voice stammers again uncertain, like there's something more he's supposed to do, to say. As though we both feel this just might be a hoax. But the moment slides by. Embarrassed, I stumble, too, "Thank you."

"Yes, 'bye. You're welcome. Take care of yourself." And we hang up together.

I stare at the phone. I stare at the sheets. The hordes beyond the windows remain silent. There's no fear in the house. I walk from room to room and turn off the lights. I crawl into bed. Collected and clear I lie with the truth and the strength of Leo's conviction, with the potency of his care and his words. The power of one word wraps like a blanket around me. Protective gossamer shroud, natural and unfathomable it flows from all quarters. Nothing and nothing haunts in the night. The world is what it is and I see it, but what damages the world is not here. I lie in the darkness and hold this — the word and the way and this truth. I call in the love, and it holds me. My sore body sinks deep and then deeper into peace.

30

Catwalk

Stealth wakes the night. Movement shifts currents, rifles sleep, pulls me conscious into the room. Held in stillness my bed settles in palpating dark. As my eyes open there is nothing, nothing at all but the room and the night and spare light. In the light dark, a flat sepia haze pulses, defining walls, desk and hanging sheets along windows, living air. All breathe the sepia overlay. Some vital subtlety exhales and I stir. Near my bed where the north wall ends is a concave with vanity, sink and hidden closet. Movement hints from the dark of the closet. Nothing. And then a brief blurred scintillation. Life force radiates across open space. A form steps into view. It propels to the center of the room.

Arresting, upright, human, not human, she is all power and savage, taut grace. Her hunched back extends to a severe oblong head, massive anterior cranial bulk. Huge incisor-ridden jaws, no flesh to them, are all bone fang snap and rend. Eyes glint from deep, boney sockets. Long fingers rake hook and claw. Twisting in all directions she prowls razor-sharp across the floor. All flows in quick, rippling purpose. Energy runs electric as her skeletal limbs take the space.

The she-cat paces and snarls.

Stalking to the wall of covered windows she strides the length of the room, back and forth, back and forth, turn and whip. Motion momentum precision penetrate the body of the house, all focus on the hideous beings beyond windows and walls. Power surges. Through wall window latch and moorings her supremacy pierces to soil. Silence defines stillness defines movement defines furious rhythm.

Night rends on the eruption of primordial screams.

The battle gone dormant ignites. Vast attack of feral forces that erupted from within me during the play pulse again now in the outer darkness, as catwoman stalks, fighting them, holding them back. Past comprehension, I watch from my bed.

Feverish, not sound itself but the result of sound, she hurls out challenge, harsh warning, lurid promise. Shriek beyond hearing tears through walls, splits past windows, hurdles rampant out onto the world. Waged out of sight, out of mind a rampage more terrible than any worst nightmare careens on the cusp of lost time. Forever the catwoman stalks vile forces that rage and riot beyond the house, hurling pace for pace along walls and windows, tempest in the flick of her will. Ferocity heaves across the skin of the world. Claw, bite and puncture rip with the thrash of her body, judder on the fang of her will. Convulsing thresholds squeal no trespass as the hideous thing cants and returns. Scars dam the whine and way out. What is out there roars back. Hosts of terror and taunt split along her watch, shred inch for maddening inch toward destruction. Nothing and nothing can pass the catwoman. Nothing passes. Nothing ever will. Night heaves back against the feral cat dance. Fabric of time and space split and disintegrate.

From the bed I have no fear. I watch, eternal marvel as she holds back all threat. Air fairly crackling attends crushing strength. What is out there is no match for the she-cat's fierce purpose. Perfect focus perfect movement strange beauty and the force of the night amplifies, contracts, amplifies, contracts on and on. I wake, doze, wake, doze and still she stalks along walls and windows, never a pause never a waver never a distraction.

Night turns on itself. Diffuse subtle light blooms through darkness. Dawn softens. At the windowed east wall, primal catwoman scans the length, sniffs and prowls, sniffs and prowls; shifts her weight. Day is coming. On a pivot, she stalks to the back of the room. Briefest pause, and she steps out of sight into dark recess.

The room settles on a last hiss of breath.

Light hints. Light sweetens.

I fall into perfect sleep.

31

Nun's Journey

There is a story of a Buddhist nun on a journey home. Along the way her traveling group is attacked by a robber baron. She is robbed, raped and left for dead.

She makes it home. Knowing the identity of the man who did so much harm to her, she invites him to her compound as guest of honor at a great celebration. He accepts her invitation. Secure in his power and false identity he arrives to discover elegant and generous preparation — a great feast with finest foods and an open-armed welcome. He accepts her hospitality in all the pomp of his imagined dignity and reputation. As the celebration unfolds she stands amidst his followers and their shared community. She names the great damage he has done to her. She understands that her karma has ripened. She bows and forgives his trespass, releasing them both. The robber baron is undone, exposed in the face of her raw transparency. He weeps into the truth that has bloomed between them. He is a changed man. Their cycle of pain is ended.

———

There was a time in my life that I thought that it was the singing on the night of our ordeal in Nevada that saved my friends and me. Unusual and unbidden like a miracle, that singing. Much later I thought otherwise, it wasn't the singing. Then I believed it was the human connection that occurred between our abductor and me that did it, opening the way for song and our eventual release. But in time I saw that, too, was not quite accurate. Then I thought the shift I made into dowsing for truth running in the current between all of us must finally have broken the spell — and all moments added up to that. Later still I understood it was my friends' struggle over the gun that shattered my fatalistic terror, so that the roles I played could come into being. It took all of us to survive. It is impossible to say — which trail, which cause, which effect had saved us — minds burdened with the terrible search for reasons.

Some say there are no reasons. Forget searching for them. Life is random. In time, when I could at last sit with the full swathe of my history and hold it, when I could cut back to the moment on the cold desert sand in the darkness when our abductor at last let us go, I saw that none of my conclusions were correct. So dense, so impermeable for so long the veils of fear, revulsion, shame, ignorance, ego, trauma, distortion and time had at last been stripped away — and I understood that none of the moments I had imagined were what saved us. At the very end the man was still going to kill us.

By the time I knew that I had peeled down to the bare bones of my history. I no longer needed time, distance or distortion to protect me from what had been. I no longer sought reasons. I no longer needed them. I simply knew how to hold my history, to be present with the full reach of what I had lived.

Then one day a friend asked about that night in Nevada. And I saw our attacker exactly as he had been in the instant he ordered my friends and me out of the van, the extremes of his rage, his madness, his military precision, the bullet of his body as he leapt out his door. His decision had been made. He was going to kill us. Every cell of him focused to the task. We would run. He would shoot. It would be over.

He'd gone completely feral.

Time popped open and truth laid itself bare. And that is when the moment that changed everything jumped into the light and I understood. Though my friends and I ratcheted and frayed against the force of his last commands, it was that last moment in the darkness where we gathered at the side of the van that brought the change that saved us, that last moment when he ordered us out, and we pulled on our packs. That last moment when we thought we would go free, too unsettled to see his real intentions.

I leaned across our small circle. I embraced him. The expansive bliss of surrender still held me, even in that last chaos. *Thank you,* I said. For setting us free, I thought. And the words that changed everything crossed my lips.

I love you, I breathed.

Three words out of a vast force made way through the tiny vessel of my youthful inexperience and poured over him. Naïve simplicity outpaced everything, expressed enormity and penetrated the moment, reaching past the outer tip of hate, pain and isolation. Three words were the instrument of our survival. Three words became the vehicle of redemption. Three words pulled one man back from the brink and the three of us with him. Three words saved us. Everything our human lives long for spoke through those words. Acceptance. Belonging. Forgiveness.

One word might have done it. *Love.*

Later, much later, this word saved my life again, opening the way to full life and greater cycles of completion.

32

Dreams

Dreams erupt. Dreams dance and dreams sing. Shattering exposure, primal catwoman, Big love. The world turns now on a different axis. A Pandora's box has been opened, emptying out long-held terror. Revealed within and beneath all of it is the love and hope of the world. There is no closing off the force of creation now. The task left is to understand what I've released. Catwoman prowls along borders deep in psyche's lost time, protection from negative intentions within darkness, the strength to bring love's potency into the light. Wild forces are waking me up. I can at last do what I know I've come to do, though I can't articulate yet what that is. What has led to all of this is my evolving capacity to at last ask for help. Three times that night — by calling my sister, by calling Ann and at last by calling Leo — I have reached out beyond old loss, trauma and fear to step past isolation and shame.

By spring of the first year of my efforts I experience a resurrection. I'm releasing myself. From the chains and the darkness of my past, I'm coming into the light in a way I've never experienced before. I begin to understand that in a strange way my shadow for many years has been the light. Through all the darkness, through entrapment, the complex difficulties of finding my way out, I've feared the light as much or more than the dark. Trapped in the dark for extended cycles, shining light on the hidden can feel unbearable. The worst of exposure occurred for me in a lightning flash — dangerous as anything. But I've made it through. Revelation is this release into light and a lightness of being.

Coming clear of a thick bank of fog that's held me captive for too many years, I feel as though it's all just in time. Just in time, and I feel the tick of time passing. Just in time, and urgency presses against riveting deadlines I can't name. I don't know what this means. I do know there is a moment in time I must be prepared to meet. There's no cushion now and no going back. Palpable, potent beyond any description, the knowing breathes into every moment, fueling a vitality that's at last fully mine.

It takes me a while to grasp that the ferocity of catwoman, no words can fully describe the fact of her, is much more than I first imagine. Beyond archetype, she's me, a full-bodied aspect of my untamed nature, living facet of my natural self. Her entry into the waking world is no dream. What has come forth is ancestral — unadulterated raw psyche, a severe, visceral power that spans all time.

Raw psyche. Beyond love, there is no greater individual or group expression in our human lives. It is life force magnified to extremes. Brute power that has leapt full-bodied to stalk my distended history is the amplification of stark survival. All the years of holding down history, of keeping the demons at bay in a lockdown at great and cavernous depths, expanded rank energies to outer limits.

Leo's gift is a force far greater, yet in a sense it's the same. Love is the force that came through me in Nevada when three innocent kids caught in the hell of lost hope opened a portal and somehow made it home. The forces on the desert that could have consumed us liberated us. A fine line saved us. Two forces that are really one, both keys in a bid for survival, are this supremacy of clashing worlds. And yet they are one, they are one and the same. In the thrall of history's claim this is my journey and I know it. How to come home, intend love, claim life side by side and awake to suffering and pain, no denial, no division. And by this, live free.

A dark hand from the past has kept a stranglehold on my family, has kept us in thrall to ensnared machinations for countless years. Revealed in terrible jeopardy that spit from my mother to my younger brother and me, it lives on in a hundred unnamed, lurid forms. I know now I must name them, claim them, release them one by one. I must go deeper to find what's most needed to make this passage. Extending far back in time, a curse, a spell, a karma — it has kept us lost and bound, mean and broken, blind. Whatever it is, I mean to break it. I can't know the full swath of the path that I'm claiming, but I know that I've gone too far to turn back now. I'm long past the point of no return. Beware the past. It holds great power. If you don't turn to face it, it will eat you alive.

It's a steep learning curve. I understand that this cat being is one expression of my inner constellation. An aspect that has kept me alive for many years, now catwoman sleeps. The night of her prowling brute force kept back the immensity of elemental, raw psyche in its multiple rank forms. With the catalyst of the play, *Extremities*, and the tango of history almost too great to bear, out she came. With Leo's naming, so simple and profound, her polar opposite has also revealed — love. Both forces served to carry me across a great threshold. And so goes the journey of years. Through alchemy, amalgamation and integration there is new form. Spirit clarifies.

External changes begin to come in leaps and waves. A burgeoning creative life takes hold. It requires that I move into claiming my role as an artist — beyond roles I've played to support other artists, my musician boyfriends, my artist friends and the graphic artist I work for. Life wants something new of me now. Old, hidden dreams begin to unmask and rise. Coming to the anvil of creative life is a calling. It is fire. A living force, it forms and reforms into newness again and again. It is never-ending. Whatever my mind might say with its history of doubt the larger me knows. I must claim this fire for myself. I must choose it so that it will choose me. Dreams tell me. Waking life demands.

Dreams come now in earnest. Not so much more dreams but with a power that is breathtaking. My facility to interpret expands. The drive to explore and participate in the world from a unique autonomy takes on new meaning. I begin to travel more and with greater frequency, as life calls me out of known ground. My sister and I expand our annual cadence, southern Utah in the spring and fall, extraordinary quests off the map. These journeys interweave collective history with personal past. Cairns and codes untangle at accelerating speed.

Many link to New Mexico. When I go there, I will go alone, always. There I will begin to discover the threads of long past lives. They do not all belong to that place, but they all tie to it, tie back to Mexico and other places beyond. What is family and rightly so, and what is individual and rightly so separates and reforms. As dream life expands I learn to hold to what is true and to separate truth from chaff. It isn't always easy. It is always extraordinary. All these realms are seductive, full of illusion and shifting phenomena, just as our daily lives are with their many distractions, allurements and projections. I have to challenge all the roles I've taken on in my life — daughter, sister, friend, employer, protector, worker, creator, promoter of others — I have to break them down, reconfigure every one. I have to learn that disappointing myself holds more meaning than disappointing others. Fidelity to spirit, to inner truth is what I must trust implicitly now. This is the essence of the creative, of an individual path that leads to clear contribution. Spirit is not logical. It requires great risk. For me it challenges every surface concept I've ever known. I understand Jung's ideas on shadow implicitly now and in particular his question, "Would you rather be whole or good?"

During this new and awakening cycle I have a dream of particular potency. In the dream I enter a house that is very familiar. I come from a place beyond the house that is lush and green. The house is a single-level building but sits on a high foundation. I've seen this house before. The house is from an earlier era, white and plain with board siding. It stands above an unpaved street on a raised foundation with steps that lead up to the front door. Yet I enter the house not from the door, but from a mystery point at ground level, directly and with ease. I know where I'm going.

Inside the house the rooms are completely bare, no furniture whatsoever. There is an uneasy feeling that permeates this place. I have dreamed of parts of this house before, of children playing and being humiliated here. But in this dream I pass by these spaces with spare notice, beyond the recognition of what they are — dark and hard-used, without windows — that is all I need to know. The room I do enter is large and spacious, plain and framed by repeating windows that surround all three walls of the house. The fourth wall behind me defines the kitchen, which lacks amenities. There's full light in the spacious room before me, not glaring but clear and diffuse. The house is old and well-used. I'm discomfited by the juxtaposition of light, peace and quietude within which lurks a sort of menace.

I step to the windows and look to the grounds outside. Trammeled to naked, hard-packed earth, all is barren. Nothing grows. From a point to my right a black horse races into view. Furious, intense, screaming; it is a thing so feral that all in its path lies in jeopardy. I'm stunned at the sight of it. The ferocity of the raging horse leaves no safe passage out of the house. It whinnies madly and spins. Danger rears in every direction. Sharp hooves flash. Even within the house I feel the pulsing threat, its rampage tearing up the earth. There's nowhere outside the house that is safe, fury from all quarters. Yet I know with certainty that I can't stay.

Within the vacant spaces of the room I begin to look for something that should be here but that I cannot see. This is why I've come. It is as though I sift through layers of old belongings, papers, hidden drawers and boxes that do not exist in time and predate my entry here, the room itself entirely vacant. Whatever I am to find, I do not find it, though it remains palpable. The ferocious energy of the black horse permeates the walls of the house. When I've completed my task I retreat to a back room, very hard used, warped floors, peeling walls. I'm drawn to the room by my need to find an exit that allows escape. Yet it is also curiosity that draws me. I know that I must find a way out, not just for myself, but so I can guide others to safety away from raging destruction — and give warning about what takes place here.

I slip into the bare beaten backroom, an enclosed porch or mudroom. Here also clear diffuse light glows from windows running along two walls. The room is small and narrow with peeling paint, an outside door, single framed windows and all a beautiful fading blue even in the decrepitude. A relaxed familiarity is tangible for me here, a knowing reference point of peace, pleasant normalcy and ease, with a sense of connection that includes but extends beyond the house itself.

Sensing something, I turn. Startle darts through me. A man stands pressed to the corner behind the door I've just walked through. His body is cramped to an extreme posture of defense and threat. Dangerous and as feral as the horse outside, head bald, his narrow, weathered face lined and unshaven, all his features strain to ice blue eyes, huge spirals of madness. He is terrifying. In his hands he has raised a glinting steel ice pick. He stares at me utterly insane — unblinking and at the ready, madness ratcheting. Yet I am not afraid of him. I am very, very wary. I am very, very awake. The black horse rages outside the house. Screaming, it pounds the earth. I look into the spiraling crazed blue of the man's eyes, into his intensity. Then I make my way out the back door. I escape the old yard by slipping away through shrubs that grow close along the side of the house. I know this route. I have always known it, and the way out. I wake from the dream.

The intensity of the dream fascinates as much as it disturbs. Some aspects are obvious, some not. It's a conundrum linked to old history that I'm just beginning to unearth. A cusp of vast understandings, it takes some time to decipher. The horse represents personal power and also the horses lined up in my past — broken, spirited, wild — all of them from childhood on. The house is the ancestral home of my paternal grandfather, a man who in desperation became a line trapper to feed his family during the Great Depression in Michigan. It also links to my great-grandfather, George Weadick, an Irish immigrant-turned-railroad-man in New York. The house is my father's childhood home. I've been to this house in waking life only once — when I was still in my mother's womb. Yet I've dreamed it time and again since infancy. It takes time for me to integrate all these dream layers. For the dream house is also a synthesis. The archetypal or literal scene of my father's unhappy childhood with its many abuses, it is my paternal ancestry home – but it is also the house in Lovelock, Nevada, where the couple was dropped off before terror reigned loose for my friends and me. And it is the house where my brother lived that I stayed in when I left my job at the tourist lodge on the brink of unraveling, after all my locked-up history bent my body in a backward bow — that first call to look back. The dream house is a place of origins, old history and odd promise. At a later date I will find a picture of the original old house of my father's family in Michigan, unnerving the accuracy of the detail that my many early dreams revealed.

The attraction I've felt to archaeology since I was young begins to find its expression. These dreams and this journey, they're all a vast dig.

The horse I must befriend and the crazed man understand. They, too, are composites and synthesis. From the madman I glean aspects of my paternal great-grandfather and grandfather; of my mother's second husband who was so dangerous; of the Nevada rapist; and the murdered woman with her spiraling eyes and her murderer husband. Later, one other will show his face — the one who exists within and beyond them all.

The kitchen in the dream is a place for alchemy. I return to it again and again in other dreams where I prepare meals, create pleasure and nourishment where there is none. A particular symbol, it is a place to evoke transformation. It is a place for the art of alteration. This is the work then, claiming the mystery of the ancestral home, the ancestral ground, freeing the lineage. New levels of conversion and incorporation, each little stage has its own epiphanies and they all lead to big ones that shake my life to the core.

———

In 1988 I travel to New York City for the first time. I've come on business. This trip sets me in place to experience two riveting portals through time that are hard to grasp with my logical mind.

One evening, about to cross a street some distance behind my companions in Soho, I step from a curb to an old cobblestone street and look to my left. The ground disappears beneath my feet, and I'm plummeting downward. The view of an old brownstone neighborhood takes my breath away. The buildings shimmer in late light, time out of time. People wander in clothing of a different era, and voices echo along brick streets. Enormous emotion wells up in me. Sudden and sharp my foot connects to old paving setts, and I stumble in near-fall. When I look again there's nothing to see but a modern cramped alleyway, the cul de sac along a street full of chic, modern shops. My companions disappear into the crowd ahead. Panicked I rush to catch them; say nothing of what I've seen.

I've dreamed the old brownstone neighborhood in repeating cycles since I was a child. I can't fit images and senses together in my mind. I push them away. Yet certainty lingers, etching dusk with a chalky finger.

A few days later, our business nearly done, we wait at a bus stop. Exuberant and restless in the late afternoon, I wander from the curb where my colleagues wait for the bus and approach a shop in a nondescript row of linked business-fronts. A sign above one window is curious. Nonsensical, yet the meaning seems familiar. The shop is closed. I step close to the large, plate-glass window and cup my hands, peering into the darkened interior. Dark objects crowd the space. They waver, unidentifiable. A tremor catches in my chest. The objects suddenly take clear form. African masks by the dozen dissolve into detail, spears and shields huddle along walls. I shudder — and drop as an elevator-like shaft plummets beneath me. The world spins. Solid pavement shocks into form beneath my feet. I stumble back on the modern city sidewalk that holds hard and sure beneath my feet. Light pales. I turn to see only the layered city, just as it was before.

———————

I don't like these experiences when they happen to me. One part of my mind goes into denial, and another part knows that what I've experienced is absolutely real. The collision of opposing realities changes everything. I've looked through one window in time and now another, and I don't know why.

The decision to come to New York on business has been in itself an unusual one. Since childhood, dreams and waking thoughts of this city have trumpeted unease in me. Yet to come here now has felt suddenly right. Why are these things happening? It is one thing to ponder ideas about ethereal experience. It's entirely another to experience them. These experiences are all somehow tied to the doors I've opened, to my progress in making sense of my past. This past, though, these pasts, what are they? I steady unwieldy knowledge as best I can — time has shifted — and return from New York riven yet somehow made more whole. Still, I resist what I've seen, and more, what I feel having seen it.

On my return home two things start to push me hard. A compelling drive to leave my job quickens. This creates a tailspin of extreme doubt and uncertainty. Five years, it's the most security I've had. Yet I'm beginning to understand that there is a fluency in my nature that requires trust in something larger than myself. It requires leaps of faith. And this faith requires everything that is true within me to trust what is being asked of me. I'm learning that right risk takes many forms and must be guided by the intuitive nature of spirit — clear, inborn wisdoms that signal, not in my mind, but within the whole of my body and spirit united. It works something like a metronome on a metric scale, fast or slow or changing, sometimes a beat with a middle cadence, sometimes radical and hard to pace. This is the way it has always been. This was my nature as a child. This is what has been nearly lost to me. All the travesties of my life are linked to missing or going against this prescience — to misunderstanding it, to not honing these skills. Prescience has always been a part of my makeup. I can track my history stone by stone, instance by instance back through the times when I paid attention, when I listened — and to those I did not. I could not control the forces around me as a child. I can take the reins in my hands now. *Moment to moment, present in the now, I can show up. I can respond.*

The second push takes form in the character of New Mexico. I need to travel there. It's a place of old convergence, about claiming myself in some way I can't even conceive. I have no idea how I'll meet the demands being made of me, how I'll survive, how I'll flourish. I know only that I must be true to this part of my nature. Understanding what it means to go against the knowing that guides me, or tries to, is a text on survival. I can look at my past and string the beads.

Leaving my job is incredibly hard. It cuts at foundations that have held me in place to allow enough safety to reclaim myself. Yet life insists, I must leave the sanctuary and lose the refuge to live the life that is truly mine. Comfort and ease take on different form. I learn that clinging to what is known will not result in keeping me happy or well. The shift that needs to come will force its way into being — or make life unpleasant, even to the point of making me ill. This part of my nature asks not only that I re-create myself. It asks that I forgo all things static. This is not like the past — all the propellants that drove me in reaction to life around me — it is not leaping to change out of confusion and pain. It is not running. This is listening. This is response. Resisting these cues means missed opportunity, vitality suppressed and life force thrown into plummet. Resistance leads only to impasse of one kind or another. Still, I struggle. But when life juice and spaciousness dim I know it's useless. Though change at this scale is frightening, if I trust what I'm learning then I must trust this. I learn to let go. Not knowing what's next, I give my boss notice. It's time.

The house where I live has a room on the upper floor, an office like a tower that's ringed round by two walls and panoramic views of the valley. It's a good place for inspiration. It's a place I go to gain a sense of perspective. I contemplate the years I've lived in this house, the deep work I've done here. Supported by solitude and beauty, security and challenge its embrace has brought me home. Here I've begun to make sense of the past. What more is life asking?

That night a new dream comes, one so vivid, so alive it's hard to shake the intensity from waking reality. The dream leads through circuitous pathways and becomes potent when I enter a theater, move to the front row and stand at the edge of the stage near the actors, dancers and action. A childhood friend stands with me. As the production completes I move to a steep stairway leading up to a high penthouse, my friend with me. The penthouse is a tower, a square, and all the living space is in one single room, kitchen on one wall and at the center a modern, sunken salon. All overlooks a vast cityscape. We settle into the luxury of comfortable cushions on the large square of sofas that take up the middle of the sunken room.

Suddenly from outside the windows the arrival of tremendous energy becomes a commanding force that takes over the room. I'm surprised to see a giant dirigible bearing down on the tower. Across sky and cityscape it hovers, massive, billowing with smoke and lightning that flashes and spears. I know this power. I have held it in my mind. But previously I have thought of it as something else — intensified or condensed or purified love. Maybe I thought it would appear as a male walking across the sky: I have experienced it like this before. I both feel and see the great and dangerous approach of this mighty force, as nearer and nearer the dirigible comes, an immense storm gathering all around.

Within the spiking violence and energy my childhood friend is unaware. She has shifted and is now a friend in my current life. She does not see or feel the ominous peril. I feel no fear. Yet I recognize that what is coming is death or the threat of death or potential death. I adjust and prepare deep within myself. But as I ready for impact I realize that this is not death. I do not have to acknowledge or welcome the approaching conflagration as death or even physical menace. I must only recognize something about it, unnamable. In this instant I'm free to move. I prompt my friend to get out of the tower. As we find our way out through the chaos that is breaking through the walls I gather up tools as I go. It takes effort to focus my friend's awareness on the danger. I pull her down the stairs just as the flaming dirigible smashes through windows and walls. As we descend I feel a terrible grief that her dog has not made it out with us, its poor, cindered form lying on the windowsill. In this life-or-death chaos, all we can do is make our way down the stairs and out of the catastrophic hit, away from the crumbling building.

We pass together through many old places.

I'm going to the Southwest, a place she has wanted to go, out into the desert toward a place very dear to me. I don't take anyone to this place, but I guide her to a certain point. There I must leave her, and this, too, grieves me. Yet I must go on alone. She cannot come with me where I'm going. I make my way to a small, worn, dear and hard-used adobe that is long, long ago. This is a place I have always recognized — special, hidden and hard to find. I go in through a black-rimmed screen door that hangs slightly askew. I enter with the ageless welcome of a small, ancient native woman in simple black dress. The conflagration cannot reach here. I pass through a roomful of many children. Though I linger with them forever, I move through another door. I must go quickly, deeper into the house.

The door leads through a passageway to a stable. As I enter, the contrast is vast. Unlike the house the stable is new and solid, though they're closely connected and the same. Through the dark entry I come into a great room of massive adobe walls white and shining. At the point of entry three women who are connected to the conflagration outside focus on three wildly nickering horses, all in a single, broad stall. The three women are trying to capture my attention, to focus me on activity in one dark spot of the stall. They're trying to convince me, show me something about the darkness. I work with them through chaotic energy. When I pull away I break free, just as each of them does in turn. And the stable fills with pulsing gold light. One of the women remains on her knees to work on one last dark spot. She scrubs at the stable floor, cleansing the final stain. All-encompassing goodness penetrates through every cell of my body, spreading across the great spacious room.

Now the women and I play together at being horses, passionate and untamed as I did as a child with my dear friend Leslie, who died when I was 10 years old. I walk to one particular stall to a large, black horse that is very wild and very dangerous, yet I feel no threat from this animal. My back is to the larger room. I face the horse and begin to whinny, nicker and neigh. The black stallion responds with me and to me. The other women do the same with the bay horse and the white. I toss my head, turn to look and see another horse across the room. He is human but he is horse. He sits in an enclosure bent over his hands. I see and sense his hands, but not what they're doing. A low adobe wall blocks the view. There is something very clear and potent about the fact that I can't see his hands, hands that work with great focus.

His head, his hair are golden and lit, shining but not blonde. They are highlighted radiance. He is very beautiful and very handsome. He is a Renaissance man. This intimidates me for a moment. But I nicker, and he responds from within. I feel his response. I feel how I can call to him. The other women are all around me, and we call to him together. We are pressed in concert into the stall among the wildly rearing horses, all calling as though we are one. I know that I have somehow made a personal connection. I toss my head and hear the others whinny, but when I whinny the man recognizes that the sound I'm making is true, it is no longer play. This goes into him. He responds by becoming keenly attentive. I look over my shoulder, and he gives another deep response from within. The energy is flirtatious, deeply erotic and connected. It is authentic. A game that is no longer a game, this is the beginning of a potent dance.

The dance is a dance of power. Facing him now across the huge stable I'm pressed in amongst the three black, bay and white horses. Calling and calling I press into the horses and express their physical force as they rear and neigh. The pitch rises into intensity until I'm called to and answered with the same passion from the man at the opposite side of the stable — though he remains as he was before, head bent to task, attentive and fully engaged in our exchange yet focused on something I can't see. These are mating calls; the neighing and rearing, the nickering power and sensuality grow to a pitch.

Beyond the horses and me and in front of the man the low, white adobe wall divides the space. On the other side of the wall where the man sits in all his elegance the room shows no physical sign of stable or horse. Slender and tall with long multihued hair the man is graceful and beautifully dressed. The wall blocks the view below his chest. Yet I know that he sits at a desk. I know that he works with his hands. The presence of the man is penetrating and physically absolute. The calls between horse, man and myself intensify further — still his head is quietly bent in utter focus. I want to know what he's doing. In particular I want to know what he's doing with his hands. He calls back in total concentration. Though he doesn't move he calls again. We call and we call and we call. The horses call and call. The transference is constant. I think the man must be playing music, a piano. Then I know he must be writing music, at the desk beyond the adobe wall. Allure bursts desire in my heart. All elegance and composure he stands. He walks to the center of the room and turns to face me. Penetrated by his piercing, clear gaze I wake from the dream.

The energy is almost too great to contain. The vitality of the man and the dream and the horses is so strong, it's impossible to separate the physical certainty of his being from my day-to-day waking life.

The mystery I must resolve is who he is, where he is and what he is doing with his hands in an adobe room full of light.

And so comes the change. I give notice at my job in a kind of agony. I have to leave old roles behind, open up options for new and more fruitful opportunity. But I don't know what will come next. Frozen and locked in uncertainty, the days before my job ends tick away. I've forgotten anything but belonging in this place. What else can I do? The woman I work for is thoughtful, smart, strong, funny and kind. She watches me suffer through my last weeks. Dragging a nasty load of anxiety, feeling unworthy, old fears and burdens begin to haunt me and gnash. Finally she offers to speak to her sister, the artistic director of the local dance company who needs an assistant. I'm grateful. I interview, get the job and accept with gratitude and relief. It's a place to start, an office position, but like so many creative endeavors everyone in the company multitasks. They need costume design and help with stage sets. I take this on along with the office demands. It's a track that at least moves on a creative edge.

When the offseason hits for the dance company, the other promise does, too. I travel south toward northern New Mexico to explore old haunts through Utah, arriving at last in Santa Fe. I don't know anyone along the route I travel, on my own in thrilled solo adventure. The quality of the light captures me. Forms, faces, colors, land, mystery, tastes and smells entice. Filled with indescribable wonder, I have little money. Intuition guides me to everything I need. This includes two nights of luxury at a beautiful hotel at off-season rates, something I would never have imagined for myself. One day I return to my car where it's parked along an old, pavered street and find that someone has reattached my loose license plate, fitted a couple of missing bolts to the door and cleaned the windows. No note no nothing, just random kindness. It's like a blessing. When I return home after a dozen adventures I feel connected, remade and inspired.

I begin to make custom story garments, each one a portrayal of land and place and with each there is a story scroll. My path as an artist takes root.

Life accelerates. The tower from the dream has shaken me down, and in truth it's still crumbling. So vivid are my dreams that I learn to step back from literal interpretation. At first I'm certain I'll find my Renaissance man in New Mexico. Then I'm sure I'll meet him in my travels. I think he must be back at home in the valley. I'm convinced he'll walk into my life out of the mystery. But I come to understand this powerful dream man from a very different perspective. He's the embodied expression of my own inner muse, my shining animus, one facet of the gorgeous gem at the crown of my life.

And he is more. In time the new awareness shocks through me with high-voltage realization. The Renaissance man is also the feral ice-pick man in my earlier dream. They are one and the same. The force that spiraled in those crazed eyes in the back room of my ancestral dream house, and in the rage of the dangerous black stallion, is also the creative force when repressed, distorted and bent. Like the three times I asked for help on the night that my inner demons burst loose, here, too, threes are a potent number. The Renaissance man, three women and three horses in the adobe stable are the resolution. Embodied personal power, they are a primal force of history, become creation itself.

33

Life Cycles

Life pushes again. Time at the dance company is rich but transitional, and I move on to claim new ground. This time I don't project all my fears on the change nor do I project all my hopes. I embrace change because I know I must. The mystery has proven worthy. With growing surety I take a job where the demands on my time are simpler, and I'm able to deepen my creative life outside of work. I spark with an artist I meet in New Mexico. As we skirt the edge of one another's lives I come to understand that his role in my life is not as a romantic partner. Rather, he is also an expression of aspects of myself that I must integrate.

Learning to identify the variants between symbolic and literal meaning of the many aspects of life both waking and dreaming is a growing skill I put to good use. It is like any sense; it must be honed and developed, or left unremarked, it atrophies.

Life places me on repeating sweeps through New Mexico and Utah. As I return again and again each journey trails to new channels of beauty, new paths of investigation. I begin to understand that very old patterns woven into these places center in a place in my heart where deepest tenderness, wonder and joy connect in profound synchronicity. And within these lie other patterns that are far less comfortable and long unresolved.

I still live in my mountain pass haven above the sweeping valley in northwestern Wyoming. One night after returning home from travels I'm at a new threshold, wrestling with the traumatic history of my early years. These are the most difficult and vulnerable passages. I leave the house, go out on the land and walk on wild ground. Among three aspen under the full moon and basking in moonlight, I lie down on the earth, listen to quaking leaves and nestle into the smell of pungent plant life. I'm seeking a way with the earth itself to understand what is moving in me. Hints and rushes of life whisper and quicken through leaf and rock, root and stem, life vibrant in the soil beneath. And what I most need to know rises from the earth itself, wisdom immediate and riveting, lost to me until this moment. I understand that the earth cares. It won't save me. That task is my own. But the earth cares. Natural forces of care speak through the earth and its many forms everywhere. Root, bough, river, soil, stone and water, all the living beings that share this place with me are taproots of life force that speak of innate change. They move through me, inspire growing confidence, and carry me deeper into the mysteries of life.

And life continues to call in its mysterious ways. It asks that I take on one more layer of family. My mother, who finally fled from the murderous rampages of her second husband a few years prior, has barely escaped with her life. She is back in Wyoming. We've been reclaiming our relationship ever since. As we slowly discover enough calm and trust to talk about our past I learn that she understands what her many betrayals have cost my brother and me. Though we speak of this history in spare detail, we do speak of it. And with that, new and growing faith is born between us. Yet she buys back the house we lived in during my late teens, a place filled with dismal reminders of loss and horror. We're dismayed by her choice. One day, with internal pressure growing in me to open more transparency with my mother, I ask her to go for a walk. Uneasy, she accepts my invitation. We traverse old neighborhoods that hold much disturbing history and memory. Vulnerable and agitated I tell her what happened after I left home at 19. I tell her about the rape. Brief but exposed I give only the most basic details. Hard for me to say and hard for her to hear, her response is clipped, her burden obvious and inexorable. Yet truth is spoken where it most needs to be heard, truth that was not safe to speak aloud before.

All of my journey to this point to look deeply into myself and bring together the broken and shifting plates of the past are bringing me home to forgiveness. This is rooted deep in forgiving myself — for not doing enough for the woman who died in Idaho and for so many aspects of my life that were out of my control but that I blamed myself for. Through this retrospective lens I'm able to see the many pressures that came to bear on other people in my life also, those who impacted me in negative ways and those who supported me. This allows me to understand and forgive, though never condone, the worst behaviors of my mother, my father, Carl, Will, the man on the Nevada desert and dozens of others. And so, I'm able to knit together fractured aspects of multiple relationships. Through these understandings my father and I also reclaim a loving relationship. I garner empathy and broader perspectives on life, refine my views and pull myself away at last from all the intensity of self-focus that has been so necessary for breaking down the brutalities of the past. What nearly took me apart in the first steps of this process has been outpaced by the power to seek help when I need it and to extend help when it is right. The power of love has returned to my life in its greatest form, integrated with the power of primordial nature. And so the pieces of my past assimilate from within deep psyche into the awareness of my conscious mind. I now have the psychic strength to be present with my mother, whose power could have helped me but didn't and, in fact, worked against me. I'm releasing not only my life from the terror of the past, but my mother from our history as well.

Over slow time she and I share more of our stories and personal experience. I begin to understand her. The loss and confusions of her childhood clarify. I see how the pain of our lives as a family began for her in Mexico and from there never really stopped. And it becomes clear that through all the years during and since that time, my mother has never forgiven my father. Neither has she forgiven her own mother for her imperfect life. She has not forgiven herself. She's made great strides, but still chooses blame and bitterness above forgiveness. Bitterness never stops haunting my mother. Though we make peace on so many levels, she will carry her bitterness for the rest of her life.

I see in my mind's eye a memory of my mother alone with me when I am a little child. My older brother and sister are in school, and I'm too young yet to go with them. My mother and I sit together on the living room carpet, lost in the motion of graphite across paper. I'm drawing in my mother's giant sketchbook. The smell of paper and pencil lead permeate our reverie. Most of my childhood memories of being alone with my mother are like this, rare absorption together in a shared solitude of drawing and imagery. In this surround of focus and imagination, images of Greek myths and varied figures grow beneath my hand, figures and forms that dance through me, alive on the page. Later, when I'm older, I'll imagine my mother as a child focused in similar pursuits. And I'll understand that for her, drawing, reading and most all her reveries were lonely absorption. But my early mastery of image and line, pulsing with life force and emotion, thrill my mother. She enters one of my drawings in a magazine contest. Later when the drawing is returned with a note that says, *This drawing could not have been done by the hand of a child,* she pushes it away. She buries my excitement and questions within her anger and disappointment. And for all her many woes, my mother never claims her earliest dream of herself as an artist. For that and for many things, she remains incapable of forgiving aspects of her life that fall short.

And so my Scorpio mother festers. I learn to love my mother beyond earliest inclinations to love as a child loves. I learn to love her with the wisdom and grace that is possible within a reflective heart. I forgive her much, but her life teaches me one other important lesson — that one who neither forgives nor claims the authentic center of their life has a high aptitude for meanness. I learn a great deal about boundaries with my mother. I learn that I must remain alert, ever wary in her presence. I learn that love, understanding and forgiveness mean neither condoning nor accepting abuse and cruelty. Great damage remains a danger within my mother's constellation, as she continues to wage her long battle for peace.

One day in the midst of these times, I throw a ring out onto the cleansing land at a private place in the valley that has special meaning to me. With all my force I cast the ring away, releasing the vestiges of old history that coil within it. This gesture closes old chapters, an act of beginning anew. Life is exacting greater risk from me. It asks me to let go of my home on the mountain pass and the miraculous place the valley has held for me for so long. This is one resolution of the long journey into my internal wilderness and the sweep of old history. Knowing I will be leaving this place with its radical terrain and vast beauty that I have loved and that loves me, I toss the ring away with all my strength and make a vow. I vow that I will find the means to affect the wild nature of this place and all places in protective, positive ways. This vow could not be more sincere as the ring flies out of my hand. The old is done, the new yet to be.

A few months before the moment that I release the ring, a call comes from an old friend I hadn't seen for several years. I remember the startle of her voice on the other end of the line when I picked up the phone. Distressed and uneasy she wants to see me and talk. She's recovering from a brutal rape that took place the previous year, nearly costing her life.

Soon to leave for one of my treks to New Mexico I plan extra time to see her on my journey south. Not long after, I'm sitting in her house, holding her hand, hearing of her awful ordeal. She tells me then that my own experience in 1971, shared with her many years before, is what saved her life the night she was raped. How I had focused past my fear — how I had connected with my attacker — how I listened for the truth and the tone and the possibility beneath the surface of what was happening — all of this had guided her through terror. My story had helped her know what to do. It helped her survive.

We talk into the late hours of the night. She reminds me of the ring that she wore every day when I first knew her, the ring she was wearing when I hitchhiked to California. The ring that burned on her finger all through the night I was raped and — though I was hundreds of miles away — held her focus on me until I finally returned, and then she understood why. She tells me also of another time of danger, of fear for the safety of her boys. How that time, too, my story gave her knowledge to help pull them all through another ordeal. And then she speaks of memories she has of another life, how as an Aztec priest she lived out the blood lust for human sacrifice. The old passions rise in her as she speaks, lurid and disturbing. I feel hands at my back ... the crumbling edge of a volcano ... endless pitch into darkness.

And pull myself back to listen as she talks of the karmic balancing within her recent ordeal, out of that long-ago Aztec life. And now, after months and months of radical counseling to break down her fear and trauma, she is almost at a point of normal function. She takes off a new ring she's wearing and hands it to me, two serpents that coil around the ring finger. She asks me to accept it as a gift.

In the weeks that follow I wear her ring as she completes her convalescence. And sometime later, at a new transition point that closes many chapters of old, harrowing history for me, I cast the ring away out onto the cleansing land, releasing our story, releasing many stories of old pain and disturbance. My vow of care and protection arcs with the ring through the sky and passes on.

Life continues to burgeon and shift. I give up the place that has been the foundation for the deepest work of my life   I leave my mountain pass home. I leave the valley. First I travel north into Canada to explore the history of a great uncle and aunt. These two were the original visionaries and founders of the Calgary Stampede, Florence and Guy Weadick — iconic myths from my childhood. From running away after each of their mothers died, they met during their early years in vaudeville, where they evolved into world-renowned acts in trick roping, riding and shooting on the Wild West show circuits. Their vision of a meeting of the cultures of the plains became an annual celebration that evolved into the Calgary Stampede. They both died in the 1950s, bigger than life. I want to learn about them, not by their fame, but through their everyday lives. I search them out in the old communities where they lived in Alberta: Longview, High River and at their old Stampede Ranch on the Highwood River. I find something of my roots, artifacts of family and history and people still alive who knew them. I learn that Florence's father, a lawyer from the late 1800s into the early 1900s, did pro bono work all his life for the rights of tribal peoples. Discovering this is a revelation that brings me to tears. I learn more about my Uncle Guy, who traced our genealogy back to Rob Roy in Ireland, though he was horrified at the thought of being related to a "horse thief." So he looked no further past that myth of history, to parse fiction from truth and fact.

I don't yet realize that these lives of my aunt and uncle are laying down one cairn after another, connecting me with a longer reach across history and time. In the lodge of their Stampede Ranch I unwittingly cross a thread that ties to the old hunting lodge back in Wyoming, the place where I worked and became ill when I was 20. The hunting lodge at Pahaska, built in 1904, has a connection to the lodge at the Stampede Ranch, built in 1920. Each lodge sits at the center of lives founded on Wild West shows that mixed cultures of the plains from the 1800s. Those old chamber pots stored in the room of the lodge at Pahaska sat at a thin spot ... a gap between places and times, extending beyond illness and death.

My Canadian journey connects deeper knowledge of family to apertures of earlier eras and hidden memory — cracks opening hints and seams into lives that pulse along thresholds of convergence, cusps on the lost edge of time. Time that flows back like a river ... to histories old and worn that begin to flesh out — histories beyond those of my blood relatives — yet histories tied directly to my life ... These parallel lives move in a restless flow, linked through time.

———

In a nearly forgotten period in the 1700s I live in the Canadian territories as a mixed-blood trapper traversing the Rockies. That time and its wilderness run deep in old remembrance. Overflowing within this life are the love and respect I hold for my full-blood mother. My father, a rough and brutal French Canadian trader, parses blankets and oddities to native peoples in trade for skins and whatever else he can squeeze from their lives. I despise him and his treatment of my mother. For me as a mixed-blood, bigotry, mistreatment and conflict play out with painful frequency, forcing me to walk between worlds ever wary. My natural inclination for solitude adds to the desire to avoid people and their habitations. I travel the wild continent, most often alone, until my life siphons into the ethers of lost history.

Time flows, and the thread picks up again. Born in 1890 to a family of French Canadian ancestry living in Los Angeles, and deeply sensitive as a boy, I mature as a painter, poet and textile artist by the early 1900s. Flamboyant, even dashing in my looks and style, I am also shy by nature and lack confidence. Because of this my life is full of uncertainty — though I push the edge of cultural norms with my wife and friends. In my early 30s I travel to Mexico out of a desire to be involved with the open-air art schools that evolve during Mexico's cultural revolution, a renaissance of its native talent. Less than two months after my arrival I die a sudden, violent death from smallpox.

In an earlier life I live an opposite migration. An idealistic Franciscan priest alongside my twin brother in Mexico we follow our calling among Spaniards, natives and mixed cultures of the time. We travel to a mission in what will later become California. There I die at the hands of the natives, after a plague of smallpox wipes out many of their people.

Deeper yet in unfathomable time I work clay and develop a method of glazing my pots that transforms the durability, utility and beauty of my vessels. I share these techniques with my people and other wandering traders, improving the lives of many. My life passes in rich connection and peaceful satisfaction, dedicated to my family, my people and the inventiveness that lies within clay's endless possibility.

Back and back and back time flows, unmeasured. I feel myself female. I tumble and plunge into a crater at the push of hands at my back. Old terror carves as I pitch into blackness. The joys and sorrows of many lives pierce through my heart as they coalesce around me, sacrifice.

And there are three lives that intersect in less conspicuous ways. They lie at the hub of what I most came to resolve in this time. We do what we do by cycling through, touched by fame or infamy or quietude that in time shred to nothing, but the need to release or make peace. And when the time to make peace arrives at its helix, we are either a haunting or we are haunted — until our task is complete. Our "good" lives sing us across time and our "bad" leave us unresolved. But in truth there is no life that plays out in exactness of one or the other, neither good nor bad, light nor dark. Lives are a synthesis. Multifacets. They are symphony. They are compost. They are clay.

It is the early 1500s and I trek as a slave through vast swaths of what are now portions of the southern United States and Mexico. The trek carries me across other lives older still that lie buried deep beneath soils like echoes outside of time, in what we now call Mesoamerica. As a male slave with midnight skin in the 1500s, from my roots and my nature and the conditions of my life at that time I'm skilled in many ways. In particular I'm skilled with the ability to read energies and the life force around me, skilled to interpret them. Male in a time when conquering means the usury treatment of people's lives (is it any different in much of the world now?) and in particular usury treatment of women and slaves, my talents serve me. I live a complex life rife with conflict. This does not free me from accounting and being accounted for in later time. I'm used and misused. I use and misuse. I die at the hands of the people of the region, caught in a moment of arrogance, misunderstanding them as they misunderstand me.

Time slips, and I live again as an effective leader of my people in the same lands. I grow in stature and power. Acute sensibilities are once again natural to me, abilities to read and draw forth energies mysterious and not of this world just as in other lives. In other times and places these capacities are called shamanism. In this life I play with power. I work for the cause of my people, for our liberation from the tyranny of invading cultures. In repeating cycles and in the face of many atrocities I'm consumed with hate for our invaders. And in time I abuse my power. The fate of my people hangs by a thread. The cause is critical. I look aside to allow for the murder of a relative on suspicion that he has betrayed our cause. His life is taken expediently toward a higher purpose. And though I do not kill him with my own hands I do not interfere and therefore condone the taking of his life. I could have saved him. A life taken is a life to be accounted for. This will bear down on my soul across time. I die of illness and uncertainty about the role I have played for my people and the outcome of their fate, though together we've changed the course of history.

In the deep south of what is now the United States there's an old plantation. Of all the pain and joy and beauty and balancing of lives, this may hold the agony that runs deepest for me. Pain runs together through time, the old with the new and in truth they are the same. I'm a little child on the plantation when my parents are lost, then a girl, then a maiden and a young woman. I'm raised with two sisters and cared for by a man who dominates us but adores me. Smart, educated and privileged, I mature to acute awareness of the inequalities and travesties of slave life. Hungry for justice, believing in balance, I work to create open-air classrooms for the slaves and their children. I have a natural acuity for sensory exquisiteness that opens into what I call spirit. As in the thread of other lives, the skills of a sensitive have different words and different concepts in each time and culture, variant expressions of the same thing.

There is a man on the plantation who also shares the capacities of a sensitive. He's a house slave. We work side by side in secret, moving our shared vision for the education of the plantation people into full bloom. Whatever name might be applied to the quality that moves through both of us in our independent natures — this spirit — it becomes a palpable presence most powerful when we come together, permeating the community and grounds of the plantation with transcendent grace. Our work progresses and expands. He is beloved of me as dearest friend and like a brother, as dark as I'm fair with my red hair and translucent skin. Even now hundreds of years past, the potency and allure of our vision, our planning, the new levels of learning and artistry that we apply to inspire our people transfer across time — something I feel with breathtaking strength and sharpness when I dare to open that old portal at all. More than any of this and woven throughout all of it is the love.

For a time, my guardian indulges and allows me my efforts. As I come of age near the time of claiming my inheritance and therefore my independence two things occur. He begins to chafe against my work with the slaves. He demands that I hold back, then that I stop. Naive with privilege and the success of our efforts I continue. He cajoles then warns. I ignore him. Aglow in the potency that wraps the plantation time out of time we are blind, my friend and I. And someone betrays us.

When my guardian threatens me without saying why, I become stubborn. One night during a tense discussion over a meal at the dinner table his sons grab me, haul me to the attic and demand I recant all my efforts. Dismayed, unable to comprehend their ill intentions, I lose my temper. They throw me to the floor. With stunning force a whip lashes across my back. Blind with fury and rage and tantrum I lash back with sharp insult. The whip bites and slices. And goes on and on, bite and slice and bite until I'm subdued. They leave me to stink in my blood and disbelief through the night. The rustlings in the house below, outcries to silence sweep throbbing and dull through my misery. In shock by morning I'm taken from the attic, cleansed and bathed, dressed and fed. I think the worst is over. I imagine a way and a place to continue the work I care so much for. I want to find my friend. But I'm settled on the front seat of a bedecked wagon for a family outing. Stomach churning, pain severe, I strain through consternation to imagine how and where my friend and I will flee. The wagon arrives in a clearing, among dozens of our neighboring families. Within a breath my beloved friend is lynched before me. Everything from here is broken memory. I never stop grieving him. My life ends with his. This agony will haunt me through centuries.

There is one life hard to locate in time. I live as a broken woman, dark and worn and prematurely aged, living on the streets of New York half-mad with pain and memory that I cannot tame — terrified, barely surviving. My life blinks out in decrepitude and misery.

Agony and then joy, beauty and then suffering, life swings on a pendulum. In a continuum one act links to another, though rarely in a straight line. History is always seeking its justice, finding its resolution. What matters is not whether we view our lives through the perspective of long cycles, as I do — or whether we view our lives as the short cycles of years, months, weeks, days, the hours of a single life or the bloodlines of our current families. *What matters is that we learn. What matters is that we love. What matters is that we reclaim and redeem. What matters is that we forgive.*

In some cycles we're restful. In some, we're lazy. In others we take on great work. Cycles are always reforming, cycles forever rebalance — cycles are always calling us home. Can we transform our lives, with all their gifts and travesties, into clarity, kindness and understanding? Can we diminish our fears and betrayals through love? What becomes of us if we cannot? Must we swing forever on pendulums of damage and undone history?

There is a theory in quantum physics of the presence of 11 parallel universes. Chaos and string theories offer new modalities for understanding our world that are nothing like the world we seem to live within, with its appearance of solidity and certainty, its hard and fast rubrics of "fact."

The accomplished biologist Rupert Sheldrake underlines these theories. Sheldrake offers a point of view that challenges modern science by proposing that all natural systems inherit a collective memory. His theories of *the presence of the past* and *fields of morphic resonance* posit larger understandings, perspectives that make sense of shifts in time and reality that I've experienced all my life. Sheldrake's work speaks to the variability masked beyond appearance. Naturalists learn to see and read in exquisite detail the land and geology of a place, the patterns of living beings who inhabit it. So, too, Sheldrake's work speaks to what is possible when we hone subtler senses to focus our attention and intention, bringing new knowledge to play on other parallel dimensions of time.

In 1989 I'm just beginning to tie all these threads. I'm at the beginning of untangling these old histories. I still know so little. During my Canadian visit, for the first time in my life, the hearts of my uncle, my aunt and her father open in mine. I sit on their graves on a sunny morning, and I understand each of them in both their great and flawed character. Through them I know myself in new ways. Expanded yet more intimate with life and myself, my time in Canada is bringing me home. And though I don't know it yet, I'm about to embark on another Canadian adventure that will take me home in ways I do not imagine. Stories thread trails in a hundred directions.

I return to Jackson but leave on a chance journey almost immediately with a friend. I break the celibacy that I've kept for three years, understanding that it's time but without knowing why. This trip will test my skill in relationship. It will be a test run for what is to come.

We travel west in my friend's well-stocked van. We camp and wind our way across Idaho, Oregon and travel on to Washington and the Olympic Peninsula. After a day and night in the Hoh Rainforest we visit a marine facility where I'm astonished and undone in the presence of a beluga whale for the first time. Some ancient recognition keens as we stare into each other's eyes. Along rocky beaches, below towering coastal cliffs, immersed in the ocean wild and old cultures of the Pacific Northwest I trek with my friend. We decide on a ferry trip from Port

Angeles to Victoria, and once we dock we drive farther and farther away from the imprint of human habitation.

A special place, my friend says.

I settle into harsh beauty opening around us, rocked by the hum of the van and the open, coastal sky. The land here runs flat to water's edge, sand to water. Curiosity piques. I sit up in my seat.

And old currents rise in a twist, surging through channels of time. Some coil of the past spreads through confusions of stimuli. We pull to the end of an eroded road and can go no farther. I'm suddenly alert to a feral presence that weaves in this place, some unnamed thing coming into form around us. A vortex begins to spin. Tense, uncertain I turn to my friend. Surly and curt he gets out of the van. I open my door and slide to the sand. I know it then. *This place, it's imbued with the same force that was present in 1971* — both at the beach in California and in the desert in Nevada.

Anything could happen.

Edgy and unsure, I feel a current twining through every movement, every breath of air that passes around us. Stretched between poles, vigilant to the distancing disregard taking hold in my friend, every instinct I have is sharp and sniffing the wind. We move down a dip in what's left of the rutted road that has turned now to trail. I follow through a copse of tall, waving willow. With a shudder I feel what speaks through this place — wherever we are, I'm on my own. We break out onto a beach along harsh, wild coastline. Nothing breaks the sand running flat to open ocean that pounds beneath vast sky. Ancient life sparks electric. My breath is lost to it.

Crossing the sand to a massive beached drift log I sit down in the face of immense, endless power. My friend sits next to me but stands again a moment later. Abrupt and careless he walks away. Sure in his knowledge of place, dismissive of my innocent confusion he strides to a bend in the coastline and disappears. I sit on the weathered, damp log and locate my cells in the enormity breathing around me. I force myself to stand. I walk along the waterline in the opposite direction, trying to get my bearings. Fearful and uncertain I feel compelled to make play at the edge of the lapping surf. Awkward I step out into cold water, climb on a slick rock, lose my balance, catch myself and wobble from one slippery, uneven outcrop to the next, moving further out away from the beach. I'm pushing against something that holds me back and I know it, against something that has held me back forever. My sense of play becomes fierce as I step from one precarious jagged slippery rock to another, further out into shallow, breaking waves. I struggle between falling and standing. A primordial power overtakes me. Waves heave and air gnaws. Overcome with the harsh, endless beauty before me I rise slowly, until I stand fully upright. I breathe the raw power. My cells split into fracturing particles. I let danger and cruel intention twist however they will. Frail and human, I lean in. Facing into the wind that blows endless off salt water, an upsurge of pulsing spray breaks over me. Searing knowledge passes through me. Wordless, amorphous it shatters through all form. The primeval extends into its eternity. Natural lightness expands, encapsulating my life in one wild breath.

In a single hour of shadow and light, I am reformed. The vortex funnels and slows. Enormous peace courses through me into wholeness. I know that some undone part of the past is now complete. The travesties and barbarities of that long-ago night on the Nevada desert are finished.

I am released from them forever.

And so it is. One penetrating night on the edge of vast ocean prepared me for what I would face in 1971. And one testing hour of wind and wild coastal immensity free me on a wuthering Canadian strait almost 20 years later. *Just in time.* I hear and feel the phrase come again. Just in time. I do not know what it means.

A few days later, when I return to Jackson, I walk a balance beam between where I am and where I belong.

I leave for New Mexico a short time later, but as I make my way south I'm called back to Jackson by a friend in need, so I return and settle in for a couple of weeks. I costume chamber musicians for a special event. I am now in place to fulfill another crossroad that lies within the valley. In the synchronicity of interweaving events an old acquaintance arrives and looks me up. It's a mystery how he has found me, since so few people know I've returned. We talk only briefly, but we're now set on a course neither of us can imagine that lies further ahead.

Seasons shift. It's late autumn when I'm freed from the responsibilities that called me back to Jackson. I'm offered an artist residency at a ranch on the southern end of the valley, and I work there on a commissioned jacket made from the skins of elk that fed a friend through pregnancy. This keeps me in the valley through the winter. I'm flown to San Francisco for fabrics for other commissioned garments. I help out friends, manage a store for a few months, complete the season. Spring blooms into early summer. It's time to leave.

Again my plan is New Mexico, but I go west before I go south to visit a family I worked for years earlier. They've begged me to come. Once I move south I don't know when I'll see them again, so I make the extra effort. Life is full of placements in time. In Halfway, Oregon, in a jewel-like valley, juxtaposed again for the unexpected, I'm asked to stay on to run their bed and breakfast. I resist, but something tells me that despite appearances, this opportunity is right. I base my agreement on two weeks away in September so I can make an exploratory trip south to New Mexico. I take on the B&B. I drop notes to friends and family to let them know where I am and include invitations to visit. A return note arrives from the old acquaintance that looked me up in Jackson the previous fall. At the close of Steve's script he suggests that I can't be where I'm going because I'm only *halfway* there. I laugh and laugh. What does he know?

The B&B is a destination-only, off-the-map place with its old Victorian house on a farm at the edge of the Wallowa Wilderness. We put up preserves, harvest eggs, chickens, fruits and wild berries. Putting food by underlines a timeless quality that is part of life here. I add new, luscious breakfasts to the guest menu and offer dinners a couple of nights a week. It feels like a step back in time. Setting the mood for the guests and meals is a pleasure. Two men close to the family make fast claim on my friendship. They both live on the other side of the state but come and go in irregular intervals. One, Michael from Portland, a bit hair-brained but smart and funny, is of Basque heritage. His humor is always welcome respite, and I adore him. We rove through wide-ranging discussions and philosophical musings that bond our friendship. The second is Peter, from the coast, a horseman and one-time commercial fisherman. He turns up hauling a horse trailer and often takes me out riding. I play it to the nines, wearing vintage riding clothes and on occasion ride his Tennessee Walker. We explore the heaven of the great wide open beyond the farm's reach and across the land above the Hells Canyon of the Snake River. It is a mood out of time. We grin, debate and laugh. Once a month when no one else is around I enjoy a fine cigar and scotch outside in the evening air, feeling into the ways this place fits under my skin. I ponder many questions that arise about why I'm here and how long I'll stay.

As late summer arrives and spills toward fall, a slower time for business, both Michael and Peter return to the B&B with greater frequency. I'm always glad to see them. Yet somehow their paths rarely cross. Michael and I laugh uproariously, play hooky and drive into Baker for the occasional evening meal. Peter and I explore the valley on foot, on horseback, talk exhaustively and compare old history. And in time Peter and I fall for each other. One afternoon with no guests in sight and the place deserted, we lie in afternoon sun pooled on the sitting room floor. Peter asks me to tell him about old loves in my life. I'm caught speechless — it is Brad who comes first to my thoughts. I hold Brad's memory close but do not speak of him. I meander through other loves, stories and time. I ask Peter the same question. Who has he loved? Divorced, a long time coming, children grown, still untangling the knots, after a while he has little more to say. He prods me again.

"There's something more," he says. "You're preoccupied. Tell me."

I've never talked about my feelings for Brad at length with anyone. I can't find my way to words. Finally I lie across Peter's chest, sink into tenderness and for the first time the words come spilling. How I met Brad in Montana, the adventure of it, how young we were, my first true love, the agony of loss. I tell Peter how Brad died. I speak of the terrible heartache. Words fall away and vibrate the air between us. I wait for Peter's words. I wait for comfort, for understanding. But they do not come. There is only silence and the dreadful ache, a vise in my chest.

There's no solace, no words at all. Peter lies still, silent.

Confused and beginning to spin on the torque of exposure, for the first time the final details of the end of Brad's life cross my lips. I tell Peter about the call that came out of nowhere, the crushing news, the horrific coldness of its delivery. I recognize all at once how close that experience was to the way my mother told me about my best friend, Leslie's, death when I was 10 years old. In the agony of association, momentarily transfixed I lie on Peter's chest, distraught. There is still no response from him. He is still beneath me. My words of bleak devastation siphon away into deepening dismay.

Peter lies more silent than the room itself. I pull away, trembling, distressed by his coldness. How could I so misjudge and expose myself this way? I start to get up from the floor. And then I see Peter's face. Chalk white under my gaze, he chokes and flinches. Fear shoots through me.

"What's wrong?" I ask, reaching out to him, head spinning. "What is it?"

He shakes his head and convulses.

Panicked, I think he's having a heart attack. I bend over him. "Are you ... are you ill?" I ask. He shakes his head. He pushes up to sit, his back to me. "What is it? What can I do? What is wrong?" I waver.

"Let's not talk about this," he chokes, his head falling into his hands.

Concern swarms out of me, paired with bewilderment and pain. I reach out to comfort him. He freezes, flinching away. Not understanding what I've done, in shock and stricken, I reach out once more. He huddles in on himself. Numb with betrayal too sharp to bear, I pull back and away.

Peter turns to look at me like a ghost from the abyss of doom. I shrink back. He blanches whiter still as he looks into my face. A hard shudder breaks over him. And then it comes.

"It's not you," he croaks. "It's not you. I'm sorry. I'm so sorry." His head falls back in his hands. I lay my hand on his chest, and his story pours out. "Years ago I was driving ... at night ... I came up on some hitchhikers ... they just ... loomed ... out of pitch darkness ... thumbs out ... I couldn't stop, only swerve ... I hit one of them ... I ... killed him."

Knifing pain daggers between us, insufferable. I swallow, staring. Filaments of light and shadow sift through the room. Life dangles on a thin stark thread. A terrible trembling comes over me. We stare at each other. I hear my voice strangle.

"What are the odds of this?" I manage to ask. Dumb with impossibility, he shakes his head.

One chance for peace, *one chance*, and we claim it. We hold each other. There are few words that can meet either of us in this place. We're the closest thing to understanding and forgiveness that either of us will ever have.

————

The circuitous pathways of our comings and goings, the convergences of our lives, are less about who did what to whom and when but about waking to the results of actions that are redeemed when we understand. It's not the exactitudes and particulars of each life that are important, but the essential nature of what the lineage of time and experience hold unresolved. Waves set in motion a long time ago, lifetimes ago, are patterns I came in this time to release: they are waters I came in this life to calm. Through every companion we find our way forward, moving toward resolution and discovery; opening the gates of the many ways we can find and offer release ... yet each of us must claim our own salvation.

34

Nathan

The strange and baffling mosaic of life with its mix of beauty and pain, mystery and wonder carry us on into late summer. Another pattern begins to clarify. Days breathe into fall. Filaments of understanding spread and plait.

Peter comes often. Michael continues to pass through and linger. I revolve through the tiny community of Halfway, giving help to the elderly when the guys aren't around. One woman gifts me an antique, purpled-glass cigar humidor under the covetous eyes of an antique dealer, who haunts the steps of her house. The guys laugh when they see how much I treasure it.

And Peter teases me about other things, like my hidden desire for commitment. "Just like all the others," he says. "Women. You're all alike."

But that's his projection. It's not what I'm after. It slowly dawns on him that I just love him and life and that's enough. This is something new in his world, a woman who isn't trying to pin him down. Summer swells into fall and begins to drop away. It's time for my trip south to New Mexico. Peter has commitments back in Eugene. But Michael has signed up for a course in Loveland, Colorado. He asks if I can time my travel plans to give him a ride there. Thrilled at the chance to show some of my favorite places to my good friend, I sketch out a map that will take us through the Black Rock Desert of Nevada, where at night you can lie on the desert pan and see the arc of the earth beneath the majesty of endless stars. Our route flows from there into Utah.

So Michael and I hit the road. I quickly discover that he's not really camp-worthy. He's also caught up in his head with constant mental abstraction. I want him to join me, put his feet on the ground and truly see with his eyes, experience the breathing body of the earth. Though we have ongoing discussions about the importance of all of this — grounding in his body in each moment and the never-ending miracle of life — I see that for him it's all just mental gyration that he rarely applies. And though it takes effort to get him to notice the world past the windows, to take in the spectacular strange country and more, still, for him to take it in through his pores, alive in his senses — What are those? he asks, ever the comedian — he does in time start to see and feel the places we travel in a new and real way.

Within all of the changing miles and vistas we have a blast. He loves to eat, so we stop for Basque meals and link his ancestors to our adventure. He gets a close, personal tour of some of my favorite secret sites across Utah. Outside of Moab a massive downpour cements our friendship through a mysterious night of rain and shelter where land and rare water sink into our bones, shared communion that reach at last past his mind. As rain pours and breathes through place and wild, history and time, Michael makes the passage into new realization about being present to the world and its wonders. It's a beautiful moment that expands. His awe spans the rest of our travels, carrying alongside our laughter and humor.

When I drop him off in Loveland I pause to put in two calls to friends in Denver. One is leaving the next day for the Middle East. The other is Steve, the man who visited me in Jackson and later sent the note letting me know I was only halfway to my true destination. He invites me to stay the night in his guest room, and the three of us go out to dinner. They're both wildly flirtatious with me, which is a curiosity since I've known each of them as friends for many years. Steve and I go hiking the next day. Rained out of our day hike early, we drop back to the city, clean up and take the trolley downtown. Outrageous, silly and full of ourselves at the Denver Art Museum, we skip through exhibits like children and come upon a simple rhyme tucked among artifacts, blankets and pottery in an exhibit of Southwest artifacts.

"The little red spiders and the little gray horned toads, together they make the rain to fall, they make the rain to fall ..."

The rhyme becomes a chant, a little mantra that stays with us as we frolic and play through hours of happy exploration in the urban landscape. The freedom to play in a city in joyous abandon is a small revelation for me. So many years of unwinding my past, and these moments give me a bellwether, marking how far I've come and my new way forward.

The child I was has come home at last, and the woman I am rings clear. Lost fragments knit together, I'm at ease in myself in ways I haven't been since earliest childhood.

Steve dwells on how much we have in common with our shared Wyoming roots. We finish the day over dinner then some dancing at an old jazz club in lower downtown. I'm glad I've reclaimed his friendship. He invites me to stay another day, but I'm ready to head south. When I get out my map reality hits me. I've spent so much time on Michael's tour and the extra day with Steve that by the time I get to New Mexico I'll have no time to linger, deepen and explore. It's a long drive back to Oregon. This has been a good trip. It's enough. I snuggle in for sleep in Steve's guest room, happy.

I have a strong dream. In the dream I'm awake in the guest room. I've painted the walls a brilliant, pristine white and clean slightest impurity from the surface of the glass of the east windows until they are sparkling, crystalline and perfectly clear. The windows iridesce with light that shines from the other side, so radiant and so clean that I understand that the windows themselves are portals. Two windows. Two portals. I come and go through these portals with great care. Something very pure waits on the other side, and when I pass through there's a deep exchange that I carry back with me, a message beyond words held within mystery. The dream is filled with simplicity, wonder and awe.

I wake the next morning feeling content and filled with well-being. Steve leaves for work. I leave for Wyoming. The dream returns to my thoughts on the drive north, sudden and bright. A vibrant dream, more filled with life force than the waking world of day, it shimmers. I can't fathom its meaning. I feel a new spaciousness that it's opened inside of me. And I feel again how lucky I've been on this trip. So many friends, life is good. As I reach Idaho and begin the drive through the long hours and miles across its width I begin to feel a turning. My thoughts arc back to Steve. I smile and move my thoughts on to other things. But they drift back again to Steve, stronger.

This pattern continues through many miles. The more I resist, the more my thoughts return to him with growing affection. I've never considered us as romantic partners. We're worlds apart in interests and nature. I try to shake away the distraction. I think ahead to the B&B and work waiting for me there. But the growing feelings have a life of their own. I quit arguing with myself. I pull over along a coursing river to take a break from driving. I let the feelings just be. Confusing yet somehow clear as a bell, they ring in my heart. It's too strange. I can't make this fit in my life. I remember the dream in the night. And I remember Steve taking his Tarot deck to work to offer readings to some of his work colleagues. I think, *why not?* I'm distracted and have a deck in the car. So I throw a spread on top of pine needles and warm earth. I'm sure this will clear my head of any romantic projections. Then I'll get on my way.

I turn over the cards one by one in lazy sunshine with low expectation. And find myself riveted, open-mouthed. When every card has been turned, I stare. All 10 out of 10 cards is a Major Arcana. Every card presents immense and powerful potency. The Tower puts me on notice that my life is realigning with new electricity and intent. The old is toppling to allow a restoration and renovation of the new. Every card tells me to pay close attention and attend to this relationship.

I'm stunned. I can't imagine myself into this. We're not a match — all of our friends would say so. He lives in Denver. I'm in Oregon *halfway to somewhere*, it's true. But Denver is not my goal. I shake off the implications. I get back in the car and drive. The sweetness of the dream, the power of what I've been feeling drop back into quiet presence. They've been seen. It's enough. I let them sleep. I know these kinds of waters. If there's anything to them, time will make sense of it. I'm in no rush.

Back in Halfway I take up the reins of the B&B. Hunting season is coming on. Committed as I am to what I've put in motion here, the old, heavy energy comes suddenly present, pressing in. I think I just have to rearrange how I handle the hunting crowd. But when I focus on that, real darkness descends out of full light. I think it's the season, winter coming on and a different chafe. I think it's a dozen things. But no approach to the weighty energy brings the shift that always comes when I get clear on what lies beneath it, whatever it is I most need to know. I can't get New Mexico out of my thoughts.

Every effort regarding the B&B turns to sudden disruption. Nothing runs smoothly. Every task I take on spirals toward problems and disarray. The heaviness starts to drag. I feel no inspiration. Nothing is simple. After a couple of weeks I realize it's useless to keep pushing forward. I turn toward quietude and deep reflection. And I see that my heart no longer belongs to this place, it never really has at a deep level. Everything is off-key because my time here is done. Life's reasons for bringing me here have been fulfilled.

It's a bad idea to stay on. Avoiding this knowledge will subsume any effort into distortion and problems.

When I acknowledge just this much I get a reprieve. When I focus on New Mexico it's like a light switching on — bright and steady. Michael has gone back to Portland. Peter is in Idaho visiting friends. We're all pulling apart. I can feel it. I surrender. I turn toward a plan to leave for New Mexico. I give notice to my employers. I've sent wintergreen from the Wallowa Mountains out to friends with preserves I've made from farm plums and apples, one box to Steve, who has kept in touch. When I send word of my plans out to my family and friends, Steve's is the first response. He calls fast with an invitation. *Why not come to Denver and drive with him to St. George, Utah, to spend Christmas with his family?* he wonders. We can include a tour through northern New Mexico to scope out my plan. I sit with this as the days tick off the calendar, and in time I accept his invitation. It will be a great way to explore where I'm going.

When I leave, I go through Boise to see Peter to say good-bye. Everything I know to trust has opened up a clear stream south. I'm focused now. I totally miss it when he reaches for a stronger connection. I believed him when he said he didn't want to be tied down, and it's not what I'm searching for.

A new die has been cast.

My arrival in Denver is met with champagne and celebration. A few days of meeting Steve's friends and we're off. Our trip is a random, gorgeous adventure that includes Santa Fe. We're falling in love. By the time I meet his family, word is out. They tease us unmercifully and fold me into their ranks. It's an enchanting, easy week. Pressed for a contribution to Christmas dinner I make apple dumplings for everyone. His mom saves hers for a private moment alone and tells me later that eating it transported her back to her childhood. I couldn't be happier.

A deep river is forming, the channels of our lives shifting to a new course. As we laugh and play life pulls, steady and true, into a new country of the heart.

Steve and I strike out for Taos, visiting wild, unkempt ruins that are favorite places of mine. We both love these explorations. Our common ground expands. We visit friends and meander through old northern New Mexico to explore possibilities for my return, then head back to Denver weighing and measuring options.

Once in Denver Steve presses hard on the fact that many of the places in northern New Mexico where I could find work run on a tourist season. That won't kick in for several months. He asks me to stay on in Denver. It's hard for me to settle in to even the thought of living in a city but I start to research intentional communities. I find some leads on cohousing. I tell him I'll stay. I launch an effort to gather friends at Ojo Caliente in New Mexico to explore the idea of creating a community together. A group of us come together there in April 1991. We start out our time there by taking in the mineral baths and get invited to the studio of a local potter that the guys have met on the men's side of the baths. When I stick my finger by accident through a pot he's building, the potter tells me the clay is calling me. Back at Ojo Caliente, we deepen as a group and exchange thoughts about what creating community together could look like. I miss Steve's efforts to throw our discussion off-track through the many ways he distracts the group. Late that night when it's just the two of us he makes me laugh and laugh. When we separate from our friends I go back to Denver in a happy haze, feeling that this group or some other will develop a strong working plan. A few weeks along, and I start to feel ill. I'm pregnant.

Shocked, grappling with the enormity, I'm stunned as the news sinks in.

Steve doesn't miss a beat, "This brings up the M word, you know."

"M word?" I stammer. "What M word ... oh, you mean mother?

"No," Steve says, smiling, "The other one. Marriage."

Marriage? Marriage has never been in my plans. Neither one of us has ever been married. Reeling, I try to fit the pieces together. I can't stay in Denver. I remind him of that. I'm looking for a small, close community. Putting down roots but not here. He tells me he just needs five years, five more years to finish his work in the city. We can search for where we'd like to live during that time. He just wants to complete what he's started. He wants this and convinces me it's good. I decide I can manage five years. So we make a vow — five years in Denver and then we'll move to a smaller place. I surrender to our lives together.

I can't settle with the idea of getting married in Denver, so we decide on informed elopement in Montana, where we have friends. Many years later I'll understand something that I cannot yet see at this point in my life — Montana is where I met Brad, a place that holds a hub of loss that still lies buried within me, too great to articulate at a conscious level. And it is here I surrender to love once more.

We visit my mother, her third husband, and Steve's parents on the way north. Everyone is ecstatic. Because of our age, both 39, we've had an ultrasound. We know we're having a son. This time in my life accelerates the deepening bond with my mother. Marriage to Steve takes history another leap forward, and motherhood takes it another leap still.

We drive to a ranch in the Blackfoot Valley managed by friends we both know. The site for our marriage is spectacular. Sandhill cranes dance in view of a thousand-year-old ponderosa pine where we'll make our wedding vows the next day — and then make them again at the meeting of the waters of the Blackfoot and Clark Fork rivers to honor the strictures of our marriage license.

The night before the wedding, everything in place, a weighty feeling comes over me. I can't shake it. We go to bed, and I lay awake restless, thinking it's some detail, something last minute I've forgotten. I think it's the excitement. I think it's overwhelm. So much change. I think maybe I'm getting cold feet. Nothing shakes loose the weight that cloys and spins. A deep and impossible sorrow like a high-wire whine clings through the night. I finally fall into uneasy sleep.

At 2 a.m. a telephone rings somewhere in the house. Our friends bring the phone to our room. It's for Steve. It's his sister. His mother has had a massive heart attack. She's survived it but barely. Though I feel we should drive south for Wyoming as soon as it's light, Steve wants to hold to our wedding plan. A few hours later he calls to ask for his father's advice. His father gives us his blessing.

So that's what we do. The next day, sandhill cranes float down and dance across the meadow as we make our vows. We marry twice, under the great old ponderosa and again at the meeting of the waters. Our friends take us to dinner and cut loose. But it's hard for me to stay in the heart of it all. I can't find my center, there's no equilibrium. Our friends set up a wedding night suite at the top of a fire tower on the ranch.

As we climb the tower to our extravagant view of the area, I feel uneasy. Though I don't see it yet, towers are becoming a repeating symbol and pattern in my life — the office tower in the house where I was caretaker, the penthouse tower in the dirigible dream, the Tower card in the Tarot spread, and now we spend our wedding night in a fire tower. I walk around the catwalk more uncertain than ever. I feel life shocking us into new cycles I can't name. Our friends have wrangled a bed up the narrow winding stairs and set up a cooler with flowers, champagne on ice. The gifts of their love and support offer a beautiful moment. Yet there is so much lying ahead that we cannot see past the panoramic view before us. The next morning we leave early to go to Steve's mother, who survives but by a thin thread.

Over days and weeks her recovery comes slow and painful. She's remarkable. She makes it. She'll be an emotional rock for me I can't imagine in the months ahead.

Life settles into a flow, my belly expands, and in late September Steve asks me to go with him on a business trip to Washington, D.C. He's changed jobs, and this is an opportunity he wants to share. There's joy and pleasure in our unfolding life together. There's also a growing distraction for me. I feel fey half the time, like I'm walking through fog. I can't pin this to anything I can name. But when I think ahead to future plans, all grows murky. I think it must just be the chemistry of pregnancy. I go with Steve to D.C.

While he's in meetings I explore museums and galleries. One afternoon I end up at an aviation exhibit at the Smithsonian. My spirits lift when I imagine the day when I'll be able to share an exhibit like this with our little son. I feel an immediate internal kickback. A razor-sharp No! streaks across my consciousness, echoing through my bones, and I feel like I've been hit by a moving train. Fragile joy and confidence rip to shreds. I take a deep breath, struggle for a sense of balance. I walk on to another exhibit, dizzy and out of focus. I understand this pattern, instinct that comes sudden and strong. I think it must mean that our child won't like airplanes. It must mean that we'll never come back to this place. This is as far as my thoughts can stagger. But there is no dreaming the future for our time ahead. Whenever I try, a heavy fog thickens. At a dinosaur diorama later in the day it's the same thing all over again. I retreat back to our hotel, shadows licking at my heels.

Back at home in Denver, Steve and I have a celebration of our marriage with friends and family and then start to think about rearranging the guest room for the baby's nursery.

We search out yard sales, but I feel strange as we hunt for the things we need. It's hard to fit shifting pieces of distraction into a whole focus inside of me. At one house we buy a dresser but it's an odd transaction. The woman who's selling it asks over and over if we really need it. There are Tarot cards spread out on her bed. She looks at me oddly and cocks her head. She asks twice if I'm ok and I nod, confused. When we're home I feel stranger than ever and go into the house to use the bathroom. Blood spots my underpants. We call our doctor. She asks me a raft of questions and tells me that spotting is not unusual at this stage. I'm healthy. It's Saturday. We'll wait and do an ultrasound Monday morning.

On Monday morning Steve has meetings. I go in for the ultrasound alone. At the clinic they ask if it's ok if I work with an intern for the procedure. This should be no big deal. I climb into the chair. The intern begins. It doesn't take long. She scans my belly. She scans it again. She scans it again. Her face crushes tight. She looks confused and starts out of the room.

"Are you all right?" I ask.

"Yes," she says. "I need to get the doctor."

"What is it?" I ask.

She walks out of the room.

My regular sonogram doctor returns with the intern. We smile and laugh. "Let's see," she says, nonchalant. "Let's see." She spreads the goo and places the monitor. Her face grows tense. She scans again. Alarm grows through view after view, and she finally half-blurts aloud, "Your baby ... his brain ... it's ... I'm sorry ...," she says, looking at me gravely. "Something's not right ...," and she strings the picture together for me as simply as she can. "Your baby's brain is nearly destroyed. I don't think we can save him," she murmurs scanning over and over.

I barely hear her. "Call your husband," she says, helping me out of the chair. "Where is your husband?" I struggle to stand. "You need to call him," she says as she guides me to a counter and phone. I'm numb. "Now," she says, and I pick up the phone and dial. The receptionist in Steve's office comes on the line. She tells me he's in a meeting. I tell her I'm at the doctor's office but going home and hang up.

"I'm going h-home," I manage to say to the doctor.

"Can you drive?" Her concern is obvious, but I'm walking out of the room. "Are you sure you can drive?"

I nod, leaving the office.

By the time I reach the elevator I can barely stand. I keep telling myself *I know how to do this. I'm practiced at this, I can do this*, but I'm falling apart. When I exit the building I can't find my car, double back to the office, start over legs rubber, sobs taking over, tears blinding. I find the car on the third try. The one thing that holds me together is a single repeating thought like a mantra, *I have to get home ... I have to get home.* And somehow, unraveling, I do. I hold onto calling Steve. I know if I go under before then I won't come back up.

When he gets to the house I try to tell him. *Steve. Steve. Our baby.*

But there is nothing, nothing either of us can do.

We walk through the maze of tests and inquiry until it's confirmed. Somewhere I've contracted toxoplasmosis, a condition rarer than rare in Colorado. We work with an expert in sonogram and toxoplasmosis — also rare — and we're lucky to have him. Kind, sympathetic, decisive he wades with us through tricky ground. But still hell unfolds. The prognosis won't change. We can't save our son. Concerned for my health, the doctor advises induced labor. I'm at risk as the pregnancy progresses. An impressive team works with us in the hospital. For three days we bare agony at a heightening pitch. For three days my body holds on. On the fourth day Steve can't take anymore. He wants us to go home. I'm worn out, shredded thin. I agree.

Through all the pain and loss and confusion, I'm coming to know something that has no words. It grows crystal clear inside me.

This is what it is to be a parent, everything for your child.

Somehow stopping the procedures and going home is right for our son. I don't know why. For another three weeks I carry him, hell all over but also making peace. Few can help me with this but everyone tries. A midwife, a friend of my sister's calls me long distance.

"Love your baby," she tells me and I do.

Through time and pain I begin to understand why the spirit of this child has come to us, has come through me, why we've chosen each other. I understand that I can give him what he needs — just a little more time being held in love, it's all he has come for. Walking through shadows barely holding on, the days seem an endless fracturing of darkness and light.

By Thanksgiving, fragmented and weary, we're at the cusp of my eighth month of pregnancy. A team is prepared at the hospital to ferry us through the final stages whenever they come. All is in place. There is no way out. No way out. There is only moving through. The isolation I feel is severe. I go out in public as little as possible. People want to pat my belly, tell me stories and pass on their many opinions on childbirth and parenting. I understand that they mean well, but they don't know what they're saying. And yet grace deepens in me. It expands alongside the agony, cadence for cadence, breath for breath.

Thanksgiving is near. We tell our doctor we want to go to Santa Fe to spend the holiday with family and friends and ask for her blessing. She resists but finally agrees with a few caveats. If there is any change while we are gone we must call her immediately. The decisions we've had to make have been grueling. We must be back in Denver for delivery. Yet we also know that we must go to New Mexico and in going all will be as well as it possibly can be. This is one clear moment of truth in the gathering storm for us. We drive to Santa Fe. The first morning Steve goes up into the high country with a friend.

I wake at first light and I know why we've come. We conceived our son, Nathan Raven, at Ojo Caliente not far from the house where we're staying. I know then that we've brought him home. This knowledge becomes both my Thanksgiving and my peace. When Steve returns in the afternoon he tells me about being on the mountain slopes looking down on Ojo Caliente. We both know exactly why we're here.

We gather with everyone for dinner. As final preparations are made in the kitchen, Steve and I dance in the living room. A strange joy of release and understanding sings in my heart. The music swells. Steve twirls me. My water breaks. Everyone comes to a standstill. When I return from the bathroom there is no doubt about what we must do. Steve and I get ready to drive back to Denver. He calls our doctor. Everyone is in a panic. As we leave they hand us an odd assortment of common household things, as a birth kit for the car. But I know there's no need.

On the drive back to Denver the contractions subside. We get home at midnight and curl into bed.

The next day at the hospital real labor begins, long and arduous. Our son dies the following morning still in utero just before 6 a.m. The doctor performs a forceps delivery. Numb lost gone even as I'm present in the room in the aftermath, we each hold our baby. As morning light swells Steve holds Nathan up to the light of day that has begun to wash through the windows into the room. I kiss our little boy, hold him, and when the nurses come I finally release him in devastating surrender.

The hours and days from this point are blurred spikes of incandescent pain. The day Nathan is cremated is one of the worst for me. That's when I know he's really gone. Steve is remarkable through it all.

When we come into the after times and it is only our grief left to manage, the going gets rougher. Steve is ready to move on. I know too well what the cost of denying grief will be. He can't bear the sorrow. I have to be with it, allow it to wash and cut through, stripping me bare, until loss is cleansed into something refined that I can hold in my daily life, not hidden away. It's a terrible time. Finally, defeated with pain and trying to move on I agree to take Nathan's ashes to New Mexico. We spread his life and his death onto the slow-moving waters of the Rio Ojo Caliente.

35

Return of the Light

The searing loss of Nathan holds me half in the underworld, hard to keep any bearings at all. I stammer through the days that twist through weeks into months.

In time I begin to pick up the pieces of myself. I put together a collective of regional artists and plan a show in lower downtown Denver. I think I'm doing fine, moving on. This is what you do. Move on. It's recommended that we avoid getting pregnant for at least the better part of a year. Nearly a year out I have a miscarriage. By December I've had another. Something inside me breaks. I tell myself I don't really want children, this was not, after all, in my plan. But the truth is that losing Nathan has taken me out at a cavernous level more than any other experience in my life. Combined with all the history stretching behind me, nothing touches this. After the two miscarriages I give up in a way I can't even name. Half in life and one foot over the line within bottomless shadows, the days melt in a sea of half-lived moments.

A dream comes in early winter 1992. In a landscape of sage, high desert and open sky I kneel next to a massive live scorpion. I feel no fear in the presence of this huge and dangerous being. To one side of the giant scorpion stands my maternal grandmother. On the other is my mother, who crouches near me and close to the scorpion's head. I lean forward over the huge creature lying passive, inert and larger than any of us. I take a bite out of the scorpion. As my teeth break through the exoskeleton, the texture of its flesh in my mouth feels as though it is cooked. Pieces of shell and flesh mix together, an awkward, unpleasant and striking sensation. From the other side, my grandmother looks on with clear interest and keen focus. My mother is not fully present, disengaged with what's going on. Her head is lowered, turned away as though in confusion or shame. The scorpion does not react in any way. It is neither aggressive nor does it show pain or discomfort of any kind.

From the center of the body of the scorpion, a large, plump bluebird rises with orange breast and chubby, orange cheeks. It looks directly into my eyes then takes flight south toward a horizon, where orange brilliance spreads across a blue sky. A swell of lush mountains outlines against vivid skyline, dark silhouette atop brilliant color. My grandmother watches beside me, attentive. The bluebird flies in a direct line to the mountain skyline. Alluring, magnetic, what is that place? It's familiar, but I can't say why. I know it, but I can't name it.

The dream stays strong when I wake and for a long time after. It remains an enigma. I have no conscious reference for much of its imagery, unusual for me with my dreams. The bird. The mountains. The greenery. I don't know if the sky represents sunrise or sunset, and this mystifies me. I puzzle and puzzle over details I can't grasp at a conscious level. I know they're specific in some way, more than symbolic, yet they remain obscure. I focus on the figures of my mother and grandmother, what they tell me, what it is that I need to know, to see.

In my teenage years, when my life at home was deteriorating, it was my grandmother's love that helped keep me from falling through the cracks. My mother resented this. How were these two women in my life speaking to me through the dream? My grandmother composed and present, my mother cowering and looking away? What messages evinced from this grandmother and mother who live within me? And what about the alchemy of the scorpion itself? Does it represent fears left from childhood in Mexico when frightening episodes with scorpions were part of my fearsome landscape? Yet there is no fear of the scorpion in the dream. I do not fear the scorpion at all nor its massive size and presence. I take a *bite* out of the scorpion. And this, the unpleasant visceral sensation, the bite — I come back to it again and again, pondering. The vivid orange sky also turns in my thoughts. What is that green place? What is the bird? The dream, like others before it, remains waiting to be understood. But this dream is also quite different. I can't put my finger on why.

In early January Steve comes home from work one day. "It's time to get out of the doldrums," he says.

"Is that what these are?" I joke.

He smiles. "We've never really had a honeymoon," he says, pausing. "What would you think about going to Mexico? I've been to Oaxaca before. It might be nice to go back."

I sit with the surprise of it. Mexico. If we make this trip, other than one brief foray I made over the border at Nogales when I lived on the ranch in Arizona in my twenties, it will be the first time back since childhood for me. Potent place, Mexico, it brings many feelings to the fore — affection, a wide sense of freedom, wonder and longing. And laced through my heart and mind are deeper complexities beyond excitement and allure, beginnings and endings that layer. All lie sleeping within thoughts of Mexico. First fear was born in Mexico. It was in Mexico that the earth burst open to me, overwhelming, endless and immense. It was in Mexico that my nightmares began. Mexico is the place where my family began to dissolve. I tasted newness, adventure, great marvel and the world in exquisite expression there. All this belongs to Mexico. It has always been Mexico, riddle and song in my heart.

"We can fly into Mexico City and explore," Steve continues. "Then go on to anywhere we want."

Intrigue and trepidation ring through my blood. The broken places inside me tremor. Yet the wholeness of me startles awake and takes hold. I smile, uncertain.

"Your childhood," he says, "it'll be great for you, for us. Oaxaca is famous for art and silver, and it's near the ocean."

I realize he's right. This trip could be a good thing. I say yes. We book a flight for late January. Packing light, I cram a single, voluminous skirt with the rest of my gear into a backpack slightly smaller than my husband's. When we land in Mexico City a few weeks later I understand how shattered I still am from loss and grief. Overwhelmed in the airport, clinging to Steve like a barnacle in the midst of mixed dialects and surging crowds, I wonder what happened to the independent woman I was. Though we intend to begin our quest in the city with museums, pyramids and dozens of sites, as we push through the crowds Steve turns to me dazed. He's almost as big-eyed as I am.

"Maybe we should start smaller, quieter," he yells, "maybe Oaxaca first." We push to a ticket counter and buy tickets to fly to Oaxaca within the hour.

We spend a quiet couple of days in Oaxaca. Our lodging just off the zocalo is a room with heavy, dark Spanish furnishings that feel oppressive to both of us. We explore the markets. The first night when we eat at an outside restaurant I feel like I'm on the edge of home or tasting the tip of home, impossible to describe as nightfall deepens. The city's alive. A wild mix of natives and German tourists fill tables, meander the streets. We nibble a queso asadero, astonished at the texture and delicate flavor. And because of that queso the next night we return to the same restaurant and sit at an outside table once more.

As we savor our meal we wonder how to go deeper past the tourist cover. We have almost two weeks. The arts are amazing but we don't want to spend the entire time doing little more than the equivalent of shopping. A couple takes a table nearby, late as we finish eating. She's petite, a brunette dressed to the nines. He's a towering man, casual with long silver hair to his shoulders. It's clear they're both from the States. His Spanish is impeccable as they place their order. Steve strikes up a conversation about the wine they've chosen. They're civil but just. We finish our meal and wander away holding hands.

Breakfast the next morning finds us at an outdoor cafe on a different street in soft, early light. The wall of the restaurant is radiant yellow that both brightens and softens the sunlight to a riper hue. The same couple from the night before is seated next to the only vacant table. We nod, take the open, sunlit seats and place our order, our backs to them. The man clears his throat. We miss the cue. A sharp "Eh, heh!" catches our attention. We turn. He extends his hand and asks if we'd like to join them. We move to their table. Fresh-squeezed orange juice arrives as they tell their story.

David is a fine arts photographer in the platinum palladium school. They live in Michigan. She works in the medical industry. He's traveled Mexico extensively over many years, and this trip is part-work, part-pleasure. His field style when solo is simple, a bit rugged for Elizabeth's tastes. She likes the finer things. They've been traveling for a few weeks. A bit bored, she's lonely for people she can talk to and they're hungry for news from the States. We catch them up on current events, talk politics and laugh through breakfast, lingering over the meal. In a startling turn they ask if we'd be of a mind to join them on the last leg of their journey, a roving path back to Mexico City.

"Give it some time," they say. "No rush." Except that they'd like to check out of their room before they've got another day on their bill.

They've got a rental car, everything's easy. David knows the country and the language intimately from years of travel and through the eyes of a photographer. He'll be shooting on back roads in small villages, and they plan to explore pyramids along the way. He's got the arts scene down in Mexico City, can turn us on to parts of Mexico we just wouldn't see on our own. It's a great opportunity. We clear out our rooms. As we depart Oaxaca, heading up over a pass out of the city, we're stopped by a military guard. Waiting to pass through the roadblock I realize it's my 41st birthday. We all laugh at this brink, new thresholds. The guard passes us on.

Since David's current photographic interest is mainly architectural we travel village to village seeking old adobe features — bell towers, old walls, unique doors in half-light or shadow. Traveling off the path to places with few roads through village enclosures, we step back in time.

In some villages we're curiosities, in others brazen intruders, not always welcome. It occurs to me that David's ease and success in traveling here has something to do with his massive size.

We explore pyramids and drop underground inside one of them to make our way through the labyrinth of its inner core, seeing clusters of old handprints and sensing the hundreds of hands that once patted stucco onto these walls hundreds of years past. All are buried now beneath the mass of the mound above us and on top of that, the colonial Spanish church reigns. The weight of these histories bear down, ancient time pressing close as we move through whispering, tight passageways, making our way back to the light.

I feel myself waking to the world again as though from a distant dream.

When we at last reach Paseo de Cortez within sight of the legendary volcanoes, Popocatepetl, the most violent volcano in Mexico, and Iztaccihuatl, or *La Mujer Dormida*, we are humbled as we study their hulk in the distance. Steve speaks of his long dream to climb them. For me the volcanoes bring ancient feelings, an inexplicable combination of familiarity, ease and trepidation that ripple out of the long-gone past. We look to our route that winds down into the Valley of Mexico and Tenochtitlan — what is now Mexico City — unaware that we stand at a crossroads and the threshold of convergence. A new arc is forming in our lives.

Within the mantle of the changing topography we slowly drive down the pass unaware that we're picking up threads that trail into the now. My heart beats a little faster with anticipation for our city exploration, the many interlinking cultures that cross and re-cross through landscape and time. David knows Mexico City well, much as he knows the country we've just passed through, and urban is Elizabeth's natural home. We find a motel, turn in the car and make a beeline on foot and mass transit for a promised gallery deep in the city heart.

The gallery is a small, elegant space filled with spectacular works. A little, enclosed outside garden of cast iron and brick opens off the main rooms, and for the first time Steve and I see original sculptures by Francisco Zuniga. Speechless in the presence of the power and grace of his incredible forms, we return to the inner gallery where I discover a haunting print by Juan Alcazar. Later we wander near the Instituto Nacional de Bellas Artes. Slipping out of the throbbing noise of the city into the quiet of a soaring cathedral, breathing in elemental sanctity old and worn, we leave coin offerings as we pass out the great doors to walk along streets that are surreal. Buildings tipped and tilted askew still hang on the last shudder of the earthquake of 1985. The sense of living on the edge is heightened, and again the next day at the Museum of

Modern Art where I'm overwhelmed by the work of artists at once startling and familiar beyond all meaning. I find myself overcome and in tears most of the time as I wander on my own. When we leave I'm tattooed with forces I have no name for. And from the deep seat of loss something knits anew, awakening and electric. This ... what, what is it? This nature, this force of nature, penetrates and follows me. It will follow me all the way home.

Steve and I say farewell to David and Elizabeth the next morning. We visit a flea market then move on to the massive inner-city zocalo. At once, as I take in the surprise of that wide-open emptiness within its surround of historic buildings and my feet step onto its pavers, I'm tossed between sorrow and joy. Rifts between recent and past history flare and spark with simmering energy. The clash of uneasy cadence layers deep beneath city crust and lost time.

At the Palacio National we're saturated with Rivera murals drenched in color and myth, story permeating stone that speaks in a tongue past word or sound. I feel bemused in the face of these murals. For Steve it's the thrill of firsthand discovery, history he has relished and read about. I walk with him through the vaulted spaces, caught between wonder and distraction. When we step back out onto the sweep of the wide zocalo its flooding past buckles, buzzing through my cells. We trek across the wide space to a small, impermanent market that clusters along one border of the zocalo, looking for food and though I'm not hungry we settle to the ground for an impromptu picnic. I feel dazed. Children squeal around us. Sky sweeps overhead. The city pulses with noise, the mash of smells, calling voices, a crush of time. Gathering our few belongings we get up to leave and wander behind the tiny market.

Eruptions of ancient hand-worked rock look like they've burst through paved surface. We've stumbled onto a partial excavation.

Upheavals of modern pavement split above the startle of carved, moldering stone and draw us forward. Steve says something I can't hear. I lean over a gap in one disturbed area. Dark earth and old hand-worked rock tumble and tunnel within a narrow, tight opening, plunging in twisting descent. I lean closer. Primal breath funnels. Alive and on the move it hisses from far below — dank and stale and denser than darkest night. Out of the disturbed antiquity, life gasps and reaches ... searching ... speaking in tongues on a long exhale. I leap back to the sunlight of the open zocalo.

It's time to leave.

I know at once that we must abandon this place and its restless history. Reaching out of the ancient past for an opening in time, something seeks new conduits for life. I shift away from the cloying nature, energy that ensnares, seeks to bind. Steve surprises me. Like me, he's ever curious in a place with old ruins. But now he's more than willing to move on and quickly, leaving the old treasures behind. As we walk back the way we've come, he suddenly recalls that he has read about ruins that were discovered just off the zocalo, beneath this old city — ruins of the Templor Mayor, heart of the Aztec empire.

We leave Mexico City the next day and fly out to Playa de Carmel, find a little clutch of bungalows along the coast at a place that feels like it has sprung up overnight and spend the night in a grass-roofed cabana. Barking lizards scamper across walls, raising a din and making us laugh. It's a party settlement, what little there is of it, and a clear offense to the locals. We move on.

Tulum lies further down the coast, an astounding lost dream towering on cliffs above the coursing ocean. From there we move inland to Chichen Itza, Ticul and Uxmal in interior Yucatan. Great, pocked bulks of stone and handwork push imagination in endless directions. Chacmools turn up in frequent repetition. Sacred cenotes dot the surrounding area, scenes of sacrifice and once the only freshwater source for large numbers of people. Somewhere along the way Palenque lodges in our minds. We know at once that's where we're headed.

In the midst of thick jungle at a strange, rambling motel, freshly deserted, doors of all the rooms stand ajar with everything inside them in place. Here we wait for a bus. The place is surreal, planted on the edge of a spare road like a living dream. Everything about the motel appears intact, yet there is no one, no one anywhere. Uneasy amidst senseless abandon, we're filled with questions. One couple hikes past, shrugging off the desertion, as mystified as we are but completely indifferent. Odd concern for them tugs through my mind as they pass us by. When at last the bus arrives we move to empty seats near the back and strike up conversation with a blonde Americano in the seat in front of us. Evening smudges into darkness. We suddenly recognize our new dilemma. It's going to be late, very late when we reach Palenque. We have no plan, no reservation. Steve latches a little tighter onto the Americano who is fluent in Spanish. But the Americano has latched onto a senorita in the seat in front of him and has no time for us.

Steve is like a fly buzzing around the couple. I can't get him to leave them alone. I feel unusually calm, but I'm also clueless about our options. When we reach ride's end, the Americano walks away hunched over the woman who is tucked under his arm. It is 1 a.m. Steve runs to him and begs for directions to a motel before they disappear.

"*Loco gringo*," the Americano jeers to the woman but barks back at Steve. "Look, I'm staying here. It's cheap but it's rough, you're taking your own chances." Then he disappears through the door of a rundown building with the woman.

We slip through the door just behind them. At the desk the couple finishes a quick transaction, and we step up. A man with a thick face and belligerent eyes looks us over. A few pesos cross the desk, a key passes to Steve, and the man softens slightly as he takes us along a hallway, up a flight of stairs and leaves us at a beat-up door. Once inside we realize there's no way to lock it, and it's probably useless anyway. We're in a Mexican brothel.

The room is spare, plain and dirty. Sitting on the bed is better than the floor but not by much. Steve ratchets around trying to make amends. It's a miserable night. When slightest dawn hints, it's like a switch has been flipped, instant darkness to light. We're out of the room and on the streets almost as fast. Light diffuse and mysterious pulses. We wander through a maze of closed market stalls. In the crazy mix of primitive and modern, we've no idea where we're going.

It's hard to describe this place. Everything starts at ground level in a way that feels like buildings and life sprout directly up from the soil. No foundations, tenuous hold, shallow roots, everything transitory. Yet human history, the force that's sculpted this area, is a long continuum. Layers stack on layers stack on layers that make time and all ideas of permanence completely meaningless. Our rippling presence blends into its dream. What we see as we wander along is just what is now, but what I feel is too vast to name.

We wander until we find ourselves facing a multistory structure unlike anything we've seen before. The lower level seems not so much walled as sewn up for the night. Mortar and cinder blocks rise in a tower above the tenuous canvas-surround of the lower walls. We step through a slight opening along one seam, dazzling into interior darkness.

As our eyes adjust we find the startle of moderate luxury, the Hotel Chan-Kah. A man steps into the room, narrows his eyes, nods. He tells us they're not open. We'll have to come back. Perfunctory, shaking his head he raises two of the canvas walls and moves back from the penetrating light. The transition is stunning. We stand in an open-air lobby, outside inside, novel and confusing. Cinder blocks stacked into rooms above us weigh in an awkward conundrum. But when honeymoon crosses Steve's lips the man seems to know what we want faster than we do. They have one room on the top floor. We're lucky. It's their best room. In a short time we're riding an elevator up to a half-panoramic view of mountain and jungle from the fifth floor. We look out over tree canopy that shades the zocalo below, jungle rippling out from town in endless green that flows up the sides of mountains. I quiver with a sense of familiarity.

Fast showers, food grabbed on the go, and we head out to the ruins of Palenque. Though once obscured in jungle and overgrowth like so many other ruins in the area, many of the old structures now stand in the light. We're mostly alone, the place nearly deserted. As I approach the remains of an aqueduct I feel plied and twisted through time, its perfect form and utility an anomaly within silence and desertion.

The Observation Tower in the palace ruins hovers above us. Stucco relieves, fragments, tombstones, courtyards, inscribed tablets, pictorial ornaments and hieroglyphs scatter across the site. Here in these ruins are some of the finest carved narrative inscriptions of Maya culture. We explore in a kind of hushed wonder and at last approach stairs leading down into a crypt beneath the Templo de las Inscripciones. As we descend we imagine the time when the chambers were built, collective burial rumored to lie beneath the final six steps. The crypt itself outweighs answer or thought. Amidst the awe and mystery of all its wonders, allure shifts to the longing for daylight. When we return up the steps it's with palpable relief.

The mysteries of Palenque bring light and happiness to my heart. At the edge of the jungle, ruins still wrapped in overgrowth catch my eye, tantalizing. I step past the border of the groomed area into the jungle keep and wander from one inscribed relief wound round with vine and plant life to another and another. I find a small stone gazebo-like structure half-exposed. It pulls me on like a magnet, and I move deeper into the vining density, entranced. Steve, shocked to find me past the jungle boundary, joins me in my reverie.

We pick up a well-worn trail. Birdcall and half heard voices pepper through crowded trees that vault to the heavens. Echoes range in and out of hearing, far and near. We wander along a meandering watercourse mesmerized with this strange, beautiful world, bend over the stream to inspect small stones and plants we can't identify. And startle when two native men come up behind us from the direction of Palenque. Their eyes cut around us sharp and probing. There are no smiles. After they pass following the trail deeper into the jungle, we recognize the foolishness of our trespass. A body of voices vaults from a distance, far, near, far, near in a rolling cascade. We hurry back the way we've come. I imagine children and families, a village tenuous and scattered in the overgrowth, voices in a spiking deluge not far behind us. We reach the groomed boundary, step out of the jungle onto the open grounds with our hearts pounding and the sense that we're just ahead of something we can't name.

We spend two nights at the Hotel Chan-Kah hardly counting our strange arrival that has now melted behind us. The world feels extravagant, close yet wide. Each night we venture out to explore the modern town of Palenque but never get far. We choose the same open-air restaurant in the old quarters for our late meal both evenings. It's a happy, romantic time. As we peruse the menu for our second meal two

Mayan girls burst onto the patio, moving from table to table. The older girl carries a basket of cloth and husk dolls. Maybe 10 or 11 years old, she's an experienced pro as she hawks her wares. The younger girl is a spinning whirlwind, all chatter and motion. They reach our table. Steve asks the youngest the name of the doll she's carrying.

"Mario! Mario!" she squeals, dancing the doll on the table, swinging it wildly about, "Mario! Mario! Mario!" I laugh into her exuberance.

The elder girl watches closely. "Can we see?" Steve gestures at the basket.

The older girl bends to the younger girl, who steps back shaking her head. The eldest stands firm. Mario is proffered into her hands, and she lays it on the table. I take Mario up and laugh with the younger girl as we pass the doll back and forth. Steve peruses the dolls in the basket.

"How much?" he asks. In a flash a transaction completes, and the elder girl takes the hand of the younger, pulls her across the patio and down the steps. Three dolls lie on the tabletop. As the two girls disappear, the dark eyes of the youngest lock on mine. My heart is in my throat as I realize that her doll is still on the table. Mario. I look up to call out, but the girls are gone, nowhere to be seen. I pick up the dolls tenderly to carry them back to our room.

The top floor of the Chan-Kah is like being on top of the world amidst birds and breeze. Open skies kiss brilliant sunset, spring into sunrise mornings. As we look over the tree canopy below and beyond, out across jungle slopes into the distance I feel how all the miles of our journey through Mexico have become a collage of perfect frequencies that plait together. Here in Palenque the heart of our travels has found exact center.

It's not easy to leave perfection when you find it, but we both know it is time. The next morning we make our way to the bus that will carry us the long way back to Mexico City. Mountains and jungle spread impossible scale as long-haired Lacandon Mayan men watch in their white xikul, smiling and talking among themselves with great animation. They laugh as they watch the strange movements of this modern world infiltrating their own. I look for the girls who sold us the dolls but see them nowhere. A clear sense of displacement cuts in and I feel the river of time, streams of interlopers, cultures usurped, building to mighty heights and tumbled down. Yet here these Lacandon remain, history sprawling around them in its loop and turn.

It's a long bus ride back to Mexico City, all night in the ever-changing populace that fills and empties at dozens of stops. In the late hours, at a backwater stop, I shock Steve by getting off the bus to purchase a strange little sandwich from a vendor waiting at the steps then eat it back in our seats in a few quick bites. It turns out that this is more checkpoint than bus stop. The only person who gets back on the bus is wearing a uniform. Everyone grows tense and hushed. I barely notice as I finish my tiny feast and look up to the rustle and fuss moving in singular motion down the center aisle. A broad, short man with dark hair and mustache ranges seat to seat with laser authority.

Steve grows taut and gives a low hiss as the man moves near. It doesn't occur to me to be concerned. He stops next to us, jerks a little, and his dark eyes stare into mine. I look back at him. His face is harsh, his eyes harsher. We look at each other for the beat of a minute. I smile a little smile, nodding. He nods back. His face changes, relaxes ever so slightly, and he moves on. It is later that I understand. He saw me buying the sandwich. I was a hairsbreadth from being hauled off the bus, drug search or for just being a woman. I shudder as this recognition blasts hard in my gut. Yet the change in the man's eyes and his mustached face as our gazes caught then parted told me many unfathomable things in that passing moment. And the most important to know is that life is good, and in this time, there are no worries.

We fizzle into Mexico City, find a generic room high up in a forgettable hotel and talk about all the places we haven't seen. Flat with disinterest and irritable with the sense of shifting currents, I feel waves bending tight to new shores. Mexico lies rich in my blood. It's time to go home.

We tumble back into our lives in Denver. I can't get my bearings. The intentional community plan sputters, unsteady flame. Steve gives lip service to my dream but doesn't engage. I start to work on a second multi-artist show. I've got energy again, and I want to use it.

A few weeks out, and I start to feel ill. I've felt this before.

It's the tower in Palenque. We're pregnant. I know at once that everything will be perfect. There are no fears with this pregnancy, not one. Light and joy, ease and laughter abound. We're having a daughter. A daughter.

I immerse in being with our child. Family pulls in close, and I see more of my mother. Our bond develops a fresh patina and from this point on is entirely new. I count cloth diapers, play with plans for the guest room-turned-nursery and begin to understand a series of things.

I remember the dream of the sparkling white walls and crystalline windows in the guest room that will be our daughter's. Through long journeys both our children have traveled to us, teaching about love and endurance, bringing blessings, wholeness and now a foundation of joy.

And the dream of the giant scorpion, it also returns to my thoughts to pester and pry. Finally I can see and integrate its many meanings. Taking a bite out of the scorpion is past, present and future resolved. I'm having a daughter, conceived in Mexico. I've taken the bite out of the biting history of my Scorpio mother and Mexico. I've taken the bite out of the shell of the past. The sting and poison of the scorpion of childhood has been converted. All of that pain-turned-meanness reaching back through generations is being transformed. Our baby is the chubby-cheeked bluebird of happiness with its vibrant, ruddy cheeks in the dream. Little phoenix rising out of old ashes, she brings old history to completion and flies into the now. The dream scorpion is also the exotic food of my childhood: the cooked flesh, awkward and uncomfortable mixed in with the shell in the dream, is the Mexican lobster my mother gave me in special morsels when I was a little child — nurture turned to agony and returned to nurture once more. I had to ingest and break down all the unpleasant, old mixed history to create the alchemy that changed one element into another, old into new. The massive scorpion of the dream, passive and inert, is the large presence of the past that has lost its power, no longer a threat. My dream grandmother is my beloved grandma, but she is also my own wise woman and astute witness, intuitive and awake. The dream mother is the shame within my mother's history, her humiliation at the betrayal of her role, and she is also my broken self bent by the loss of our son, Nathan. The dream was prescient. Lush green mountain silhouette against flaming sky portrayed the jungle and within it, Palenque, where the little bluebird of happiness flew to await its rebirth. Did the dream portray sunrise or sunset? The dream portrayed both. One cycle completes. Another begins. Every day. Every month. Every year. Every generation. The cycles go on. What began as dissolution in my childhood in Mexico has traveled full circle, and it is Mexico that has returned new, verdant life.

Our pregnancy is flawless, exquisite. A beautiful Scorpio daughter is born with great ease nine months after her spirit joined to ours in that southern realm, new dream begun.

36

Diminuendo

And so a child is born, a girl child utterly loved. In the link between then and now, time being a river, a meadow, a moment expanding, much could be said. But the simplest to say is that life is a calling. To remain true as both mother and woman, I have to answer its call. Unlike my mother before me, I do. The muse will not let me rest.

Life remains simple for us for a while, full of the joys and sorrows that life brings, rich with great happiness in our child. Yet there is a vow my husband and I have made. It is the vow, before our wedding vows — our commitment to live a life outside of Denver.

And alongside that something else rises.

I at last understand what the Renaissance man of my old dream was doing with his hands. He was writing a book. Writing has called me for a very long time, long before I arrived in Denver. Since I was young I knew I would write a book. But like so many aspirations buried in my early years of travail, this path has not yet been realized. In the two years before Steve and I came together, ideas for the book were forming. It was a main focus when I met him. One of the first gifts Steve gave me was an elegant writing pen. Later he built a simple pine desk and bookcase for a sunny nook in our bedroom. And yet again tragedy followed tragedy, so that in our early lives together writing was lost in the margins. Buried out of sight and out of mind, the book lay dormant. When joy bloomed in our lives as parents we deepened into wonder, and still story slept. But in truth it was ripening into new form, gathering new threads.

Our minds are often unaware when we cross the deepest threads of our history and the open doorways in parallel time — these occur in repeating patterns and frequently with no conscious awareness at all.

But once reference points exist for this kind of experience, patterns emerge at a conscious level and new challenges arise. One of the biggest is to investigate what's been revealed, yet remain neutral and clear of projection. It's a tricky dance.

When experiences of this nature shift from disturbing to intriguing or cross into thrilling, it's easy to get carried away, layering projections onto what has occurred. All of our dreams and ambitions, emotional reactions, fears, desires and hopes flood in, opening us up to new possibility but also the risk of gross misinterpretation — all the tantalizing ways imagination takes hold. Projection can help give us wings. But getting carried away with projection can deter understanding the truth that is trying to reach us at a conscious level.

Like any deep work, these touchpoints, openings and passages require us to sit with ourselves and face truths that are difficult in one way or another: unresolved grief, incomplete cycles, unrequited love or hope, instances of disregard for ourselves or another, unfinished patterns — patterns we've avoided, refused to embrace or kept at bay, often for a very long time. Some are painful. Some are joyous. Whatever we have not been able to embrace and integrate, in these lie our liberation. It's fierce work.

In 1993 a new repertoire of gateways into parallel time open and build for me.

Starting with our trip to Mexico this cycle will last throughout my pregnancy and into the early years of our daughter's life. Within — or apart from — these occurrences the natural flow of daily life moves on. Some of these gateways I barely recognize for what they are, in the fullness and demands of everyday life. And of those I do, many seem to carry no correlation to anything I can piece immediately into whole cloth. Often I do little more than acknowledge a moment when a cue or clue unfolds. Yet I do fold in threads and curious connections unleashed during this cycle, following them as I can, riding the current, attentive and grounded in the normalcy of our lives. Subtle, like a dance of changing partners invisible to the eye and most surface senses, I've been in these kinds of patterns before.

Cascading stories within the many loose threads of clues and cues begin to interweave, undeniable. And still the task remains — walk in the everyday, feet on the ground, attentive in observation, not seduced by projection.

Within the traces that begin to connect in a larger whole lie important pieces of a puzzle that has been unfolding in me for years — aspects that relate to the facts of my history since childhood. Unresolved fragments to the enigma in these patterns — and particularly to the violations I experienced in my late teens and early twenties — revolve toward a greater need for clarification. On the surface, they're the strings of cause and effect of my current history that need to be completed in some way.

Though I've shared broken fragments and segments of this history with close friends, my husband and family, I've never spoken with anyone about what I've lived in a full and connected arc. Events out of context do not make for wholeness. They remain disjointed. Over the years of our shared lives together I've tried to talk openly with my husband about my history but with minimal success. He knows only some broken segments. The need to share my history with my husband grows. Exposed and tender I try to give voice to the truth of my life. He refuses it outright.

"I don't know what I can do about it," he says, gruff and withdrawing.

Agonizing to attempt in the best of circumstances, I don't try often. My efforts to share with him are shut down. So a key part of me is forced underground.

Though my husband is bright, funny, creative and generous with a wealth of great qualities, he is not capable of holding the space for deep pain or something so glaring as my past beyond a few fast-ticking seconds and maybe a pat response.

I've brought most of my past into the light through deep work before we were married, but I have not linked the beads of my history in a full continuum. I've released an immense swathe of demons. I've pulled myself from the fire. I've taken hold to embody a creative life grounded in authentic autonomy. I've shifted patterns that have changed the arc of my life and my relationships. And I've put together the many pieces of my history into a loosely bound whole. But I've yet to knit the full continuum of relatedness within each string of what has occurred. Divisions that protected me for years by keeping old events in separate compartments still exist inside me and this can no longer serve. *History understood as disparate events does not hold the integrity of true completion. And history presses for its wholeness.*

Apart from all of this, as a writer I can feel that a story is rising, and I know that I have to find its living voice. I also know that this time it will not be denied. But I do not imagine that the story I will write will be a story of my life. As deep creation pushes for its form, I don't understand what life is asking of me. I don't grasp that the first voice of the story will not begin on paper, flowing from the tip of my pen. The living voice must begin — and exist — in the core of my life. The core of my life is the center of my most intimate relationships — the relationship with myself that I have worked so hard to realize — and my relationship with my husband.

Life carries on. I don't keep count as the years of our marriage unfold. Five years, Steve said, five years in Denver. Our marriage and our daughter have my full attention. Those five years pass and flow on. Life is full. I imagine now as I look back that my husband must have thought that the life he'd claimed in Denver and that held us there for a while could take precedence over our vows and our many agreements. It was not so outrageous, I suppose, that he thought if he played his cards right I would sleepwalk past old dreams, as many people do, as my mother did before me. But both of us made a vow. I can't speak for my husband, but my vow was born from the heart of my being. It sprang from the core of my life. It carried the essence of all that life had taught me. My vow was entrusted to the heart of my husband. A vow like this is not something to be taken lightly. A vow like this has a life of its own.

And life would hold us to it, true to intent and laid down over time.

Our vow cannot be fulfilled living life as it is in Denver. Five years pass, and then two more. In this time Steve disavows his agreement to join the intentional community that I've invested so much of my heart and dreams in, the original vision that convinced me to stay on in Denver. I let this go. Waters are shifting. There's a new current building, and I trust it. In the seventh year our vow picks up its own timeline. Though I don't understand it, I feel the sure beat of change moving beneath the daily rhythm of life. I'm surprised when I begin to feel drawn back to Wyoming. I've never considered a return to live there. At first, I think the pull north is simply about spending more time with friends and family. With my husband's blessings I make many trips to Wyoming with our daughter, at first for short visits and later to explore communities where he agrees we might choose to live. I don't yet see that the life we're living in Denver is an illusion couched behind broken promises. I trust the ideals and dreams I think that my husband shares.

Yet something refuses to be sidelined. It flickers and burns beneath the surface of things. I begin to feel a growing vacancy in our lives. I try to fill it with things — random novelty, money spent in a thoughtless cascade, cause and effect dulled in a tidal pull I can't quite name.

Philosopher Eric Hoffer once said, "You can never get enough of what you don't need."

Money and things can never make whole a person or the inauthentic refuge of a heart. Things and money and weightless promises are not what I need. What I need is caught between poles of divergent forces — our lives in Denver are no longer true. And a larger call is emerging.

My husband is a good man and so charming when he wants his way. He is also unnerved by change, inflexible beyond his personal desires. This is nothing rare in the history of relationships. But in our case it is the thing that brings us to a brink.

Is it inevitable that these differences will break us down and break our marriage? It's impossible to say. But what I do know is that we all make our choices and as he makes his I begin to make mine, moving toward what is genuine and rings true in the core of my being.

Grief, an agonizing part of life, becomes unwieldy in relationships over time without great care. Just as we have already been sorely tried, the path that is calling now tries us again. Though I don't understand what is taking hold I do know that I'm held by deep guidance. I've learned to trust it with implicit care. Whatever the facts of our lives, the writing life that calls can never become whole in life as we're living it.

During this cycle we choose a woman for counsel who practices a method of Hakomi, in order to work through tensions building between us. This method is based on the assumption that people carry their answers within them. My husband does not take part in the work we should be doing together — because of your history, he says. But I'm glad to do this work. I know the rich ground of the inner life. I know the rewards that exist by facing its challenges. It does not take long for me to come full circle. For the first time with another person in my life, I string the events of my story into the continuum they are. Hakomi has done its work.

Life carries on, and the pull toward Wyoming intensifies. During one of my treks north it is a dream that foretells the way. My daughter and I stay a few nights with an old friend in Jackson, the valley where I lived for so many years. I wake on the morning of the day of our return to Colorado, stunned by the visceral potency of the dream.

A frog being, tall as a human and walking upright, moves along an earthen path carrying a child frog tenderly in its arms. The little frog's head rests on the adult frog's shoulder. The green skins of these two are so fresh, so moist and so porous they are impossible to describe, delicate sensibilities that beat with exquisite receptivity. The adult frog approaches a downslope in the path, carrying the child. They descend into a verdant grotto, beauty shimmering beneath the earth's surface. Within the grotto a lush world sparkles green upon green upon stone upon water. A pool of great depth winks and within it life pulsates, swirling with turtles of every possible kind. On mossy banks an unkempt woman sits weeping, her hair stringy, unwashed. The distraction of the woman's grief blinds her, though before her turtles swim and dive and turn in crystalline water. The woman cannot see or feel either turtles or the vibrancy of life held in this place.

When I wake I feel the vibrant green skin of the frogs as though it were my own. And I know the woman. She's a friend, a writer in whose home we're staying. Why does she sit unkempt and weeping at the edge of the gorgeous pool, ignorant or indifferent to all the beauty around her, the rare and fecund life swimming before her?

I can't place the dream into waking context. I try to unwrap its meaning into my life. I understand the cleansing symbolism of frogs and turtles in their many aspects of protection, pacing, abundance and carriers of the Earth, but the dream is speaking of more than these qualities. It seems sprung straight from the heart of the Earth herself. I think the dream belongs to my friend, not to me — to this land and the place where she lives. With regret I release the exquisite beauty of the dream to the place from which it sprang. I imagine I will leave it here.

I ready my daughter to leave. We pass from house onto the land, pack up the car and drive away. Up the incline from Snake River bottom to the upper plateau, my girl sweet in her car seat behind me, the dream holds. I feel it swarming around us. It breathes, pulsing and seems to expand. Like rain filtering through exquisite frog skin, it holds close as we top the plateau. I drive slow ... slow ... then slower to the waking beat of the dream. The dream embraces the full sweep of the valley. When we are half way across the upper plateau it suddenly springs to sparkling life all around us. In one breathless moment the truth explodes. I stop driving. This valley, massive rough-hewn bowl of elemental forces, this valley is the verdant grotto of the dream. A seismic quake moves through me. I pull over to the side of the road. The dream is prophetic. We're going to move back here.

I reel with the thought. It makes no sense, no sense at all. We have a life already in place. I've never imagined that our lives will shift back here. I try to shake off the implications. I can't understand them. It's impossible to fit our lives into this riddle. There's no logical sense to this at all.

I shrug it all off. I think I can resist it. I think that it must be symbolic and will unfold other meanings. Yet through chance and synchronous events the change comes. It breaks our marriage. It isn't the valley or the dream that does the breaking. I remember the moment of no return exactly, something seemingly small.

Late in the fall, on a return trip from St. George, Utah, to visit Steve's family I ask that we stop for the night in a place special to me and not grind the whole drive out in a single day. My husband agrees. Our daughter is young, long drives are grueling for her, and Utah is a mystical place of the heart for me — compass point and beloved opportunity for respite and inspiration. My husband is aware of all of this. I grow sleepy and ask him to wake me when we get to San Raphael Swell. I fall asleep.

When I wake we're miles past the Swell, miles past the turn to Moab, Steve blasting his way toward Denver. He turns to see reality hit in my eyes, the stun, the effect of his casual betrayal. A small thing, a large thing, a terrible thing, it glares. This moment aligns, perfect symmetry with the full swathe of life with my husband to this point —

promises spoken, broken, ignored; intentions espoused, cast away, laid aside. The rhythm of these things empties out. I watch awareness bloom in his eyes. I see his attempts to mask it. We both feel the cost. He knows what he's done. And that's when I know. This is how it will always be. This is the way my husband lives his life. What is in him is his way. That is all. It's the most important thing to know in this moment. We don't speak of it just then. We don't dare. But this is the beginning of the end. Life as we have known it moves now to a changing rhythm. Things could go differently. But the net has been cast. It begins to play itself out.

A small house in the valley up north in Wyoming opens up, and a friend lets me know. I've already dreamt the house and will dream it again before I ever see it. I resist its lure, but a strange thing begins to occur. Often and out of the blue I feel the presence of mountain lions moving in close all around me. Over time I began to feel stalked by this feline nature. The feeling grows when we're in places most important to my husband, an uncomfortable, unforgettable sensation. Unnerved I brush these occurrences aside, turn away from their unsettling sensory expressions. And when I do the feelings intensify. So I begin to pay close attention to each time the feeling of mountain lion presence appears. I notice when they soften and recede. A pattern surfaces, paints a picture and begins to make sense.

The day that I give in and rent the house in northern Wyoming the mountain lions settle, turn friendly, come in close to sit by my side and in time fade from the scene.

I still think we'll make it, my husband and me. But I know I can't deny my life by compromise based on half-truths.

The house in the north is simple, funky and has great light. In my dreams before I ever see it, a fire pit is central to the middle of the main room. Within the fire pit a snake coils, shedding its skin. Snakes are symbolic of transmuting poisons at all levels. They represent powers of creation, transitions from birth to death, cycles of rebirth. In the dream, people come to the little house for immersion in healing and creative rebirth of the essential nature of their soul's calling.

I have another intense dream back in Denver. In it I wrestle a massive serpent coiled around my husband's neck, choking the life out of him. I fight in the dream for his life with a prayer that he be spared from the fate he's creating, that he survive this ordeal, that he retain his well-being and the full autonomy in his life. I pray that kindness will survive within our journey.

When I at last visit the house in northwestern Wyoming for the first time, there's something indefinable about it, mysterious. When I move some of my grandmother's belongings into the house in 1998 the quality becomes palpable. Later, in a startling moment, I suddenly understand. I feel safe in this little house. For the first time anywhere in conscious memory I feel safe. Until this moment I have no reference for understanding that I have never, at the deepest levels of my life, felt safe. The home with my husband in Denver is restful, secure. But not like this. When I understand the nature of this house, what it offers, I begin to know many things. This is where I will do the work that has been calling me. I understand that this work will be demanding. It will mean ever-greater challenge and risk. This house is where the something I have no name for will be born. Last shattered bits of myself begin to journey home. It's sometimes strange, what brings peace.

We shift between Colorado and Wyoming. Over the years of living in Denver I've spent much of my free time exploring the Black Arts Festival there, its events, literature and community.

On one trip back to Denver on a return from Wyoming my husband and I attend a performance of the Cleo Parker Robinson dance company. A faux African market has been set up in the theater lobby. We wander through booths, looking over wares. At the end of one row I turn a corner and enter a last booth almost tucked out of sight. I stop to read a poem on a poster that is curious and moving. I turn, nod at the artist and turn back to look over his leatherwork arrayed along the booth walls. Bewildered I'm startled to tears at the image of a slave lynching, embossed on a leather bag. Enormous emotion washes over me. My husband is speaking with the artist. I struggle for composure, keep my back to them and move from one African holocaust scene to another, interspersed with work that portrays varied celebrations and beauties of African cultures. As though walking between worlds, I struggle to keep myself in one place. As we ready to leave I turn to the artist and tell him I'd like a poster with the poem but will come back for it later. Shaken, I take his card and we return to the performance. I don't go back for the poem.

Six months later my marriage unravels. I live in the little house in Wyoming with our daughter. In the overwrought vise of waiting to receive the final terms of divorce from the courts, which will determine everything about where we will live and so much else about our lives, I sit on my bed one afternoon while my daughter is in school and grapple with the many unknowns that lie ahead. The faith I've placed in trusting the myriad risks that life has exacted from me feels overwhelming in this moment. I lean against the wall at my back and pray for calm in the face of what will come. I pray for the path that will be best for us all. I pray for release from tension and uncertainty and a way forward that will sustain us.

The wall behind me dissolves. As though from the roots of the earth itself in a cavernous deep below, a force of nature incarnate rumbles through legions of black drummers beating out a rhythm. I see the men. They sit along earthen walls, their hands beating the heads of drums held between their legs, chests bare. The force of the drumming builds to a powerful cadence and breaks in a pitch to drop back beneath the surface of things. A great peace floods through me. The vision fades. The strain of my mind against the borders of worry and fear is shocked open. I sit with what I have seen and heard and have no idea what it means.

I know not to chase this experience, to not be distracted. If there is more that I need to be aware of, it will come. My responsibilities are great, and I go on with the normal tasks of my day and evening. And the following day I receive word. The decisions of the courts grant my daughter and me our lives in Wyoming. We settle into life in the northern valley, maintaining a solid bridge to her father in Denver. Time makes its pass.

I recounted the instance of the drummers to a friend recently. He said he could see how such a vision would be comforting, concocted by my mind at a stressful juncture. Yet experiences like the one with the drummers are not comforting. In and of themselves they are disturbing. If they can be held and not denied, they can transcend a moment until it transfers something purposeful. The peace that transferred from the drummers through their drumming carried a deeper message to me that in time would reveal itself.

My livelihood, based in coaching and consultation, turns out just as my dreams foretold. Many people come to the little house for help and perspective, and I begin to develop programs within my community. Whenever my daughter is with her father I travel to New Mexico and step up pursuit of my life as a writer. And to build on the deeper guidance I follow, I develop a program in Wyoming focused on diversity and tolerance. I create writing programs that I take into schools and the public library. All of these efforts are interlinking agencies to develop awareness and well-being for many.

When I go to New Mexico, pulled by specific landforms that act like magnets to my core, I follow threads that bring me into alliance with a quality much larger than myself. As this accelerates I begin to find the voice of my story. It comes like an eruption of volcanic magma that I allow to burn and move through me, linking all the eras of my life into a solid whole. At home in Jackson the poem by the African artist whose work I saw at the dance performance in Denver begins to press in my thoughts. I finally send him a letter and ask how to order the poster with the poem.

On a day sometime after this, my daughter in school, I work in my kitchen and something catches my eye. I turn from the sink and look toward the dining table. Just above its surface an ephemeral white veil wafts as though in a breeze through an open window. There is a strong presence behind the veil, familiar yet undecipherable. The veil dissolves to reveal two clasped hands blacker than night, dear and ancient beyond comprehension. These are hands I have known forever. A stab of joy mixed with longing and sorrow pierces through me. The hands, lined and beautiful, reveal nothing else. Unfathomable knowledge transfers to me with a tenderness that impales my heart, room penetrated with love and the awareness of something beyond time. And then the opening is gone. Nothing but the light, the table and the chairs remain, locked within normalcy, yet tenderness and sentient alertness have imbued into everything.

Questions and awe, puzzlement and wonder rifle through my next days, but any inquisitiveness that I bring to what has occurred is for naught. There is nothing more. I let it rest.

A short time later my daughter and I are invited to the birthday party of a friend at her boyfriend's house on a high butte cast among stars. His nephew is in town and she wants us to celebrate with them. As we arrive the sky is a crystal-clear, sparkling immensity, luminous and charged. Stepping out of the car into the high altitude night I'm instantly alert to the convergence of elemental forces pulsing around us. The stars and sky are imbued with precise clarity that brings all my senses alive. I feel an unusual kind of happiness. We walk the descending path to the house, deliciously light and free for the first time in weeks, liberated for the moment of all concerns. I've felt this before. We're on the cusp of a perfect moment coming into form. Somewhere there will be a flash of experience that holds exact keys to unlock doors of questions I haven't begun to ask.

Inside the house we put our coats in the bedroom and join the party, move among guests making light talk, my daughter shy among the very normal exchanges of a very normal gathering. I don't intend to stay long. I want to get her to bed at a decent hour, happy to share just a bit of this celebration with my good friend that will probably go on into the night. Gorgeous in her birthday glow, my friend is laughing as she turns to introduce me to a man standing behind her. He reaches out, takes my hand in both his hands and looks directly into my eyes. An electric current courses through my fingers. His skin is dark, and I look at our hands clasped together, his warm, brown fingers folding close around mine, pale in lamplight. I look back into his eyes slightly bemused, smile and nod, then turn back to my daughter. After cake and ice cream I go into the bedroom to get our coats. Suddenly the man is by my side, like a gentleman helping me to put on my coat. We laugh, his attention flattering, and I gather my daughter to leave.

A couple of nights later, my birthday friend and her boyfriend come to our house for dinner and bring the man with them. He talks about his life, his work and the house where he lives in the East, flirts openly, our attraction palpable. He and I meet for coffee a couple of times, and when he leaves the valley to return home there are a few phone calls. I suddenly remember the hands that appeared through the veil in my kitchen. Were they foretelling the moment his hands would take mine at the party? An attractive thought, yet something shifts as this crosses my mind, and I shudder.

That night I have a dream. In the dream I'm in a house like the one the man has described to me as his home in the East during our phone calls. I find my way through circuitous passageways to a back stairway. I know that I'm not supposed to be here, but when I hear him call out I climb instead to a doorway that opens out onto grounds of a vast estate. The estate surrounds his house, nothing like what he described to me. I wander, uncertain about what I'm doing here. I come to a place where secrets lie buried. Nothing is what it seems. I wake and know immediately that I need to break contact with him. When he comes to mind after this, a heavy weight grows murky and clouded. I relinquish all thought of him.

Two months or more have passed since writing to the African artist about his poem, and I've forgotten about it. One afternoon I get a call from him. He apologizes for his delay in getting back to me. He's been traveling but would be glad to send the poster and poem. We talk about his work. I talk about the diversity and tolerance work I'm doing in the valley. It's a nice exchange. I send a check for the poster with a letter describing how haunting and powerful his work was for me the night at the performance in Denver.

Life, full as it is, carries along. I go on with developing my work, keeping time on an even keel for my daughter, and continue to write. But something is trying to push up from my subconscious. Clues and cues rise to the surface about a place and people I've never met. There is intensity to feelings that arise, related to whatever this is. Finally I find a spare moment for solitude when I can sit undistracted and contemplate what the feelings and clues relate to. I feel into a force that grows sharp, pressing from just beneath the surface of life.

And instantly I'm looking into a small, close room like an attic as though through a window, but not exactly. It's more like a wall has dissolved, and within the room I can see a red-haired woman with green eyes lying on a rough floor, yelling amidst a boom of male voices above her. With sudden shock a whip cuts into the skin of her back. Her confusion and rage and the pain of the lash meld with the chafing voices of men, brutal and demanding. She struggles against them. The whip cuts again into her back, and a cacophony of sensations, feelings and pain rupture across time, and I am this woman's agony. I am her confusion. I am her rage. A flurry of images bursts through me. The brutality in the attic, whip cutting into flesh, agonies of incomprehension break through my heart. The world starts to spin. Her skin is my skin.

And I am back in my little house. Panting through panic, disbelief and eruptions of throbbing grief, I'm overcome. Within the grief everything comes crystal-clear. I know what comes next in the attic: the agony, the confusion, the long night of suffering. I know what will follow. As through a vast fissure ripped in time I'm laid bear all over again. Searing pain cuts through my soul.

As the enormity of what I've seen and what I feel at last subsides and I can gather myself in the here and now I'm shaken to the roots of my being. I suddenly understand that the hands that grasped mine at the party are not the ancient hands that appeared through the veiled portal above my kitchen table. The hands that grasped mine at the party are the hands of a man from a plantation hundreds of years before, the hands of a guardian who brought about the death of my beloved friend; they are the hands that cast my life aside for the benefit of his. As history integrates, the old grief takes me apart. When at last I can hold it, when at last I can accept exposure to this parallel life, the first wave has done its work. I'm awake in a way I have not been before.

The ancient hands in the portal are love beyond time. They've prepared me for what I must know so I can lay the past at rest.

Shifts in the fabric of the world, openings in parallel time that have occurred before have happened with a naturalness that is often so quiet as to make them easy to step away from, or almost miss and I could doubt what had occurred. Not in this instance; there is no missing this. I've come too far to close the door now and I know it. Just as in my earlier life when I opened the buried history of my younger years and knew when I reached the point when there was no going back, so it is now. There is no shutting the door or turning away. Life wants me awake at new levels I can't fathom. As with previous thresholds in time, I've crossed into the immediacy of another. And all of this, it is just in time. Again the understanding comes … just in time … just in time.

What is symbolic in our lives? What is real? Different experience and different talents require different kinds of intelligence, fortitude and awareness to unfold and prove useful. The way the man at the party took my hands is the same way that Brad took my hands 30 years before, two hands clasping my own, what are they telling me? When is now? Hands clasping, hands held, hands reaching, hands tender, hands doing great damage, hands professing love, hands hiding their purpose, hands signal, hands closed, hands open they stream through my life. The hands in the portal are ancient beyond imagining. The hands in the portal encompass all. They hold the beginning.

Sometime after this shocking episode the poster with the poem arrives. I write to thank the artist and he calls. We talk further about our work. A friendship builds. We start to discuss working together on a project I've developed. As time passes I tell him about my experience with the ancient hands. And I tell him about the split in time to the life on the plantation. He accepts these experiences as normal, nothing unusual. They are natural expressions within the fabric of life to him. He feels no personal connection to the life cycles I describe, but we both acknowledge the potency in relation to our work and our different cultures. He comes to the valley to bring his artistry and his cultural lens, springing open connections in students and valley residents that catalyze new thought on old bias, bigotry and opinions, challenging cramped attitudes. Together we awaken creative thinking and creative life in people who believed they had none. By our work and our friendship, a long thread of history reignites and lays to rest.

Time flows on. My grandmother's belongings that came to me as she simplified her life set the foundation for our little valley house and helped make it home. They surround us like a daily blessing, reminding us of our shared history and her love. About two years after we move in I'm home alone one day when I hear the wax and wane of a loud buzzing like the beating of enormous wings whirring over the house. I check, but there are no planes flying overhead, nothing to make sense of the sound. Two nights later I lie in bed, and the same sound returns and intensifies. Lying in darkness I see and feel the underbelly of a massive bee larger than the house flying very slowly overhead. I think I must be dreaming but I'm not. As I lie awake a profound majesty exudes over house and land, and the massive creature passes. In the morning I consult a dictionary on symbols. I read that bees in this context represent the passing of a soul. The telephone rings. It is my mother. She's calling to tell me my grandmother has died in the night.

In the first splintering moments of grief, I collapse on my bed. My little daughter climbs up with me, and we weep together. She climbs down from the bed, gathers every comfort she can find in the house related to her great-grandmother and our shared lives. She brings them to the bed and spreads them all around us. We hold each other tight. Not long after this we work old grief once more. Her Christmas tree, planted outside in a snowdrift after the holidays for the duration of winter, stands in view of our kitchen windows. One evening a huge bull bison ambles into our driveway. He scratches and scrapes on the little tree, shattering branches. We look on heartbroken. Many tears are shed in the night. The small pine — symbolic of many things, wonder and loss interwoven and that life is full of impermanence — still stands in the early light of morning. As we leave the house in biting cold to walk to school my daughter approaches her small pine with greatest tenderness, gathers the broken limbs together, tucks them in at the base of the tree and pats snow into place to close off the path of the bison. And then she walks the length of the drive beside me, her head bowed, hands held in prayer.

And that is how it is done. We hold our hearts in the heart of the world, finding our way each day into new life. New seasons. Let us pray. And so we do.

Several months later I open a box. Near the bottom a photograph lifts from darkness to light. As though hit by a runaway train and thrown across eternity, an explosion of pain rips through my heart from the inside out, as the image comes clear in my hand. Brad. This vision of him, almost impossible to hold, takes me apart. Everything that has led to this moment allows me to stay present, but barely so. Pain buried deep beneath pain beneath pain beneath pain is finally released. What I have unraveled with my mind and long effort comes unstrung at last from my body and heart, the loss of him buried away in the middle of so much. I begin to lift free. Over time all the far-flung pieces of myself have come back home to join in full life.

So go origins. For years I carried a lingering sense that there was a before that I had to uncover, but before what before when before why I could not say. Now I can sit and take in the full journey. Before murder, before rape, before rank betrayal, before threat, before loss, before Brad, before terror, before Mexico and within Mexico there was love. A long time before, my parents were happy and for a while there was joy. The joy and the love of the world live in me too. This joy and this love are not something to have. They are something I am. Before, between and within everything there is love. The broken threads have knit together to make whole cloth. I find the brief time in childhood when the world was all one, joy blooming wonder to laughter filled with belonging and close warmth. My mother is there, ripe with contentment, filled with delight. And there, too, is my father in all his youthful well-being. Their joy and their love sing in me. What was broken I now have made whole through understanding.

And Brad? Brad has been with me all through the years, presence and guide who remained and held fast. The third presence that drove me from my boyfriend's house so many years before, that was Brad. Once I had made the leap of moving back into the mountain pass house, without knowing what was guiding and pushing me, I was awake to everything that could and did follow.

I have made it to safety. Brad knows and now it's his time. And the moment arrives when he needs me to let him go. We're both ready, no longer bound. And so I do; I let him go. I remember the day and the hour and the moment and the place where he finally moves on. I know, too, when down the river of time he chooses life once again. Time is a river a meadow a moment expanding.

The claiming of time, the claim of history, slowly the fingers pull back and release. The dark hand recedes. It has no claim on me now.

37

And So It Is

By 2004 my vows have been fulfilled. For Thanksgiving, my daughter is with her father as I hike alone in a 14 mile arc across the Pajarito Plateau in northern New Mexico, a pilgrimage that pulls between cultures and times. This is mountain lion country. The journey completes a cycle of lifetimes that speaks through the wild regions of my heart.

This trek is one of many acts that lay to rest old, incandescent sufferings, through celebrations of the mystery and beauty of life, the wild integrity of this dear world. It is also a pilgrimage of gravitas.

As I hike across mesas, dropping in and out of arroyos and canyons, I contemplate the politics of destruction and war that take place across the earth, the unnatural disasters. I consider my role — where do I bring relief, when and how do I contribute to these realities, the many ways the subtleties and actions of our lives are complicit within the larger scale of time and events. Nearby lies Los Alamos, heart of the Manhattan Project, site of the creation of the atomic bomb. Walking this country is an act of balancing extremes. The challenges of this one-day trek require me to overcome old fears. Mirrored in minor key are aspects of the journey of my life, its shifts across time and space, history and place.

I hike alone on a demanding trek into wilderness in early winter with no certainty of how long my journey will take. If I can, I need to make the distance in a single day. The physical demands are great. My route is not a straight shot across flat ground. I drop deeper and deeper into canyons, elevation loss that I must regain again and again. At last I stand on the lip of an immense and tight canyon. Slick with hidden ice, switchbacks hewn into rock twist and drop into shadows far below. I gaze into the depths, open my pack for water and food.

And a massive boom reverberates, shocking me back, like the beat of a distant drum striking somewhere across the canyon.

Echoes buckle and roll, rumbling to a shuddering standstill. As vibrations shimmy through brilliant chill air, crossing the mesa into the distance, I stand in awe and wonder. Who, what could this be? Voices out of nowhere filter and recede from the far side of the canyon. Mystified I stow my water, heft my pack. When all has dropped back to stillness I drop to the switchbacks cut into the canyon walls and begin the long descent into the canyon bottom. Will I meet people on the other side of the mesa? I've seen no one through all the miles I've hiked. When I reach the bottom my legs tremble with fatigue. In the solitude of the close, cold canyon there is no one. I read the topography, walk down canyon, seek the way up and out the opposite side. It seems impossible that there will be a trail. But when the canyon softens and opens, I find one.

I step onto the first switchback — and stop in my tracks. Above the second switchback a massive landslide has taken out the trail. Boulders, rock, the upturned roots of juniper and mesquite, ravaged bitterbrush and primrose hang among heaved earth and paddles of torn prickly pear. On the last settling catch of the upheaval the fresh disruption of soil breathes into crisp air. The slide is fresh. It just happened. Stunned, I gape. And understanding breaks through me. This is the huge drumroll that burst forth when I was at the top of the canyon — the pound of ancient rhythms pouring across mesa and time. My heart skips ... I take a deep breath ... so close ... so far.

And next awareness breaks. I can't go on. I can go no further. I'll have to turn back.

I marvel at the slide, feel my disappointment, turn away. And deep conviction stops me. I survey the damage above, the crazy tilt of disturbance, the upended trees and rock. I listen to the settling of the earth, feel into the breathing life around me. And I understand that what has called me is still calling. I test the footing, feel into my core — and begin to scale the slide, scrambling upslope, feeling my way by instinct and invention. Roots of juniper and mesquite snag at my pack as I struggle around upturned boulders through a tenderness of soil porous, soft beyond imagining — first exposure to light and sun in how many years? The climb is arduous. It requires complete attention.

At the top of the canyon, I step from the shifted soils of the volatile slide to the upper mesa. Voices whisper and call. The very earth seems to speak. I walk forward. It feels as though I'm walking into a village vibrant with daily rhythms, spikes of song and laughter, the buzz of communal life. But the voices fade into a stand of close-growing cane cholla that hover a few paces ahead; thin columns absorb faint impressions of movement and sound. I shake my head, pass around the cactus and walk on. Not much farther a wild ruin opens before me. I stand in wonder.

The ruin is large. I gaze across the scattered hump and thrust of old walls and mounded earth and drop my pack. And there, right next to my pack, is a cluster of fresh-picked immature yucca pods. Like an offering in plump, jade green, they glisten in the sun, jewels gathered in a small concave bowl of eroded stone. *Oh*, I think, *someone's just left them. In this sun they'll desiccate in minutes.* I look around, enchanted. But no one, no one is there.

Near this place lies the heart and purpose of my journey. I refresh myself, explore the ruin, leave my pack and walk on. A bit further, in a private act of surrender and sacrifice I quietly complete another cycle. Holding the world in my heart and my heart in the world, I return to the ruin, make my farewell and travel farther into the unknown and the long trek back the way I've come.

————

Over the next few years, life carries on with its many demands. Within them I continue to keep a writing life. The book I thought I would write has been usurped — I now have a partial manuscript that deals with the story of my life. Yet as the calendar page turns over to January of 2008 it's time to set this life story aside. It has done its work, brought my history full circle, clarified and complete. I can lay it all down; let the past rest. It's time to move on. I shelve the manuscript. I begin research on a different book.

And the U.S. economy begins to tank. Work is hard to find. Apprehension about livelihood and my daughter's well-being rise, and as I search for work, winter deepening, January closes on one cold winter evening with nothing certain for our road ahead. Caught in a rotating blur of concerns, a blue mood holds me in its grip. I know from experience that this kind of mood is core guidance trying to break through into awareness. I suspend all my projections until the perspectives and understandings within me can unfold into my grasp.

And with this, a sudden revelation breaks in a cascade. It tells me that not only is the history of this one life of mine complete, put to rest — transparent, rebalanced and freed — the cycles of hundreds of years of many lives are complete as well.

All is clean, the past resolved.

Stunned I wonder what this can possibly mean. A void opens before me — the emptiness that precedes all new beginnings. But this time the scale is shocking. In this emptiness there is nothing that cues about how to move forward at the most pragmatic level. It is a time of suspension.

No catalyst exists to strike on the flint of old patterns. There is no new promise to light the way.

In the face of such vast unknowns I face reality along parallels of deep winter and uncertain times.

A few days later we're at the library, a favorite place for my daughter and me. While she grazes through her own interests, I wander through the stacks random and restless, pulling books off shelves and barely looking at what comes into my hands. When we get home I see that I have three biographies on Carl Jung in our bag.

I remember many years before, when I was just beginning to crack open the intensities of my past. At that time I had an old copy of one of Jung's books that was always present on my bedside table. It was a used book that I must have picked up like so many others, in a random moment of curiosity. I never read it. I kept it at my bedside because it felt like the presence of a great-grandfather who was always near, supportive and loving. The book was a comfort to me through those years, like a touchstone, a talisman or cairn I trusted but that held no logical meaning.

Now, I have three biographies on Carl Jung in my hands. I let curiosity sweep over me. I begin to read.

The first biography helps keep my mind engaged between searches for work and daily demands, turned away from anxiety. This biography is poorly done. It lacks objectivity, and the author seems to have an axe to grind. When I've finished it I grab the next, only to keep my mind clear and focused beyond worry. This second biography is more engaging. I finish it in a few days and read the third. The most contemporary of all three, the third biography is dynamic and well done. Each of the three books brings to the fore different details of Jung's life. By the time I finish, I feel great satisfaction with the discovery of connections and information that interlace a greater whole between all three renditions of his life.

The day I finish the third book I sit with my mounting concerns and ponder next steps. Work remains hard to find. A kind of prodding is present, pressing from within my subconscious. I let thoughts and impressions sift up from subliminal planes of awareness. As they break surface I understand that a deeper truth is telling me to let go of the ideas I've had about research for the new book I'm planning to write. This awareness has a sharp edge of disappointment, but I shrug it off, small in the face of my other concerns, though it adds to the featureless void. I feel curious in the face of this discomfort, this next expression of the unknown.

And suddenly the blue mood that has hovered around for weeks blasts open, arcing into consciousness clear as a bell, message succinct.

Your history is done. So now you will tell your story. It's not about you anymore.

Shocking along my nervous system this reversal tingles and pops, vibrant and awake. No answer to my practical concerns follows. But certainty rings true and absolute. When the next revelation hits it nearly knocks me off the couch.

The crossing that Jung made in his life from 1913-1915 parallels the same crossing you made through the work you did in your thirties, the same work you have done throughout your life.

A sensation like steel filling in along my spine catapults me to standing in the middle of my living room floor. I gasp.

A snap of emergence sparks through my cells and my mind at the same instant. The quality is irrevocable. It vibrates through the room. I flinch in the face of the audacious nature of this assertion. But I realize it's true. Many people have made the passages Jung made in those years. People have been making these crossings for a very long time.

With no certainty of how it will be done, I accept the work as it has been laid out before me. I must turn again to the story I've shelved — the story of my life that is no longer about me and yet must be carried in the vehicle of my archetypal experience. I understand that I must trust this, offer my life in service within a book on a timeline I cannot imagine. Life asks me to risk again at a level I know I will not fully comprehend until this new cycle is complete. The shock of this awareness and its demands penetrate, imbued with absolute authority. I must claim what I now know to be true. Without Jung's background or training, I navigated the extremes of my life and made the passage through the darkest inner landscape to make a similar crossing.

The question that has troubled me all my life forms again: Why do some make it and some not? Jung's methods were fierce and demanding as he evolved them, his patients at risk throughout. My own path has been fierce, rife with risk. Why was I able to make it?

Over the next few years I will find myself in circumstances unimaginable to me on this cold winter day in my tiny house in Wyoming, with few options available to sustain our lives. But in the moment that cognition breaks, it's enough that I acknowledge what life wants of me, to accept and surrender to this challenge.

Though Jung was far from the first person to make such navigations, he was original in his thought about the process — and in his methods of cataloging, analyzing and translating them through a rigorous lens. Yet there is another body of his work that was far less well known. He kept private much of his most mystical experience, including his work with astrology. After he died his family repressed and buried these aspects of his life even more, out of the public eye.

Beyond this, the efforts he made in 1913-1915 were the work he asked of his patients. He knew when his own psyche fractured that he had to make the crossing of the darkest inner landscapes within himself, or his theories and practice held no truth and validity at all.

Over the next years, life opens doorways to me that appear impossible in the winter of 2008. Journeys foretold through vision and dream will traverse wide geographic sweeps that carry me across old paths, through adventure and out into time out of time. Within months of my startling epiphanies, life will test my capacity to show up for the unusual in a whole new way.

Through an odd twist of fate, I'm accepted for a course in California though I don't truly have the credentials to take part in it. The professor is a legacy bearer of Jung's later work — the astrology Jung used with his clients in his later successful years as a therapist. These astrological keys will give answers to some questions about the hows and whys of the individual struggle to survive in the face of a fractured psyche. And because I'm in California for this course, I travel home across Nevada and there re-discover the sites of the old ordeals I shared with my friends. Through this unexpected chance of fate I release the last vestiges of the damage of that history as it dissipates out of my cells and through my hands into the same ancient desert sands where we dug our graves on that night so long ago.

During the next years and cycles, friends and family gather around my daughter and me to see us through hard times, a circle of help where once there was none. Out of this time the mosaic of parallel lives and staggered historical eras reveal to me in growing detail, their story at rest but their purpose now clay to be re-worked into new form. My daughter thrives. We both do. Life carries on. And again, time makes its pass.

Stories must complete before a new story can begin.

In 2011, a young woman launches on a journey. In northern California she'll begin a full scholarship program in the Bay area, writing and arts, a precursor to college about a year out. She's seventeen. Within a year, college in New York City will claim her again. She's opening a gate now, passing through. I'm waving her off, heart full and shining. Seasons are shifting. Parallel time.

Author's Note

Why tell a story like mine? I have no interest in continuing the legacy of titillating, gratuitous and voyeuristic violence that too much of our literature and media have borne into our lives, our culture, our world. My interest is in how we move on. How we create other kinds of worlds, new stories, how we come through the agonies of life to creative revelation, to love and care. My interest lies in how we become more than the awfulness our agonies make us prone to, how it is that we heal, how we make art of our lives.

By the time I wrote this story, it was no longer about me. I had moved on. This story is bigger than me, and in its own right, it claimed one last tithe. It demanded to be told. And so, with some resistance but ever the grateful student of a larger intelligence that has guided and kept me alive, I surrendered. There is always the chance that our stories will illuminate, inspire, that they can serve. That is the point of story. Cruel, mean-spirited story used as superficial entertainment makes of us all immature children. Beware the culture that treats story so.

The questions come. How did I live all of this and make it through? Surviving extremes is nothing new to human experience. My experience is more horrific than some but far less so than others. Yet each individual talisman of survival leaves a cairn and can be useful. My story as told in the previous pages is a partial story. We can only attempt to portray the arc of a life through timelines that link through its heart for a particular purpose. Each life has many threads, many arcs. This story is a catalyst, a provocation, an invitation to the inner journey, the journey toward peace and creative living. Whatever in life keeps you from wholeness, take courage and investigate its wild frontier. The last true frontier that we have as human beings is the inward journey. All others pale in comparison. The distortions created by what we refuse to see about ourselves, by all that we push down out of sight, by what and how we hide from our true nature, are the territory of the inward journey. What we fear rules us. By deconstructing our fears, just by the act of naming them, we become liberated. We are wild. Each and every one of us is wild by nature. All effort to keep parts of ourselves hidden sets that wildness against itself, gives energy to what is hidden, repressed, until aberrant monsters grow out of all proportion. The journeys we make in the external world are child's play compared to the risks and dangers, the sheer beauty and luster, the novelty and expansive wisdoms of the provocative inner realms.

The inward journey is arduous. It demands total presence. The jewels and treasures we seek in the outer world are mere baubles compared to the evanescent wonders present within — there is nothing that compares. Every success and every loss of our living, however small or great, call us to explore the inner mystery, the depth and breadth of meaning within ourselves. When we ignore or suppress that call, the cost is great. This is the place where all wars must be fought. In that is our only salvation. Until we bring ourselves home to ourselves we project our pain and our suffering, our embattled egos and our terrible wounds onto the world, playing out in hideous repetition one upon another. Come home, come home and know thyself. Life calls us to this. Come free. It is the only way to intimate relationship with this fabulous world, to know the world by knowing the self and by knowing the self, to understand the world.

In the arc of my story I dwell on dream work, not in all of its complexity but presented simply as a realm of deep meaning and a tool. Each of us has particular talents and capabilities to guide us. Of the many skills I put to use to find my way, dream work was, and is, profound. It is critical to understand that no one holds the full set of keys to another's dreams, to the particular language and symbol of the individual other than the individual themselves. These are unique to each of us, a pattern language that lives within. Archetypes and symbols rich in the collective unconscious are important. And seeking the wisdom of others' experience and knowledge is good and natural. Yet it is imperative to learn and return to the originality of your own inner landscape to fully understand the puzzle. We carry our answers inside of us. We must learn to understand and speak in our own tongue. The individual language of symbol, image and tone carries unique nuance that meets and weaves the world in an artistry all our own. Vigilance is part of the process. Vigilance to speak biting truths to the self cuts through seduction and distortion. But ultimately the process comes to nurture and love. These qualities expand in us with self-knowledge.

I have a keen sensibility for recognizing patterns. We each have our talents. We need only apply them. I became adept at recognizing patterns that mirror to me in the outer world. There is an adage that holds true, as above so below, as within so without. One type of pattern that carries great meaning for each of us is the power of anniversary experience. Anniversaries hold enormous potency. I came to understand that the weight I felt at certain times of the year, the emotions, confusions and magnetisms that played into my decisions, interactions, perceptions and engagements, could inform me in new ways about the old story I held buried deep in my cells. With attention and great care each layer and resonance of many anniversaries revealed patterns I needed to acknowledge, deconstruct, understand and integrate so that I could finally release their hold on me, their effects that limited the flowering of my life. This kind of work takes time. It takes great patience. It requires a recipe of fierceness paired closely with exquisite tenderness. We must be ferocious to prevail. And we must be kind. We must be tender. We must be generous with ourselves.

Curiosity carried me forward when nothing else would. I wanted to know, I wanted to understand, I wanted to get inside the inner workings of what had happened to me. I wanted the truth — not the veils time, confusion and fear had passed over it. My range for certain experiences in life was limited, and I wanted to know why. Curiosity carried me into danger when I was young and poorly guided, yes, but it was also curiosity that drew me out of danger, toward understanding of what kept me bound. What had happened to me? Why? Not the stories I repeated to keep the phantoms at bay or to assuage my ego or to create an acceptable persona in the world. I wanted to know what had really happened to me. And that required unveiling the whole story from childhood on and then assimilating even the poison to transmute it. Profound curiosity paired with need drove the investigation that peeled it all back. I discovered so much more than I bargained for. I learned great truths about strength and weakness. Within our strengths are our weaknesses, and within our weaknesses are our strengths. I learned that everything at a certain level is really the same. It is energy. It can be worked. Expression, perception and interpretation are all faces. They are not the whole. Anger bespeaks pain. Pain bespeaks loss, or perceived loss. Anger and loss constrict the heart, the cells, the spirit and the body. Violence and violation constrict like a vise. The way through is by slow expansion, the process of revelation. To reach the other side of pain, one must eat it whole. Too much expansion too fast and the heart, the spirit, the cells burst or collapse. Balance and caution, yet risks must be taken. And that is a dance always refining. Breaking the heart opens the heart. Or not. The choice is always within us. My dance was often awkward, sometimes a shambles and, as often, elegant. We learn the steps as we go.

Guide and ally all through my life has been music. It pulled, called, seduced and moved me. I had projected that muse onto others, like the minstrel boyfriends, as the thing outside. But like any other form or expression, I had to understand its structure within me, as me and its unstructured aspects as well, the muse that can climb through mind, emotion, spirit and body with a force like no other. Someone once said that music is not sound — music simply utilizes sound to reveal itself. This is a truth that breathes in my soul. In the many years of clarifying my life I realized that I have always been a tuning fork of sorts.

Several years after primal catwoman's appearance, I met a woman in Denver, a practitioner in a particular therapeutic form. It was a time when tragedy brought me face to face with new veils that had to be lifted, more layers peeled back from history's stronghold, each layer, each in its time. My husband and I had lost our son and were beginning life anew as parents with our little daughter. The tragedy of severe loss paired with great joy, and also the great vulnerability of having a child in the world, brought to the fore many unresolved feelings between us. Because I had already done so much inner work, I had certain fluencies. In a few sessions this wonderful woman was able to help me make sense and string the patterns I needed most to understand. In the beginning with her I was not able to speak many parts of my story out loud, so I wrote it down. Once this was done the real work could be completed. I already had the tools I needed for the rest.

Yet one important exchange between us differs and stands out. I had told her of my experience when the forces of wild psyche opened full-bore in me. At the time, her response was very confusing. She told me with some anger that I had no business all those years ago taking on my history by myself. I sat in her presence stunned, dismayed, dumbfounded. I felt certain she hadn't grasped what I'd shared with her, the real extent of those harrowing times, my isolation. Where would I have possibly turned for help? I felt her assessment wrong, ill-informed. But I came to see in time that we were both right in our way. I had little-to-no-choice, out of both what experience had taught me and what was available to me. The avenues I had to choose from for help were arrogant, ignorant or cruel, so they sealed me off in deeper isolation. The accrued damage was great. If I was going to make progress at all, I had to do it on my own. Yet in time I came to see the point this woman was making. Such journeys into wild psyche are dangerous as anything. I barely made it. It's good to have help. For me, mine was the journey I had to make. Yet caught in cycles of danger, dangerous risks can be hard to identify, and cycles of unnecessary risk can be difficult to break. This is an important code to the process, learning to identify old patterns that can lead to more problems. And there is another important key. In our very human need to feel special we can make the mistake of identifying ourselves as special through over-identification with our ordeals, their pain, our traumas. After all, we've survived them. Yet the only way to move beyond is to lay them down. Or they become Gollums, our precious. This we must also break with, to be truly free.

In a session near the close of my time with this woman, she suggested that I call up feral catwoman any time I needed help with problems in my everyday world. I looked at her as though she'd lost her mind. I immediately understood that she had not grasped the nature of primordial catwoman. She did not have any real understanding of primordial wild nature at all. This was the point in our work when I had to trust my own learned wisdom. Wild nature like that does not domesticate. Feral wild nature is a force beyond. Uncontrollable, savage, it is unto itself. Catwoman is life-and-death feral at the extreme. She has no place in the day-to-day. She is not a flat archetype, nor is she imagined, idea or figment. She's full-blooded and raw. There is nothing more raw than nature at this extreme. Original, elemental, severe, one must not call out such forces lightly. I had to come into relationship to find my way to wholeness. Feral psyche does not nurture relationship. I had to sense the truth and answers about this through the metronome I carried within. We need each other for comfort and love, the humanity of shared stories, the eloquence of shared paths. We need each other to be heard. We need to listen. We are built for story. It is how we learn. It is how we inspire. Story breathes our lives. It holds our song. Refined senses, the engagement of instinct, intuition and deep listening brought me to truth, and truth rings out the music of the soul. This was not catwoman's territory. For this, I did not require her nature, the purposes of her great and dangerous self.

The strongest and longest thread of my life relates to prescience, since I was a child, a fact of my nature. My grandmother had it before me. This was not something I was encouraged or schooled to know or to trust. I had to discover and learn its workings through trial and error. Embracing and understanding this informing guidance is the most important elemental language I know. And of course, that is the story.

And there is this — the rich and beautiful tapestry of my daughter's life that finally and fully informed my own. I could understand in new and profound ways, through each stage of her development, my own experiences as a child and young woman. The model of her life gave many gifts of new insight into what is possible through nurture, commitment and care. And revealed to me more profoundly than anything possibly could the stages of my life when I was young; where I was at what age and what was happening to me in the immense landscape of change, exposure and disturbance I faced in my childhood, youth and young adulthood. Through her growth I understood myself at new levels that released the past, claimed the present and brought me all the way home. And greater than all of this, she is love incarnate, the greatest blessing to spring from my wildest dream.

Until my own inner cyclones abated, until the raging-hot magma burst forth and cooled, I would be at the mercy of storms inside and out. Storms are cyclic. They arise and they abate. They disperse. We are natural elements, all of us, filled with natural cycles. We must learn to read our weather, navigate the wild regions, make it home to our contemplative and reflective natures that align us with new cycles, new journeys that hold the keys to the art of our lives. Then we can know and find our way. Then we are one with the world.

Thanks for walking with me, all the way home.

Acknowledgements

For all my deep love and gratitude for my daughter, I also give many thanks for her contributions of skilled genius and editorial insights that have enhanced this book. Greater than all of this, there could be no brighter flame in a life than she is in mine.

There is always a larger circle that sustains our lives and our creations, in direct and indirect ways. So many have contributed to the realization of this book, it is impossible to name you all. Your numbers are great. You know who you are. Your lives fill mine, and I am the lucky one.

There are several people I must name specifically. For my sister, Colleen, I am endlessly grateful for all the ways she has supported this effort — a believer from the beginning, she contributed in ways too numerable to state here, and to my life in endless concert with all that is good. For my brother, Tom, tech wiz and loyal enthusiast, his curiosity and steadfast additions are beyond compare. For my youngest brother there will always be endless love. For my beloved grandmother, Berniece F. Hooley, I cannot imagine where I would be without her. Her love both made and saved me. For my parents, Joyce Ann Hooley and Allen Bernard Cabot, now long gone, I cherish our long paths and our resolutions within them, their lives far bigger than this story allows. For my brother-in-law, Norman Farquhar, there are no words for the many ways he has put ground beneath my feet when it seemed there was none. And within the circle and lineage of my larger family, the echo of belonging to all of you carries through the deepest regions of my heart.

For Maria Hajic, dear friend, cartographer-in-spirit and so much more, who helped map this story almost from the start, you hold a central place in the creation of this book and in the weave of love that defines what is best in the world. Through your hundreds of connections and discerning clear eye, great effort has evolved into clear form. For Sandy Leotta, friend since childhood, who carried the torch and kept the light for me as I navigated these pages, muchas gracias, mi amíga. Karen Skaggs, I could not ask for a better friend to sustain the dozens of discussions that balanced doubt alongside the fires of creation, your heart is all over this book. James Mathieu, it's been a good long path we've shared and your constancy, support, musical genius, wide perspectives and big love have helped me keep rhythm throughout this effort. Lisa and Charlie Feitel, if I say Tikkun Olam, you will know exactly what I mean — you have truly helped me repair the world. Cindi and Steve Kestrel, your many-layered support and belief in my efforts have burnished my wings in this and so many endeavors. I bow to our good friendship. Karen Brighton, our trails go a long way back. Whether on the Pacific Crest Trail or bound to a French fry basket in Pinedale, Wyoming, or within the big arc of far-ranging adventure, the vein of our friendship runs deep, your generosity to me like a miracle. Lyn Dalebout, your varied insights, friendship and love are my blessing. Jane Gallie, Debbie Schlinger, and Susan Thulin, you have held a candle and kept the faith for me in more ways than one. To Dana Vanburg, from field science to the pages of this book, your support in my life is immeasurable. For Guy Rocha, great friend and genius of research, your contributions to my life and the birthing of this story are varied and cherished. To the Teton County Library staff (and libraries everywhere), I have boundless gratitude.

To my dear readers, who brought unique viewpoint and strong critique to this book, your devotion, enthusiasm and grace have not only made this book better, you have made me better in my pursuit of the truth at its heart: Karen Brighton, Alison Brush, Christian Burch, Stella Cabot-Wilson, Colleen Cabot, Tom Cabot, Lyn Dalebout, Lisa Feder-Feitel, Charlie Feitel, Gina Freschet, Jane Gallie, Laurie Gunst, Maria Hajic, Jenny Johnson, Susan Juvelier, Cindi Kestrel, Steve Kestrel, Patty Klauer, Sandy Leotta, James Mathieu, Linda McFall, Dina Mishev, Debbie Schlinger, Karen Skaggs and Susan Thulin. Thank you for your varied and composite dedication, professionalism, love and friendship, they reach beyond the stars. When it was down to the wire to get this book across the finish line, there were many who helped carry it home: Terrina Beatty, Keith Becker, Karen Brighton, Alison Brush, Colleen Cabot, Jenn Castro, Lyn Dalebout, Lisa and Charlie Feitel, Laurie Gunst, Mary Hartman, Lanie Hicks, Jenny Johnson, Cindi & Steve Kestrel, Magdalena Koob-Emunds, Ann Ladd, Sandy Leotta, Frances Pollack, Karen Skaggs, Guy Rocha, Bill Sloup, Susan Stone, Susan Thulin, George Vlastos, and Dana Vanburg. To you I am ever grateful. Tim Sandlin and Steve Ashley, so much appreciation for your seasoned advice at critical junctures.